TWEEDDALE

D1179413

DARLINGTON

PUBLIC LIBRARY

DARLINGTON
PUBLIC LIBRARY.

NEIDPATH CASTLE AND RIVER TWEED

TWEEDDALE

BY

WILL GRANT, F.S.A.Scot.

Author of "The Call of the Pentlands,"
"Pentland Days and Country Ways," etc.

BRITISH LIBRARY
LENDING DIVISION

- 1 AUG 1979

W 56/6272

OLIVER AND BOYD

EDINBURGH : TWEEDDALE COURT
LONDON : 98 GREAT RUSSELL STREET, W.C.1
1948

007243872

FIRST PUBLISHED 1948

Peebles

BORDERS
REGIONAL
LIBRARY

The spirit of Romance dies not to those
Who hold a kindred spirit in their souls.
(MEREDITH)

My chief passion in those (adolescent) years was for the
Border countryside, and my object in all my 'prentice
writings was to reproduce its delicate charm, to catch the
aroma of its gracious landscape and turbulent history, and
the idiom of its people. . . . I found in its people what I
most admired in human nature—realism coloured by poetry,
a stalwart independence sweetened by courtesy and a shrewd
kindly wisdom.

(JOHN BUCHAN, the late Lord Tweedsmuir,
" Memory Hold-the-door ")

DARLINGTON PUBLIC LIBRARY		
DATE 13.4.48	CLASS V 390	LBLD.
ACC. No. 84537	DEPT. Lend	CARDED
V.D.R. Holmes	C & T	LETTERED
PRICE 12/6	STPD	CTLD. K

V 3989

PRINTED IN GREAT BRITAIN
BY R. & R. CLARK, LTD., EDINBURGH
AND PUBLISHED BY OLIVER & BOYD, LTD.

DARLINGTON
PUBLIC LIBRARY.

FOREWORD

"NATURE I loved"—No one could have used these words with more sincerity than the writer of this book. Mr. Will Grant was a great lover of Nature in all her moods and ways, and he writes of them with deep insight and understanding. In the words of Principal J. C. Shairp, whom he so greatly admired, he proclaimed anew that " Nature is not a dead mechanism, but one informed by a vital life which moves through all material things and makes them instinct with unity and beauty." These pages tell of his communings with Nature among the hills and glens of his own countryside. . . . To see him set forth for a day on the hills and heights, with knapsack, strong tackety boots, long stick, and with the light of anticipation in his eyes was a tonic ! One knew that great things were in store for him : from some hilltop he might see the grand sweep of country from the Pentlands to the Borders ; in some glen he might watch with delight the dash of a wild mountain burn, or on a quiet moor he might follow the course of a gentle stream meandering through the heather. He would have a grand day, and at the close of it there might be one of those magical sunsets which he so vividly describes.

Such sights and doings would be part of his day—but only part : for his humanity was as great as his sense of the beauty of earth and sky ; and " Never was there a footpath yet that did not pass something of human interest." Along with his sense of the mysterious and the beautiful was his understanding of the lives and doings of the country folk, his admiration for their steadfastness and fidelity to duty. " Man goeth forth to his work and to his labour." The ploughman and the shepherd and their like he held in high esteem—he realised what interest they put into their work—and what a spirit of enjoyment : " I've seen mair fun at a clippin' than ever I saw in ony toun," said a young shepherd. [Incidentally it is heartening to read that there are probably more young shepherds on the Border hills to-day than there have ever been.] He writes, too, of those " helpers and friends of mankind," the horses and the dogs. He has many

v

tales to tell of the sagacity and devotion of the sheep dog, and he gives a delightful picture of a ploughing match and the victorious team returning home.

No part of Scotland is more rich in history, legend or romance than the Scottish Border country " where every ruin is history and every glen a song " ; and a book like this will surely help us to realise afresh the richness and the beauty of our heritage.

LILIAN ADAM SMITH

DARLINGTON
PUBLIC LIBRARY.

CONTENTS

vii

DARLINGTON
PUBLIC LIBRARY

ILLUSTRATIONS

ix

ACKNOWLEDGMENT is hereby made for permission to
reproduce the following illustrations :

Charles Reid   Plates I, III, XII, XV, XVII, XVIII,
                              XIX (upper), XX, XXII

Walter Brydon   ,,   IX (lower), X, XI, XIII, XXI
Robert Adam   ,,   IV, XIV
Francis Caird Inglis   ,,   VIII
The British Council   ,,   V, IX (upper)
Ian Smith   ,,   VII, XXIII
Sir Duncan Hays   ,,   II
Dr. A. Wood Smith   ,,   VI
G. W. Marshall   ,,   XVI
James R. Marshall   ,,   XIX (lower)

DARLINGTON
PUBLIC LIBRARY.

INTRODUCTION

THERE is a glorious wild tumble of hills, dear to the heart of walkers and hill climbers, in the elongated stretch of country bounded by Tweed from its source to Innerleithen, and by the road from Traquair to Moffat by lone St. Mary's. It includes Tweeddale and the Tweeddale hills, the Tweedsmuir hills and the Hart Fell range. Hundreds of green rounded hills are contained in the district, connected by high-backed ridges, wide-spreading valleys, deep ravines and sequestered places, whose very loneliness is their deepest charm ; and almost all of it is given over to the rearing of sheep—one of the most important sheep-grazing areas in Great Britain—and to the pursuit of game. The ranges lying in and around this area comprise the Southern Uplands or Southern Highlands of Scotland, stretching from the Cheviots to the Pentlands, the Moorfoots, the Lammermuirs, Broughton Heights and the Hills of Ettrick, Yarrow and Eskdale-muir—the Borderland of Scotland.

Geographically considered, Peeblesshire is largely the dale of the Tweed. The romantic name " Tweeddale " by which Peeblesshire was known from early times is an appropriate one for a county of which the main natural feature is the river Tweed, with its attendant hills and waters, valleys and watersheds. The name occurs in ancient charters, in State documents (Tuedal), in Wyntoun's *Cronykil*, *Peblis to the Play* (Tuedell syd), *Blaeu's Atlas* (Twee-Dail), and a " Symonem a Tweddell " was made a Baron by Malcolm Canmore at Forfar in 1057 (*Genealogie of Sainteclaires of Rosslyn*, p. 3). Tweed is named in the " Marches of Stobo " (A.D. 1200) ; " dale " is of Scandinavian origin, and the name " Tweeddale " is as beautiful as the land it describes, and is as preferable to that of Peeblesshire as is the ancient name of Linton Roderick to that of the modern West Linton.

In Tweeddale there is a hill for every fancy, a glen for every taste, and for all who study the character and personality of hills by which they make their appeal, there is ecstasy and delight in the making of new friendships. In this glamour-haunted land, love is increased by knowledge of the hills. The fascination, the glamourie of those wild pastoral solitudes is twofold. There is that communion which comes from surrender to the gracious spirit of Nature, specially manifest in Tweeddale, and, that which is of human origin—the whole phantasmagoria of life from earliest time that has been enacted in this district, strong deeds, strange visions, haunted moors, human passions and heroisms, a tremendous human background, surprising the wanderer to joy and sadness, beauty and terror, wonder and awe.

Although the hills are all under 3,000 feet in height, all are diversified in glowing colours and graceful contours, and afford fair prospects and far views. It is not so much size as variety in form and colour that counts in the beauty of hill scenery. Line may give the sense of nobility or grace in form, colour gives richness and stirs emotion, qualities that inspire not only the artist and the poet, but also the ordinary wayfarer in search of impressions. Sir Archibald Geikie, writing of these Southern Uplands, says : "Nowhere else in Scotland can the exquisite modelling of flowing curves in hill-forms be so conspicuously seen. . . . From the skyline on either side, gentle but boldly-drawn curves of bent-covered moorland sweep down into the grassy meadow on the floor of the valley. These are architectural forms and remain distinct at all seasons of the year. But their beauty and impressiveness vary from month to month, almost from hour to hour," and speaks of the lovely annual phases of tone and colour, the glistening greyish green of bracken, the smouldering purple of heather and the deepening sunset tints of brown and gold before the frost begins to bleach and stiffen them into their winter immobility.

The green and gracious valleys of Glensax, Manor and Drumelzier are counterparts in some respects of many a Highland glen ; the mist gathers round the high hills and trails across the pine-tree tops, the burn brawls beside the nibbling sheep, the path winds up the glen to the shieling and the cottage.

Of the valleys of Megget, Talla and Gameshope, each is different from the others, the constituent width of the valleys, grouping of the hills and the skylines, and the view from the hill-tops contribute to this variety ; while Gameshope (Gyemsop) of solemn gloomy grandeur, with its succession of deep gullies, thundering cataracts and black cauldrons is perhaps the wildest and weirdest of all. Here the water rises quickly in flood, as the surroundings are mostly of rock and retain little moisture, while the river's own deep springs never fail. It seems as if the giants had strewed the glen with gigantic boulders, and, disturbed by the Brown Men of the Moors, suddenly left them, while at play. Gameshope is as much identified with giants and covenanters as Drumelzier is with fairies and with feuds.

All have their historians and story-tellers, and some of the stories are eerie, like the Brownie of Bodsbeck which begins— " Aye," says Chapelhope, " it will be a bloody night in Gemsop this " ; a story which John Buchan says " may fairly be regarded as the classic of that wild triangle of hill between Tweed, Ettrick and Megget."

" If ye're for peace, and a day that will haud for ever—gang up Tweedsmuir, yer laddie an' you thegither—in Fruid, ye'll mend yer soul," so sings Gilbert Rae, the poet of Fruid ; and if you are not for the angle, but have a mind for Hart Fell and " The Crown of Scotland," then here is the way of your going, and rich will be your reward. For the wayfarer in search of natural beauty, and the Feeling for Nature [1] in hill and glen, with peace in his soul and tranquillity in his heart, Tweeddale is a land of subtle allurement and charm.

On Tweedside we shall meet Mistress Dods' fishers, " pawky auld carles . . . that cam' hame at e'en wi' the creel fu' o' caller troots," and Fisher Jamie " at gloamin' tide . . . wi' saumon on his back gaun linkin' doon."

And up among the high hills, as well as in the pastoral valleys, we shall often meet the shepherd and his dogs actively at work —the hardest workers in Tweeddale—not " asleep upon a sunny knoll with his face to the sky," which Dorothy Wordsworth and many others since her day, considered the normal " happy picture of the shepherd life."

The quietude of the hillside gloaming, so instinct with movement, will touch the deep cords of the heart. We shall stand transfigured, listening to that prosaic twilight song of Tweed, singing to the faint stars as one by one they become visible ; and see the night descend, and the hills be wrapt in sleep.

As we ascend the upward track over the hills, eye and mind become alert and enquiring, the spirit of expectancy is awakened because the ascending road is ever provocative and intriguing, ever exciting, and pleasures of the imagination constantly intermingle with those of actual sight.

[1] Professor John Veitch, *The Feeling for Nature in Scottish Poetry.*

It is one of the offices of Nature that while we are humbled in her sight and feel ourselves of little esteem, and our successes and failures small things compared with the spaciousness of our surroundings and the sublime plan of the world, yet she too exalts and enriches us with her wealth of suggestions. On the silent hill we are in close contact with Nature, we feel a sense of union with a new life that is pure, noble, inspiring, a sense of exaltation, it may be of spiritual elevation, seeing that mountains have always possessed the power of evoking religious feelings, and influencing artistic and literary powers.

We love the hills for their strength, their endurance and their thrilling power ; they reveal us to ourselves and give to us a philosophy of life that is more dignified than that to be obtained in the valley. Days spent on the hills are remembered for hope and courage. Memories are among the greatest gifts bestowed upon us by the hills. How precious the Silences, and the memory of the evening stars, when we found ourselves repeating Blake's magical words :

> Speak silence with thy glimmering eyes,
> And wash the dusk with silver.

It is sometimes wise to turn away and close the eye when viewing certain stages of land or sky or cloud scapes, dawn or sunset pictures passing to highest expression, so that the perfect picture may be retained. Perfection, like happiness at its height, lasts but for a moment. To gaze fixedly at the most beautiful object in Nature is to diminish the pleasure. Ebb and flow is of the essence of life : it is better to catch the full flow and let the ebb pass by. "The art of life is to know when to look away, when to leave," said Arthur Symons ; and Ben Jonson put it this way :

> In small proportions we just beauties see ;
> And in short measures life may perfect be.

Strange experiences of body, mind and spirit may be ours on the high hill-tops. We are then free of the encumbrance of bodily weight and fatigue, mind and spirit are dominant, and there is a secret community between the high hills and our own inner heart. Problems resolve themselves, a right perspective is regained, spirit is restored to a keener edge and open to every impression. Truths inspired in such moments not only test and confirm past experiences, but make for us beacon lights for guidance in future days. The opportunity of obtaining such gifts is worth all the gold of Ophir.

This value of the mountain-top in men's lives has often been stressed. Gilbert Coleridge in *Some and Sundry* has a quotation from Mark Theodore Bourrit on the mountain-top as the place of reconciliation :

It is, in fact, the mountains that many men have to thank for their reconciliation with their fellows and with the human race ; and it is there that the rulers of the world, the heads of the Nations, ought to hold their meetings. Raised thus above the arena of passions and petty instincts and placed more immediately under the influence of Divine inspiration, one would see them descend from their mountains each like a new Moses, bringing with them Codes of Laws based upon equity and justice.

We remember the part that the mountain solitude and the " place apart " played in the greatest story of all time : " The mountains shall bring peace to the people, and the little hills, by righteousness." In placing the shrine of Apollo under the cliffs of Delphi, and his throne upon Parnassus, the Greeks testified to all succeeding time that they themselves attributed the best part of their intellectual inspiration to the power of the hills. And what lover of the mountains and hills would not endorse what Ruskin wrote of " The mountain Glory " :

They seem to have been built for the human race, as at once their schools and cathedrals ; full of treasures of illuminated manuscript for the scholar, kindly in simple lessons to the worker, quiet in pale cloisters for the thinker, glorious in holiness for the worshipper. . . . Great cathedrals of the earth, with their gates of rock, pavements of cloud, choirs of stream and stone, altars of snow, and vaults of purple traversed by the continual stars.

Often it may be that when resting in pure contemplative pleasure surveying some sublime or tranquillising landscape, stray thoughts from past reading come before us, especially as we ponder Nature's beauty and appeal, " the sense of a heart in things speaking to the heart of the wayfarer."

One such thought from Principal Campbell Shairp's *Poetic Interpretation of Nature* strikes a helpful note, namely, that as both Nature and the soul of man proceed from God, man must come to the spectacle with the thought of God already in his heart.

He will not get a religion out of the mere sight of Nature, neither from the uses it subserves as indicating design, nor from the beauty it manifests as hinting at character. Neither morality nor religion will he get out of beauty taken by itself. It is useless to seek in Nature alone what she never intended to give. What we get out of Nature depends on what we take to Nature. Nature is visible thought, and in Nature the Highest pours Himself out for our soul development.

At times we may be so conscious of the Feeling produced in us by Nature that we can tell immediately we are touched by its uplifting power. It is a real experience. We rest our faith in it ; and search the poets and the seers to confirm the experience, for their witness to the presence of the divine in human life is part of our enduring inheritance. " I am convinced there are hours of Nature, especially of the atmosphere, mornings and evenings, addressed to the soul," said Walt Whitman. Words-worth testified to it also. The exercise of that elusive quality which is termed Imagination—a combination of the intellect and emotion—has brought many, as it brought him, to a consciousness of mysterious presences in the sky and in the hills ; a great world that could only be comprehended by this quality that transcends mere reason ; or what Wordsworth termed, " reason in her most exalted mood"—a combination of reason and emotion; for where reason may fail, the higher forms of emotion—a kind of imagina-tive instinct—may be a reliable guide to truth. " The highest use to which Imagination can put this visible world," said Campbell Shairp, " is to gather from it some tidings of the world invisible." " Hope hard in the subtle thing that's Spirit," said Browning. " The development of the soul ; little else is worth study." And who is he who would dispute with Keats that " The world is a vale of soul-making."

In the following sketches the desire has been to convey some-thing of the pleasure of the pastime of hill walking, to interpret the atmosphere and Nature influence felt amidst these rolling hills and valleys where the burn-heads croon and the wild birds cry, and to tell not only the joy of companionship with Nature but with those who spend their days and win their livelihood amidst the open spaces of hill and moor and glen.

Happy are all who have full control of limbs and lungs, and possess the desire to enjoy all such exercises. Strokes of mis-fortune and physical infirmities often curtail the usefulness of the individual through no personal fault, and are a severe test of endurance, but for the most part there are compensations. There are still open, avenues to the contemplation of the beautiful in Nature, and the delight of sensing first impression of " atmosphere." And there is reading, and the reading of all great literature in its true poetic and spiritual content, is to raise the thoughts above sublimary cares and pleasures. So may we enter into full possession of our true self, and attain happiness and dignity although precluded from active service. In writing this book I have had all such in mind, as well as those separated by distance. May it assist to a fuller realisation of how much we owe of delicacy of feeling, culture and refinement to the gentle things of Nature appealing to ear and eye ; and to that world of the spirit, intangible but no less real, that lies around us in this wonder-land of Tweeddale, so rich in historic, literary and legendary lore.

The name " Tweedie," famous in local history, is unconnected with either the river Tweed or the commodity of that name. Its derivation is from a place in Stonehouse parish, Lanarkshire—Twedyn or Tweedie—which belonged at the time of the War of Independence to Finlay de Twedyn, ancestor of the Tweedies of Drumelzier. The fabric name " Tweed " arose early in the nineteenth century (1826) through the erroneous description in an invoice quoting " Scotch Tweeds " for " Scotch Tweels," despatched by Border manufacturers to London merchants. When the invoice arrived in London, the merchants considered the name " Tweeds " had commercial possibilities, and henceforth ordered " Tweeds " instead of " Tweels," with the result that the Border manufacturers wholly agreed with their London correspondents, and from that time Tweeds became popular, and the world trade designation is far renowned, the present demand for such goods exceeding the supply. Check tweed trousers, black and white, called " shepherd tartan," such as those worn by Sir Walter Scott, were first made in Peebles ; indeed this was the initial form of the manufactured article, along with that of the travelling cloak.

" Tweeddale Court," Edinburgh, was so named by the Tweeddale family—the Hays of Yester, Earls of Tweeddale (Neidpath Castle)—whose town house was situate there, being first built and occupied by Dame Margaret Ker, Lady Yester, daughter of Mark, first Earl of Lothian. Born in 1572 she married James, seventh Lord Yester, and bestowed the mansion on her grandson John, second Earl and first Marquis of Tweeddale, who defended Neidpath Castle against Cromwell's troops. The last of the family who resided there was John, fourth Marquis, and Secretary of State for Scotland, 1742–45. He died in 1762. The British Linen Bank occupied the property from 1792 to 1808, followed by Duncan and Alexander Cowan, paper-makers, till 1820, when it was tenanted, and later (1829) owned, by the present proprietors, Oliver & Boyd, Limited, publishers. Thomas Oliver began printing in or about 1778, joined a few years later by George Boyd ; and prior to settling in Tweeddale Court they were at Fountain Well, High Street ; Netherbow ; and Baron Grant's Close, High Street. The house was described as stately, with a fine old garden which descended by a succession of ornamental terraces to the Cowgate, where was the carriage entrance. A plantation of lime trees, shown in seven rows on Edgar's Map (1742), is mentioned by Defoe in his " Tour." The garden site is now partly occupied by the company's printing and binding works. The first branch Bank in Peebles was that of the above Bank, opened in 1825 under the agency of John Welsh, W.S., Sheriff Clerk of the County, and brother of Robert Welsh of Mossfennan. Sir Walter Scott, " R. L. S." and other Scottish authors were interested in this Bank with its romantic early history as a Linen Company, incorporated by Royal Charter in the year after the 'Forty-five, while the public mind was still agitated by the events of the recent Rising ; and the writer spent forty-five years in its Head Office.

Some of the chapters have appeared in whole or in part in various journals, magazines and Broadcast Talks, but such have been either rewritten or amended, so that all the material, including much new matter, appears in its present form for the first time. I acknowledge my indebtedness to the *History of Peeblesshire*, 3 vols., edited by James Walter Buchan, M.A., LL.B., and Rev. Henry Paton, M.A. (1925–27), representing the work of twenty-three contributors, which is a mine of information, while the earlier records and authorities have also been consulted, and are acknowledged in the text.

WILL GRANT

EDINBURGH, *July* 1946

DARLINGTON
PUBLIC LIBRARY.

I

TWEEDDALE HEIGHTS

GLENSAX, THE HUNDLESHOPES, GLENRATH

To get an idea of what Tweeddale is like, the best way is to climb either physically, or in imagination, to the summit of the hill ridges that abound on all sides, and survey the glorious scene.

The ridge of high hills to the south and east of Manor valley which includes the Hundleshope, Glenrath and Blackhouse Heights, Dun Rig and Stake Law, forms part of the watershed between Manor and Yarrow, and encircles one of the most beautiful glens in the country—Glensax, which until the beginning of the sixteenth century was part of the Forest of Ettrick, and as such was royal demesne.

It is possible to walk along the tops of these high hills without descending much below the 2,000-foot contour line. Beginning with the Drove road that rises from the Gipsy Glen, a mile and a half south of Peebles, we soon sense the allurement of this old track that winds like a green ribbon over the rolling hills by pine woods and heathery hill-tops. Looking Tweedwards we see the Hydropathic at Peebles, first built in 1878, like a Swiss chalet among the hills, Kailzie and the valley of Kirkburn, and the heights above Cardrona and Traquair, while up Tweed's silvery stream towards Lyne and Stobo there is a grace, a wild loveliness in the green vale amidst moorlands and hills that is always associated with Tweeddale. This old road to Yarrow and the English Border has many a charming viewpoint. From Dun Rig the county boundary goes along the watershed over Blackhouse Heights, Black Law, Broad Law and Megget. Northwards from Stake Law the watershed sweeps round the head of the Glen valley, and descends to Newhall Burn at the summit of the pass through which runs the road from Innerleithen to the Gordon Arms. The Quair Water runs northwards from the slopes of Dun Rig and Stake Law through the beautiful valley of Glen renowned among the Borders.

I

Reaching Dun Rig, at the head of the valley, we may complete the circle of Glensax by traversing Glenrath and Hundleshope Heights and arrive at Bonnington and Cademuir in the vicinity of the beautiful county town of Peebles. It has been said that the prospect from these hills is one of the finest in the Border country, for it includes a vast variety of hills. Great sweeping hills like Atlantic breakers become static, beautiful in contour, graceful in outline, diverse in colour, many of them rising sharply from the glens by which they are surrounded, some bare and rocky, others covered with grass and heather and bracken. Rivers, meadows and woodlands lend variety to the scene that satisfies the eye and kindles the imagination, not only with its natural beauties, but also with historic interest and romantic glamour. Indeed Tweeddale is excelled by few counties in Scotland, if by any, in the variety of its scenery and interesting historical and romantic lore. Every bit of Scotland, every mountain, hill and valley, every mansion, cot and farm, has its own story ; and so it is with this little bit of Border country that surrounds Glensax. The whole is comprised in the estate of Henderstoun, renamed Haystoun by the noted Tweeddale family of the Hays of Smithfield and Haystoun, who purchased the lands in 1635. The manor-house was built in 1660, as the armorial stone shows, and occupies a charming situation on a knoll overlooking Haystoun Burn, surrounded by fine old trees and homely parks. Sir Duncan Edwyn Hay, tenth and present Baronet, is one of the most popular and well known of Tweeddale lairds.

Newbie farm is overlooked by two pointed hills known as Newbie Kips ; and Newbie has a story that will last as long as any legend. About the year 1772 the tenant of the farm found that from time to time several ewes and hoggs were missing. Complaints also came from Grieston, Colquhair and East Dawyck. One day a sheep returned to Newbie with the Ormiston mark upon it. The clue was duly followed up, and the missing hoggs and ewes, so far as not already disposed of, were found on the farm of Ormiston (Glenormiston). It appears that Murdison, the Ormiston farmer, and Miller, his shepherd, engaged in their nefarious practice with the aid of a sheep-dog Yarrow, which they had trained stealthily to cut off the desired sheep, watch them till nightfall, and then, under cover of darkness, bring them to Ormiston. The Newbie shepherds easily identified the missing sheep, although the marks were defaced. A Peebles Burgh record of 27th July 1772 records that Murdison and Miller, charged with sheep-stealing, were " lodged in the vault of the steeple, which, being very insecure, needs to be guarded day and night. The Council orders new locks and a guard." They were tried in the Justiciary Court in Edinburgh before a jury, the trial starting on the morning of Friday, 8th January 1773, and proof continuing until five o'clock next afternoon. The jury were empanelled at eleven o'clock and dismissed at five o'clock on Sunday morning. Both accused were found guilty, and ordered to be hanged in the Grassmarket on 24th March. Objections were made to the verdict on the ground that it was signed on Sunday ; in the circumstances it was deemed " a work of necessity." This was the first time that an arrest of Judgment was moved for on that account. The Judgment was appealed against to the House of Lords, but the appeal was judged incompetent. Accordingly, sentence was carried out in June 1773, when, as narrated in the *Scots Magazine* of that time, the misguided farmer and his shepherd " showed signs of penitence and behaved as became persons in their unhappy situations."

It was to better purpose that Robert Hunter of Polmood set his dog Algiers, when not rounding up his sheep. This faithful animal, it was said, with money in a napkin tied round his neck, would be sent off to Lamington, ten miles away, for snuff, and refusing to pay any attention to passers-by, duly returned with the message executed. On another occasion a purse was tied round his neck ; the dog swam the Tweed, and brought back tobacco from the Crook Inn. It was also said that he could take a letter to Edinburgh and bring back an answer. His fleecy coat yielded a pair of stockings every year.

It was near Newbie, Dr. John Brown tells us, that he once assisted in " burning the water," after " having been on every hill-top from Muckle Mendick to Hundleshope and the Lee Pen, and having fished every water from Tarth to Leithen Water." And it was in Haystoun Water, so the local fishers will tell you, that a sixty-seven pounds salmon was caught, and embedded in one of its fins was a silver shield telling that the fish had been placed in the water in Spain ! The water bailiffs offered five pounds for the shield, but the fishers were coy.

The glen also enters into Border romance and minstrelsy for it is not unlikely that it was down the Glensax burnside that the lovers in " The Douglas Tragedy " travelled in the moonlight when they came from Blackhouse Tower on Douglas Burn, by bridle-path, up the Black Cleugh and over the shoulder of Dun Rig. The ballad brims with life and incident ; the hero carries off his beloved by night from the Tower, which probably belonged to the Douglas family—Ettrick Forest belonged to the " Good Sir James " in 1321-2. Then follows the deadly conflict in which the lady's father and seven brothers are slain—" the Douglas Stones," supposed scene of the combat, are in Risp Syke not far from the Tower—the maiden stops to staunch her father's wounds—the struggle between loyalty to her family and affection for her lover—the continued flight, and the tragic close :

> Oh they rade on, and on they rade,
> And a' by the licht of the moon,
> Until they cam to yon wan water,
> And there they lichted down.

> They lichted down to tak a drink
> Of the spring that ran sae clear ;
> And down the stream ran his gude heart's blude,
> And sair she 'gan to fear.

> " Hold up, hold up, Lord William," she says,
> " For I fear that you are slain ! "
> " 'Tis naething but the shadow of my scarlet cloak
> That shines in the water sae plain."

> Oh they rade on, and on they rade,
> And a' by the licht of the moon,
> Until they came to his mother's ha' door,
> And there they lichted down.

> Lord William was dead lang ere midnicht ;
> Lady Margaret lang ere day ;
> And all true lovers that gang thegither,
> May they have mair luck than they.

The Hundleshope Heights next claim our attention. The name means " Hope of the Houndswell "—grave, stern hills rising steeply from farm lands below. They lie to the south of the famous hill, Cademuir, with its hill forts (Cadhmohr, the great fight), whose story has been told by Dr. Christison in the Society of Antiquaries' *Proceedings*, vol. xxi, where will be found a description of the sixty-seven ancient forts in Tweeddale.

Prehistoric remains of Upper Tweeddale are very numerous, and many of the hill-tops have stone forts of circular earthwork, which add to the interest of the wayfarer.

For over two centuries the Gledstanes possessed Hundleshope, and many a fight they had with the Burgh of Peebles over the pasturage rights on Cademuir. In 1357 the owner was John " Trumble " (Turnbull), who had a charter from David II, said to include free isché and entry in the common pasture of Cademuir. His daughter married Sir Wm. Gledstanes from East Lanarkshire —of the Gledstanes of Cocklaw. Their territorial name was taken from an estate in Roxburghshire, and from them has been traced the lineage of the famous statesman William Ewart Gladstone, whose father, John Gladstones, obtained in 1831 a royal licence to drop the final " s." In 1303 its owner was William de Dureme, English keeper of the Royal Castle of Peebles, which disappeared soon thereafter, and the name " Castle of Peblis " is an early designation of the thirteenth-century Neidpath Castle, over the courtyard entrance of which is the crest of the famous Tweeddale family of the Frasers. (In 1618 Hundleshope became the property of Scott of Harden.)

There is an interesting note about Hundleshope that connects it with the 'Forty-five. David Scot, the last of that name in Hundleshope, was the Jacobite friend and kinsman of John Murray of Broughton, the Prince's Secretary, and Murray gave orders to him, prior to the Rising, to remove from his house at Broughton his strong-box, with its " papers of a very dangerous nature," in order that he might secrete it. The box contained " the Cypher by which I wrote to the King and Prince, with all the letters I had received, and copies of such I had sent, together with a short journal of all that had passed from the time of my being first engaged in the King's service, and likewise a full account of the whole, which I had made out that summer from my memory and the short journal."

The instructions were duly carried out, and the box was buried in the Hundleshope garden (now Hallmanor), and cabbages planted above it so that Scot might " free himself of any uneasiness he was under from having it in his house " (*Memorials of John Murray*, Scottish History Society, vol. 27).

Out of the Hundleshope Heights comes the Waddenshope Burn that falls in a succession of cascades from the bare heights through brakes of heather and fern, and deep birken glens till it reaches the pastoral valley and joins with Glensax Burn to form the Haystoun Burn. The former name was Walthamshope, which appears as early as 1262 on the occasion of a dispute between an early Saxon settler named Robert Cruik, or Croke, of Cruikston, and the burgesses of Peebles regarding the right of digging peats in the Moss, but where the Moss was no one seems to know. The lands of Crookston lie between Maddenshope and Hundleshope, spelt Hundwaluchishope in the deed of 1262 contained in *Peebles Burgh Records* (1165–1710), p. 5.

Waddenshope means Woden's Hope, and as Woden and Waltham are synonymous, and Woden is the Saxon for Odin, the chief of the gods in Norse mythology, it is likely that the Saxons lived in this valley before the Scandinavians came, and gave the name Glensax, Newbie being the Settlement. The Scandinavians probably arrived in Glensax by way of the Douglas Burn.

To the south of the Hundleshopes are the Glenrath Heights, a high ridge separating Glensax from Glenrath, the latter having a story that goes back to the morning of Tweeddale's history. From the summit of the ridge there is a far view down Glenrath at the entrance to which stands Woodhill, or Woden's Hill, a mound rising in the middle of the valley, 200 feet high, and 1,000 feet above sea level, fashioned by moving ice and moraines deposited by converging glaciers. On the top stood the traditional Castle of Macbeth, or Malbeth, the twelfth-century Tweeddale Sheriff; more probably the stones are those of a disturbed cairn of a British chief.

On all sides of Glenrath the hills rise abruptly, are high and steep, bare and storm-gashed; scree abounds with bracken and heather and grey-lichened stells, and the burn, after tumbling and brawling through rocky clefts, wriggles like a cobra along the floor of the glen, upon which converge no fewer than nine hill ridges. The outstanding feature of this long-drawn glen of wild and rugged grandeur is the evidence that abounds of primitive occupation by some ancient tribe. Cairns, circular settings of stones, carved foundations of huts probably made of turf or wattle and daub, extending for half a mile, prove that in early times a large population, probably of the Cymric tribe of the Gadeni who inhabited Peeblesshire before the Romans came, found a home in Glenrath—the Glen of the Fort—where now stands but a lonely shepherd's cottage at Glenrath-hope. Notes on the ancient remains in Manor parish and other districts of Peeblesshire are contained in vol. xxii of the *Proc. Soc. Antiquaries, Scot.*, while the volume for 1940-41 refers to the " Medieval dwelling sites and the primitive village of Glenrath," where excavations were carried out in 1939. The records of travellers, collected in Hume Brown's *Early Travellers in Scotland* before 1700, agree in describing the dwellings in Southern Scotland as very rude, with roofs frequently of turf or heather, coming down so low that sheep could graze on top of them.

It is wild hill country on the tops of the Hundleshope and Glenrath Heights, and I have recollections of bracing winter days there, experiencing the full blast of the icy north-west wind, compensated by fine visibility. Provided you are on the lea side of a dyke or pine plantation, there is a peculiar joy in listening to the fury of the wind as it raves across the hill-tops, and soughs through the deep dark glens, while on the rock faces of the cliffs it resembles most the thundering roar of an express train. Looking down from Hundleshope Heights into the dark ravine, we could see the partly frozen Hundleshope Burn that joins Manor Water opposite the Black Dwarf's cottage, and as we stood, a blast of wintry wind blew up the abyss and whistled about our ears. Springs, mosses, lonely lochans and peat hags were frozen, but we found one of winter's secrets in the exquisite colours of sphagnum mosses, caked and frozen as they were ; they glowed a mosaic of bead-work in pink and green, yellow and grey. At no other season does the sphagnum wear such captivating colours. Up to about 1823 a series of lakes filled the valley between Cademuir and Hundleshope which by some is thought to have been an ancient river course.

One of the commonest and sweetest names for a valley in Tweeddale is " hope." In Celtic it means a small valley between mountains ; in Iceland *hop* is haven—shelter ; in Anglo-Saxon *hof* is a farm and a house upon it, and in the Hopes we find the shiel or shieling, from the Norse *skali*, a shepherd's hut, and as Professor Veitch points out, the people who named the hopes built the shielings. The earliest dwellers in Tweeddale were of the Cymric branch of the Celtic and they must have been a numerous body.

Here among the Tweeddale heights and glens the world is shut out and forgotten ; here there is peace, where the solitude, the dignity and the silence of the enfolding hills may fill the soul ;

sheep bleat far up the hillsides ; the raven, the hawk and the heron fly over the heights, whaups whistle and peewits cry in the glen, and the fisher angles up to the very syke head. Here we may feel the thrill of the hills, and be charmed and nourished by a meditative spirit, enriched by that " subtle lore that Nature brings unto the reverential mind." Sunrise and sunset and the pearly grey of the weather-gleam lead to that attractive land of Faerie to which the Ettrick Shepherd pointed the way. Much there is to attract and inspire the hill walker to venture forth in search of Nature's gift in this part of Scotland's Southern Uplands, for :

> Scenes such as these . . .
> Compose the passions, and exalt the mind.

II

THE SECRET OF THE HILLS

HILLS are to landscape what inspiration is to poetry and style to prose, they give to it that arresting dignity and splendour that raises it above prosaic mediocrity. So it is that up here on the old Drove road we have mentioned, with its imaginative appeal and its stirring scene outspread before us, we feel that we may freely give ourselves the pleasure of endeavouring to solve the Secret of the Hills. That there is a secret, and a revelation, the wanderer among the hills knows only too well.

The westward outlook from this road includes the hills of Manor Vale. Near by is Newbie Kips, with a fringe of tall pines like spaced-out marionettes marching over the crest, a blue-and-white sky shining through the lacework. Northwards is a forest of larches, their winter glow as charming as their springtime glory, while from the valley below rises the sound of rushing waters. A delightful odour comes from the pine woods. Pleasant, too, it is to the foot to break the " bone " of the half-frozen turf, upon which zigzag markings speak of the amusing antics of the vole.

The winter colouring of the pastoral countryside on this day of atmosphere and sunshine has its own distinctive appeal, and it is interesting to observe the power of reflecting light possessed by the earth, and varied by different soils and by vegetation. Heather is a soft, velvety brown, bracken has a reddish hue and variegates the carpet of the hills ; under black dry-stone dykes snow wreaths form an unbroken line striating many a hillside, while in the valley rich red soil contrasts sharply with the vivid green of the half-ploughed field, the line of plough-land straight as a ruler. Colours abound also in the woods. A film of delicate grey is on a line of three single ash trees, lemon-coloured stacks bield the farm buildings and, sweetest note of all, a line of milky wood-smoke rises from farm cottages and trails across the olive-coloured pines.

Not only the eye is charmed, the ear also is captivated. A farm-yard symphony rises upon the still air—the jolting and creaking of a farm wagon, the cackle of fowls, the barking of a dog, the chopping of wood, a ploughman talking to his horses while he " louses " them, the champing of iron shoes on cobble-stones as they amble to the stalls and, nearer, a grouse rises and shouts his irritated cry, " Go-back ! Go-back ! Go-back ! Gurrh. . . ."

How good it is to stand upon the hill-tops and look down, listening to the sounds coming up from below. Or just to be among the hills, to feel their impress upon the spirit, to gaze on beauty, and to feel the same spirit. Beauty is eternal and its imprint remains as a possession for all time. " The spirit of man on Beauty feedeth " sang the poet-laureate Robert Bridges. It is a continual feast enjoyed by the walker who is also the nature-lover, a sacrament, if you will, in which feeling replaces thought. Not a step in the journey but has its replies. Beauty and music are on every side. Our greatest adventures are not those we go in search of. The things of beauty and of the spirit often come unsought.

With the declining day came a quick changing of the clouds. Westward the sky cleared—a pale blue ; clouds in the eastern sky turned mauve, and pine-tree tops were bathed in pink. But these colours changed momentarily, the evolution of the cloud-land went on. Storm clouds gathered in the west, leaving a weather-gleam on the southern front through which the daylight shone—green and blue and pearly white. But the storm clouds onwards rolled, and the window in the sky disappeared. Snow-ribbed hillsides of the glen became black as Erebus, and the wind blew, moisture-laden from the hill-top snows.

But, look ! the pageant of the daylight in the east is changing to a deep lavender colour, then purple, and gold. Advancing dark clouds are sailing onwards for seas of blue and white, in which float islands chased in gold, whose duration is fleeting. Sunset effects follow hard upon each other. In the gloaming a solitary hoodie crow sails down the glen, with thrice-repeated cry, a cynical bird, friendless.

Grey rifted clouds from the west vignetted new enchantments of form and colour. Over a western ravine, which held more snow than any of the surrounding hills, a strange unearthly glow of electric-blue light came through a break in the sky, bidding

"Good-bye" to the parting day, for the climax came at sundown.

Some strange interplay of forces was at work. The ravine became a volcano out of which rolled livid smoke-like mists, writhing and fuming as if escaping from the tortures of a nether region, and rushing to embrace with passionate arms the snow-white summit of "The Rig." In every hollow and ravine night was gathering : eastward the sky was a blaze of pink and purple, while across the intervening sky raced a panorama of tumultuous clouds—hills of cloud, rugged peaks, dark valleys, bluff head-lands, animals of grotesque shape with large ears and bulging eyes, wild cats and unicorns, then filmy fragments of cloud that trailed gossamer threads, followed by giant airships, more ships, a fleet of ships, argosy upon argosy, the fleets of heaven that know no haven.

Suddenly, through a rift in the racing clouds, a crescent moon appeared, and we bade our sister the moon " Good-evening," and our brother the sun " Good-night." The air grew chill, " hoar frost flightered down the night," it was time to descend from the high hills to the valley. But, no ! One could not leave the hill-top just yet. One became merged in the surrounding scene, embraced it with the mind, became a part of it ; it held one fixed, it fascinated.

With sunset, the stormy pageant ended, peace came to the hill-tops, the skies were at rest and Nature arranged the picture. She swept the sky clear, and painted it blue, and set a crescent moon above the highest peak, the apex of a vision built up of a few sweeping lines.

But, ah ! how fair and beautiful she looked :

> That fair orbèd maiden with white fire laden
> Whom mortals call the moon

" chaste, serene and meekly tender," but three days old, slim, shining, scintillating, girdled with pearl, and her light shone upon the windings of the river in the darkened glen, and they gleamed like strips of the silvery sky :

> Far up the sky with ever purer beam,
> Upon the throne of night the moon was seated,
> And down the valley glens the shades retreated,
> And silver light was on the open stream.

The stars also appeared :

Mortal though I be, yea ephemeral, if but a moment
I gaze up to the night's starry domain of heaven,
Then no longer on earth I stand ; I touch the Creator,
And my lively spirit drinketh immortality.

(PTOLEMY)

In such moments thought takes wings and soars to unimagined heights ; one spirit is over all ; spirit blends with the Universal Spirit, we become a part of the whole, one with heaven and the stars. That is the secret of the hills' fascination, the thrill of every experienced hill-man.

Man lives primarily by the resources of spirit ; and after strenuous climbing, the last heights are conquered only by the power of that spirit. Hours spent on the high tops have immortal value. They are often the Mount of Vision where human life and destiny are viewed against the background of the eternal values which are the thoughts and purposes of God. The icy blast may make the blood tingle in the veins, and we may return cleansed, and with a corrected perspective, that are part of the joys of exercise on the hills in winter, but in the glories disclosed may be felt a vigour in one's sense that is all spirit ; an inspiration and reassurance to the soul for further wayfaring on the plains, and the work of the days :

Thy work with beauty crown, thy life with love ;
Thy mind with truth uplift to God above :
For whom all is, from whom was all begun,
In whom all Beauty, Truth and Love are one.

III

SUNSET OVER TWEEDDALE

" Man's happiness, his flaunting honey'd flower of soul, is his loving response
to the wealth of Nature. Beauty is the prime motiv of all his excellence,
his aim and peaceful purpose."

(BRIDGES, *Testament of Beauty*)

THROUGH the revolving seasons in the glens of Tweeddale Nature paints for her lovers pictures of strange and
marvellous beauty. Her winter pictures are of exquisite
loveliness, for in winter Nature is a master artist however severe
—witness her work in the rigid woods, strung for music like a
harp, keyed up by frost, the water-courses and the hill horizons, the
mountains chiselled of marble, and the deep-blue sky ; and marvel
at the frost's own dazzling wizardry, snowflakes and crystals.
Nature has for long risen into an equality with humanity as a
subject of art.

If summer appeals to the affections and the sentiments, and
fosters enquiry and the art impulse, winter is a bracing disci-
plinarian, of heroic cast, addressing the intellect, and " reason
in her most exalted mood " ; and in winter the moon is more
triumphant, stars shine more brightly and the heavens are high
and great with an enlarged simplicity. While of the interplay
effects of winter winds and clouds and sunsets, no picture, either
in words or on canvas, can portray the daring of such artistry.
Wherefore, welcome, winter-time.

Our entrance to Newbie glen broke the silence. Sensing our
presence, a herd of black cattle in a far-off corner came bounding
along, heads down, tails up, only to draw up suddenly just short
of us, and stare enquiringly. Charlie, the pony, also came to
greet us ; and Robin was there, his glowing waistcoat vying with
the colour of the beech hedge. Robin was some distance away
on a paling stob, but he saw the crumbs we threw, and hopping
on each intervening post he came to rest opposite ; one glint of
his beady eyes, and in a flash he was off with a beakful.

Walking, we realised just how still and deep was the silence

in the glen. Gay winter sunshine reflected colours everywhere.
Gallant Scots pines contrasted with autumnal tints, red, yellow
and ethereally pale ; beech hedges made ruddy setting for
glistening furrows in garnered harvest fields ; but, most charming of all is the high corner of a field covered with white rime,
dotted with clumps of copper-coloured bracken, under a coppice
wood of larch, and over it all hangs lightly a soft blue gossamer
haze. A delicate part of the hillside this, and magical. Tinker
Bell is there with the Fairies.

The day calls for exercise, hill-tops are snow-crowned, but
low-lying parks are green, sunshine has tempered the frost, and
ploughing is going on in a near-by field ; real work this, that only
darkness terminates. There is little sunlight in the glen in winter,
the high hills shut it out, so we take the Waggoners' Road, or
locally " Lady Blair," being named after Lady Elizabeth Hay or
Hunter Blair (*d.* 1859) with whom it was a favourite for morning
riding exercise. It edges the pine woods, and skilfully winds up
and along the hillside and over the hills into the sunlight, to
where in years gone by woodmen plied axe and saw, and denuded
the hillside of her towering pines. Heavy must have been the
wagon loads, for wheel-marks are broad and deep, and glorious
must it have been to view, from some vantage-point apart, the
motion of gallant horses straining every muscle to breast the
steep incline.

Nature has been busy on the old track ; it is now a lovely
thing, storied, intimate. No part is more picturesque than the
nook at the five-barred gate where a spreading beech over-arches
it caressingly ; each gate-post embedded in wine-red leaves, the
lichen-covered wall sprinkled with powdered snow, and the
sides evenly heaped up to half their height. But it is the beech
leaves on the frost-bound track that claim our interest—there
they lie just as Boreas left off playing with them as they fell last
night—snatched in short eddies, each bunch of leaves, each single
leaf, so richly dight, arranged with perfect artistry ! Nature's
treasures are illimitable.

Ere the track breaks from the roadside, a fretwork avenue
of naked beech is seen, set against the winter sky ; and at the last
outpost one lone feathery birch, exquisitely beautiful, gathers to
herself the whole horizon. And where the track lies in the open,
a throng of bracken-shadows lines each green bank along the
track—plaided ghosts of noble horses in motion.

DARLINGTON
PUBLIC LIBRARY.

GLEN SAX

DARLINGTON
PUBLIC LIBRARY.

WROUGHT-IRON MINISTER'S GATE, SKIRLING

Old tracks are lovable things ; and if the journey's end be silver, the gold is in the going. Good it is to follow on, experiencing the emotion of the forward view. Yonder lies Tweeddale's comely county town clustered in the meeting-place of four broad valleys, a Royal Burgh since the time of King David I, and its name Peebles (Peblis) signifying in British " shielings, or the encampment of a nomadic people "—the Cymric tribe of the Gadeni—(Renwick's *Historical Notes*, p. 182), with an honourable history of strenuous endeavour and splendid achievement, friendly, independent, Scottish, with brave colours—red and

ARMS OF THE BURGH OF PEEBLES
(Matriculated in the Lyon Register, 18th December 1894)

white, and a gallant motto, " Contra Nando Incrementum "— increase by swimming against the flood—success by overcoming difficulties ; the armorial bearings showing three salmon in natural colours, one above the other, the centre one represented as swimming against the stream—going up Tweed to spawn, while the resultant increase is typified by the other two going downstream—swimming in the opposite direction. Tea-time is drawing near, a thin blue haze lies over the house-tops ; beautiful for situation, set amidst the rolling Tweeddale hills, whose high tops glisten white in the winter sunshine. So clear and vibrant is the air, I can hear the town clock chiming the hours.

As sunset draws near, the sky moves to a deeper blue ; already a faint blush gilds the east, and streaks of pearly cumulus fill the west. Two hours yet till the sun sets, but already things are happening. We hasten our steps, for our powers owe much of their energy to our hopes ; then suddenly, awestruck, we pause. What scene so terrible in beauty is this ! (" That beauty, which, as Milton sings, hath terror in it." Wordsworth's *Prelude*.) High above the horizon rises a billowy cloud, snow white, and in the centre of it a rose, pearly pink ; and the edges, jagged like Alpine peaks, are green and purple ! One of Nature's pictures, of which Whittier wrote :

> Aloft on sky and mountain-wall
> Are God's great pictures hung.

Followed immediately a sky of clouds wind-riven, later torn to shreds by elements that raged in fury high above. The panorama passed. The cold grew intense ; action was necessary, and yet, the sky pictures held one fascinated. Strange feelings filled the soul. Walking seemed an idle thing, inane, inexpressive of our feeling ; the urge was to climb, to mount, to see with vision unimpaired those mysterious happenings.

Up through the old plantation, over snow-covered twigs and trunks and the roots of ancient pines, over the boundary wall and up to the summit with its weird outcrop of rocks—here was vantage-point indeed, here was amplitude for sense and soul, whence one might parley with the helmsman of those stately argosies of air, and in such solitary places to " taste the pleasure of believing what we see is boundless, as we wish our souls to be " (Shelley).

Fell a great silence. The farther horizons were reflecting the roseate light of sunset, first one part of the heavens, then another ; cloud vessels were lit up as they passed through seas of pink and purple, green and yellow, to harbour in amethyst. Brief was their passing : highest impressions are fleeting : life is an ebb and flow.

Then the setting sun burst through—blazing with strange unearthly light, and instantly it shone upon a far-off hill-top, a rig or shoulder over Posso, and flood-lit a whirling spiral of snow as it danced along the rig, a ghostly sprite, and vanished into space. Another of Nature's pictures.

Far across the sea of hills the fires burned, casting lurid lights on every side. Edges of pearly, opalescent streamers irradiated fires of flaming gold. From this spring of radiance flowed a sea of blue and yellow and red gold. Again, the fury of the wind, and gorgeously tinted filmy tendrils became as fine lace-work, a golden comb, a spray of fire. One moment, and it was gone. The contending elements destroyed each other. Such glories of sunset are for a man to remember with delight all his days.

Soon the Frost King gripped the earth with icy fingers. Long after sundown a violet-and-crimson hue filled the western sky ; the familiar road up the glen shone faintly through the growing dusk, but the far-stretching road to the Hundleshopes gleamed like silver : it pointed westwards.

IV

THE MORNING OF THE YEAR

I. SPRING COMES TO THE GLEN

> " Look ! Look ! the spring is come :
> O feel the gentle air."

ALL seasons shall be sweet to thee, says the poet ; all are beautiful and inspire joy in the healthy soul—winter with its bright stillness, and its clear pastel patterns, spring with its birth of life and song, summer with its bigness and luxuriance of growth and autumn with its golden harvest ; the day reveals untold wonders and the night enfolds us in mystery.

Winter is much beloved by the hill-man because of its silence, in which he finds contact in a oneness with Nature, with the hills and the Eternal Spirit. It is a gift beyond the price of pearls. But to-day the silence of winter, when stilled was the voice of birds and running water, has gone ; it fled with the coming of the south-west wind :

> But now the North wind ceases,
> The warm South-west awakes,
> The heavens are out in fleeces,
> And earth's green banner shakes.
> (MEREDITH)

Early in the morning the spring came, heralded by an outburst of song. All the countryside is vocal once again ; the time of the singing of birds is come, and the voice of the turtle is heard in our land : all the woods are ringing with bird-song and the cooing of doves : over hills and parks and fields curlews and peewits are diving and circling, and the girding alarms of cock pheasants come from the brakes. Soon the woodlands will be changing colour, larches will burst into green like a cheerful song ; " the mountains and the hills shall break forth before you into singing, and all the trees of the field shall clap their hands."

Winter is over in the glen, and nothing now can hinder the

march of spring. Green and yellow will take the place of clarets and browns, olives and greys. High above the pine woods snow lies in deep patches, dyke-backs are filled, and above the line of trees mist covers the hill-tops. There is no sky or cloudland to-day. All is mist-crowned. But perhaps this is not all a disadvantage ; it keeps the attention to the lower slopes. As I pause, a pheasant alights on the top of the dyke in front of me, gives one glance, then glides down to the field below. A pair of blue-tits come to the rowan tree : thrushes, chaffinches, wrens, ousels, all are active, full of life and movement, the spring-time urge will not be denied. In the woods the turtle-doves are cooing, and over all the voice of the burn is dominant as it pours down from the melting snow in the corries far up the glen, laughing all the way—the gurgling laughter of spring. Yes, there is laughter in Nature for those in tune with the spirit of creation which is joy and laughter ; the laughter of the dawn on the rosy hill-tops, the laughter of the setting sun when it turns the streams to gold ; the stars also dance. Joy is the note of the Divine laughter ; and laughter like music runs through all creation. Soon the cuckoos and the swallows will be here again, and all the loveliness of spring and summer days.

The soft wind has brought rejoicing, and melting snow is making food once again abundant to birds and beasts of fur and feather. The storm-cock (missel-thrush) is louder to-day, whistling and shouting without restraint, in great abandon, from the topmost branches of the highest trees, challenging the woods, defying the mist and the voice of the waters. He is the trumpeter of spring.

There is a field on the hillside that is almost covered with sea-gulls ; they are remarkably silent ; strange that they should confine their attention to this one field. All are on the ground ; they have seen my approach ; they are all in the air, a great white cloud of flapping wings. Then as suddenly they plane to earth again ; once more the field is silent. Now they have moved into the far corner. There is something there they must find good to feed upon. I shall ask the shepherd. Gulls are clumsy on their feet, and not infrequently are frustrated in their endeavour to secure that upon which they fain would pounce. A robin comes out of a beech hedge, and struts over the snow till he comes to the melting edge ; he too finds something to eat. Rabbits find something also ; they scatter at my approach.

So light is their tread, they leave no trace on the snow surface. While I examine this the bird music in the copse-wood suddenly ceases. Strange it is that all the wild things, beasts and fowls of the air that here enjoy happy, free and unmolested life, are so shy of humans, and immediately fly away. Man is the enemy, yet how often we long to get near to them, with no evil intent. While I retrace my steps, the music starts again, as if they agreed—" Yes, he's gone." Most of the birds could not have seen me ; they must have been " wairned." " I feel it would be better if the birds would sing ; that gives me more conviction of the existence of joy than anything," wrote Grey of Fallodon in a winter of depression.

This copse is closely planted, it is dark and silent, yet the warmth of the sunlight overhead is felt within, and the sweet healing smell of the pines is as delicious as the incense of the wood smoke I inhaled as I came by the shepherd's cottage. Exquisite are the beech leaves in April, after the winter storms have bleached them ; a light shade of brown like a walnut shell ; the bud is alive in its sheath, and soon the new leaves will push off the old ones. But what a joy their bright colour has been during the winter months ; and who can forget the cherished memories of how the beams of the car lamps lit up the beech hedges of the country roads as we returned homewards after a day on the hills.

The trunks of the trees in the beech hedge are knotted and lichen-covered, grey and green. There is a friendliness about them, like old folks who have long since made their peace with the world, and so the gnarled branches twist and twine and embrace each other, and the tree becomes the stronger for it, so that it can withstand the wildest storms. Although they attain no great height, they are like little folks often strong and sturdy, and full of character. Moreover, what myriads of things they hide in summer. You never know how much there is in hedges. Under the thorns, dead leaves lie huddled, packed by the gales, and in and out the small wrens glide.

Proceeding farther up the glen, many noisy burns come bursting down from the mist-crowned heights. Here comes the young shepherd, broad-shouldered, strong, his cheeks the beautiful golden-brown colour of superb health—" clothed with the sun " is Alice Meynell's phrase ; only those who live in the sunshine and the open air can attain to that tint. As we chat I ask him about the sea-gulls. " Yes," he says, " now that you mention it, there's ay sea-gulls in that field—there must be some kind o' grub they get there, an' naewhere else ; na, I never see them on the hillsides, but in that field, aye, often ! " The recent storm ? " Oh, aye, it was bad, but we had the snow plough up the glen, and that helped ; we were able to reach the cottages lower down, and got stores as usual." Had he lost many sheep ? No, not many ; he rescued several that had slipped down through the snow into a deep narrow burn, and a few had been drowned. He had taken precautions before the storm broke. Experience teaches these wise young fellows to act quickly in such circumstances, and almost always they snatch security and victory out of the jaws of the devouring storm, to their own credit and their master's welfare. Theirs is a faithful service in which duty is nobly done.

The glen road is interesting ; little of it is seen at a time. The hillside falls away on the one hand down to the burn, and rises on the other to a height of over 2,000 feet. A " hoodie " crow flies down the glen uttering his raucous cry, hunting for dead sheep and lambs : the pariah of the hills. Conditions at the head of the glen are still wintry, and mist has flung his robe on shoulder-heights of snow. Here the winter silence seems to reign ; no, there goes the birling of a whaup, and his call is oft repeated, a far-away sound, eerie in the thick mist. Silence once more ; and again the curlews call. Yes, spring has come to the glen. A week ago it was here that I saw Reynard, in good condition, with a splendid brush, too near for shepherds' peace of mind, as he slunk between green patches on the snowy hillside.

There are no gladsome sounds of lambs up here, as lower down, where they are gambolling, jumping and running races. It is too early yet for Blackfaced ewes on high ground. Many are gathered at the head of the glen, where hay (" keep ") has been stored ; they do not bleat, they stand silently and stare somewhat piteously, patient mothers.

On the hillside, winter storms have taken full toll of the old trees. One stalwart pine, 150 feet in height and straight as an arrow, with foliage only at the top, has fallen against a giant silver birch, and together they form a triangle on the skyline. Pines and birch have little grip on Mother Earth. All around is evidence of the unequal fight with winter winds and giant trees. But to-day it is interesting to view the delicate tracery in birch and elm and oak and ash silhouetted against the grey mist.

We learn more about the trees in winter as we watch them through storm and frost and snow ; more intimate are the bare trees than in the glory of their leaves, and how refreshing the colours radiated in winter sunshine on silken beech and silver birch. Very near to the heart of Nature-lovers are the trees. " I know all the big trees, and have come to a social, silent under-standing with most of them," said Walt Whitman : and Victor Hugo, poet and philosopher, also felt a strange affinity with trees, a kinship and understanding. Woods and forests and the magic beauty of the world were an inexhaustible wonder to this mystical lover of Nature so gifted with imaginative vision, and " eyes of bronze-gold like the eyes of an eagle." Gautier compared him to a forest oak, and Flaubert declared he was " one of the Forces of Nature, and that there circulated in his veins the sap of trees ! "

The glen seemed a different place to-day in its misty shroud, but had one dropped down into it ignorant of the time of year, one would have known the season, for the whaups and peewits, the birds and the lambs would have proclaimed that spring had come to the glen.

The shepherd whose hirsel is on the low ground was going out in the darkening, accompanied by his young son, soon to become a shepherd and being trained by his father to the most important branch of the " hillside business "—" the laumin' tim'," when I met him at the field gate with his long crook. " Aye, it's the busiest tim' o' the 'ear ; I'm hauf through wi't noo, but we're at it frae mornin' licht till dark, an' whiles I'm up through the nicht as weel." And what of the storm ? " Weel, I'm no quite sure yet what effect it's had on the ewes, but the gimmers (two-year-old lambs ; mothers for the first time) aye gie a bit trouble. Them that has twa lambs often leaves yin o' them, an' if I'm no there, she jist leaves it ; ye see, they ha'na the mitherly instinct of the auld yowes." The two black-and-white collies sat with head erect and listened as if they under-stood it all.

When spring comes to the glen it means much genuine, honest toil to the shepherd. But then his philosophy of life is born out of the silences in which he lives, and the keynote of it is sincerity.

How we had longed in the darker days of winter for the

coming of spring, and watched for the first signs. Then came the " venturous harbingers," the first green of deciduous trees, and daffodils

> That come before the swallow dares, and take
> The winds of March with beauty."
>
> (*Winter's Tale*, iv, 3)

The scent of wood smoke was sweet and satisfying, but how we yearned for that first faint opalescent haze fragrant with the odour of muirburn (heather burning). At last we inhaled the first breath of spring-time air blowing soft from the moist hills, and knew that spring had come. " God renews his ancient rapture." The miracle of spring surprises us all ; yet, the promise is eternal. That which was dead shall be made alive.

II. SUNRISE AT LAMBING TIME

> " Never for me the lowered banner,
> Never the endeavour lost."
>
> (SHACKLETON)

Another lambing season among the Border hills and glens has come and gone ; once again park and haugh and hillside are dotted with the yearning ewe and the bleating lamb, and over all is heard the lamb's innocent call and the ewe's tender reply.

The arduous toil and anxiety of the shepherd are almost over for another year. It was upon this that I meditated one day as I walked up the glen, and thought of all that had contributed to the care and well-being of the numerous flocks around. Often all night long eager shepherds had been out among the sheep, " twisted shepherds, brown and old, full of memories " ; sturdy, athletic, eager men with weather-beaten face ; and young herds keen to learn the hillside business, all are in service at lambing time. It is cold during the dark hours of night when winter lingers in the lap of spring, so the shepherd is usually well clad in tweed and woollen garments. With his crook in his hand, and lambing satchel strung over his shoulder, in which to carry home the weak and the orphaned ones, and containing milk and medicine, he sets off on his rounds, now here now there, looking over the expectant ewes and satisfying himself that all is in order. And when the time arrives he knows no rest. Long days and difficult nights are his while lambing lasts, and he knows no sleep for long periods, and meals are at infrequent intervals.

Just then the shepherd himself came along, and we had a crack. " Man," he said, " I wish ye could write something for us about the sunrise at laumin' tim'. Ye ken it's as true to-day as it was twa thoosand years ago, as we read in the Book ' shepherds keep watch over their flocks by night,' first in the parks and the fields for the low-ground laumin' in early March, and later for the hill lambs in April. Then, it was for fear o' the wild beasts that came down from the hills ; now, of course, it's just that the puir beasts need a doctor, the same as ordinary folk, an' it's better to be on the spot when it happens. Aye, and it was to shepherds that the guid tidings o' great joy were first conveyed," he added.

And after we had talked for some time, and he saw I was interested in what he was saying, he spoke in confiding tones : " Man, it's stern wark ; warkin' away in the dark and the freezin' cauld ; often wi' drivin' snaw an' sleetin' rain ; warkin' amidst life an' death, among animals that ha'e nae language but a cry. I ha'e ma ain thochts then, an' they crood in on me. I wish I could tell ye o' them."

Truly the shepherd is Earth's foster-child, so close lives he to her, and to him she reveals her secrets and her tears. " Often," he said, " a sough o' dool draws ower me as death an' difficulty are met wi' in the dark hours when life is in the balance, when vitality rins low, and there lowers the solemn, unrelentin' sky ; often I'm sair owercome."

He paused for a moment. Then his eyes gleamed, and his voice grew tender as he continued, " But when the first faint flush o' dawn draws near—it's different ! "

The loneliness and the requirements of the shepherd's life demand that he should think things out for himself. The solitude of his days has gone to make him independent and self-reliant. This detachment and simplicity of life and outlook conduces to strength of character. But you don't often hear the shepherd's own point of view, because he doesn't talk much or readily. It's easier for him to think than to speak, and perhaps that's to his credit. He has a philosophy of life that is the fruit of experience in his work among the silence of the hills and the stars. His greatest pride is to see his ewes graze and his lambs suck, and he will risk his life to save a sheep without any thought of reward. He is acquainted with every aspect of outward nature, and knows the face of heaven and its varying aspects better than anyone else. Who so familiar with " the sky," the breaking light that heralds the sunrise, the quick change in the face of Nature as the morning hours draw nigh, when sheep begin to move, and break their fast on dewy grass ?　Alone with hill and sky, these airy sights are beings with a permanence of life, their very names are vital with a sense of personality, they people all his solitude, and thus within him grows the unworldly heart ; perchance the impassioned soul.

So with this experienced man with whom I talked, as he continued in the soft, lowland tongue : " What wi' the darkness o' the nicht, the hard wark, the want o' sleep, th' enfeebled vitality in sheep an' men in the oors afore the dawn, and that feelin' o' despondency whan things dinna gang richt, man, can ye wonder that we prize the risin' sun ?　Whan the first sign appears, whan the licht creeps ower the hill, the load somehow is lifted, and renewed strength and poo'er come into ma airms. I wish I could tell ye how much the sunrise means to us at laumin' tim'."

Sunrise to the Nature enthusiast may be the symbol of Eternal Youth, but to the shepherd as he watches and works among his flocks by night, it is the very embodiment of a new hope, a new courage, by which he is revitalised to pursue his labours in the saving of life among the sheepfolds.

V

DRUMELZIER IN THE LAND
OF MERLIN

PROBABLY no parish in Scotland has so much history and romance identified with feuds and raids, as well as wild beauty and mountain grandeur packed into its twelve miles by three as Drumelzier, pronounced Drummellyer.

It forms a narrow strip of territory bounded by Tweed, and divided from Manor and Megget by hills and ridges. In shape it has been likened to a boot, with Kingledores as toe, Polmood as heel, and the estates of Stanhope, Drumelzier and Dawyck forming the leg; the whole being dominated by an endless jumble of rounded hill-tops linked one with another by high broad-backed ridges, with deep cleughs and hopes cut by mountain torrents and raging streams, a wild, solitary mountain land with no fewer than twenty peaks rising to a height of over 2,000 feet, and burns innumerable flowing to every boundary.

The history of the old-world village and parish is linked with the families who lived there, and the parish kirk in which they worshipped.

The Frasers were the earliest known proprietors, although the Monks of Melrose were landowners in Upper Tweeddale in the beginning of the thirteenth century. Then came the Tweedies in the fourteenth century. King James IV was a familiar guest of James Tweedie, who promised faithful and lifelong service. The family prospered; of retainers they had many; they controlled the Tweed valley. Ambition knew no satisfaction; they quarrelled and fought with their neighbours. With the Geddes family their feud continued for many years, as did that with the Veitches of Dawyck.

From the end of the fifteenth century deeds of violence and of bloodshed were synonymous in Tweeddale with the name of Tweedie. Two Tweedies—William of Drumelzier and Adam of Dreva—were implicated in Rizzio's murder (9th March 1566), just as John Hay, Younger, of Talla paid full penalty for his part in Darnley's murder in 1567.

The King intervened in the Tweedie-Veitch feud, and in the Proclamation of March 1611 it is stated that all the other feuds except this one had been settled. For sixteen years before this, the King had been moving for peace among the lawless Borderers, and ordered some offenders to appear before him and his council at Holyrood. James Tweedie appeared and found caution for £10,000. Ten years later, in 1606, the King succeeded in getting the principal offenders over to his way of thinking, and James Tweedie is named as one of those " weill disposit to the peace and quietness of the estaite."

But the leopard cannot change his spots or the Ethiopian his skin. No more could James Tweedie. One summer night in 1612 he met the laird of Dawyck by the side of Tweed ; they fought, and Drumelzier fell, his blood staining the white blossoms of the hawthorn spray. Such was the nature of Border feuds and hatreds, that lasted for so many years.

The part that Drumelzier Castle played must have been an important one. It is a sixteenth-century building, and in structure shows the transition stage from keep to modern house. It is a stern, cruel-looking building still, with mortar as hard as the whinstone of which it is built, large windows, iron grilles and shot-holes below the cills. Doubtless this castle, set amidst such peaceful surroundings at the bend of the river, witnessed many a scene of tragedy and woe, as well as of feasting and of song. Could it but speak, what a varied story it would tell !

Very little remains of the fourteenth-century Tennis Castle overlooking Drumelzier Haugh, but the round tower and bastion were more completely developed here than elsewhere in Tweeddale ; a strong castle that played a dominating part in the life of the times. It is worth while climbing up the hillside to visit it. All who travelled this way in feudal times, says Dr. Pennecuik in his *Description of Tweeddale* (1715), must needs salute and pay homage to the haughty Baron Tweedie, or else go back the way they came, not without some marks of disgrace.

The Tweedie motto was " Thol and Think," a fine old family tradition, little emulated by the later generation of the sixteenth century.

The memorial to the warrior baron James Tweedie in Drumelzier kirk reads : " Hic Jacet Honorabilis Vir Jacobus Tuedy De Drumelzier." The weather-worn stone was replaced by a duplicate of the original, complete with inscription and coat of arms, in 1911 by Colonel Balfour of Dawyck, C.V.O., D.L., F.R.S.

The Tweedies were succeeded in Drumelzier by Lord Hay of Yester (afterwards Earl of Tweeddale) who held the estate for two hundred years. The Veitches held Dawyck from the end of the thirteenth century, and of this family was the late Field-Marshal, Douglas, Earl Haig of Bemersyde and Viscount Dawyck. His mother being Rachel Veitch. Naesmyth of Posso succeeded the Veitches in 1691, and in 1897 on the death of Sir James Naesmyth, fifth Baronet, the estate was acquired by the Balfour family.

One of the Veitches, William, who held the land in 1602, was called the " Deil o' Dawyck " ; no one ever survived his sword thrust. He was an intimate friend of the " Hoolet of Barns," who could see as well by night as by day, both men being of great physical strength, and took part in many of the feuds and raids in the Drumelzier hills and the English Border.

In 1930 Colonel Balfour made the experiment of importing capercailzie from Finland and Aberdeenshire, and setting them free in Dawyck Woods. Since then the birds have become definitely established and have spread throughout the county. In May 1937 two nests with eggs were found at Dawyck, and a nest and chicks discovered at Stobo in 1938. They have also been seen at Rachan, Glentress and Drumelzier. Capercailzie were strange to Tweeddale before Colonel Balfour's experiment, existing only north of the Forth and Clyde. Indeed they were actually extinct for many years, but were introduced to the woods of Taymouth Castle from Norway in 1837. A clutch of ptarmigan eggs was also tried at Dawyck, and one bird at least is said to frequent The Scrape. Both capercailzie and ptarmigan were common in the Megget district in the seventeenth century. The estate has roe deer and a herd of Japanese deer. The Dawyck heronry is of ancient date ; James IV got herons from Dawyck in 1497, and there are still nests on the estate among silver firs surrounded by a grove of beech and sessile oaks.

To-day the collection of trees and shrubs at Dawyck is perhaps unequalled in Scotland ; it is a Mecca for all arboriculturists. Linnaeus, the famous Swedish botanist of whom Sir James Naesmyth, second Baronet, was a pupil, is believed to have visited Dawyck. Among famous trees are Pacific Coast conifers, such as Sitka spruce, Western hemlock and Douglas fir, planted from 1840 onwards, beech and sessile oaks of 1720–30, and the well-known Dawyck fastigiate beech, late seventeenth-century silver firs and survivors of the original 1725 larches—"the oldest larches in Scotland," the Dunkeld larches having been planted in 1738 (Loudon). The specimens of *Picea Breweriana* from the Siskiyou Mountains of Western North America grown at Dawyck helped to save them from extinction. There is also a fine collection of miniature rhododendrons, of which Colonel Balfour was very fond. This noted arboriculturist died on 2nd February 1945. Stobo Castle is also famous for its fine trees, and of the ten gean trees, visible from the public road ; the largest had a spread of branches 70 feet in diameter, a girth of 10 feet and a height of 64 feet, twenty years ago.

Drumelzier Kirk on the banks of the Powsail Burn was founded more than a thousand years ago, and its walls were old at the Reformation in 1560. Its history has been told in *The Church of Drumelzier*, by Dr. Gunn (1931). Here are a few items from the records (1531–1930). Evidently a relic of sun-worship still survived among the inhabitants in early days for there was trial of those who in 1598 made " bane-fyres " on the hill-tops at Beltane. The persecution of witches and warlocks, in which hundreds were put to death, continued for many years in the district. When the King took a hand in subduing Border raiders he summoned the Tweedies of Dreva and Drumelzier and Veitch of Dawyck to meet him and the Privy Council at Falkland (1600) : and John Tweedie and his retainers had to place himself in Drumelzier Castle, and William Veitch to do likewise in Dawyck Castle. Fifty years later Cromwell appears and Neidpath Castle is captured : the Drumelzier minister is " in a fleeing condition " for two months " because of the English putting garrisons in the country." Steps are taken to prevent Conventicles of Covenanters in various houses in the shire (1674).

Sabbath-breaking occupies much space in the records—carrying a handsaw from one parish to another ; reviling the Kirk Session and calling them a parcel of false knaves ; killing a fish with a stone and riding into Tweed on horseback to take it out —fine and imprisonment. This happened not during the prevalence of Presbytery, with which Sabbatarianism is usually associated, but during Episcopacy (1673). One of the elders forgot it was the Sabbath day, entered his barn and began to thresh. He was sharply rebuked and exhorted to be more circumspect, and suspended from the eldership for seven months (1732).

Henry Calderwood of Polmood also forgot the day, and lead peats on the Sabbath.

1703 : " Drink to be sold on Sundays to country persons only between sermons. No shopkeeper to sell pipes, tobacco, candles or other merchantware except for the sick, under penalties." 1707 : " 7/– to a poor scholar to buy shoes, and 2/– to buy the Book of Proverbs for him." (The Book of Proverbs and the Shorter Catechism were once bound together and systematically taught in school in Scotland, for our forefathers insisted upon religious instruction, believing that all learning must be hallowed by the Word of God, and this received testimony in the character and personality of our ancestors. But the Education (Scotland) Act, 1945, makes no provision for religious instruction, although there are certain safeguards !) 1714 : Two trees from Dawyck to make a bridge over Drumelzier Water, £5 : 16/–. 1725 : Bridge over Stanhope Burn for children on the west side to go to John Batie on the east side for education, £10 Scots. 1742 : Dawyck suppressed. (A chapel was built on the site of the old church in 1837, in which are the original font, the old bell founded in 1642 and memorials of Dawyck lairds.) 1745 : Sunday, Nov. 3. A party of Prince Charlie's Highlanders marched from Peebles through Stobo and Drumelzier. At Peebles, where they camped in the field west of Hay Lodge, they compelled the mills to be set agoing to provide meal for their commissariat. (Tradition asserts that Eddleston Mill (Kirktoun Mill : *Blaeu's Atlas*) also was kept grinding all Sunday for the same purpose.)

In 1726 a schoolmaster was appointed " as he had a good hand of write, and skill in arithmetic and music, could teach Latin and sing common tunes " ; but alas, four years later he is accused of going to Peebles and drinking there for several days. In reply he said he had been " stopped at Stobo by the bigness of the water, which was true." He is " admonished to walk circumspectly." 1738 : Rebuked at intervals for being drunk and neglecting his duties. 1742 : Drunk at a penny-wedding, and warned. 1743 : In a similar condition called and made outrages at Glenholm manse and Drumelzier manse, and is reminded of previous warning ; craved time " to take up his defences." 1749 : Dismissed from all his duties, schoolmaster, Precentor and Session Clerk. Six months later, said he was unwilling to demit on account of the circumstances of his family. 1780 :

THE SLOPES OF DRUMELZIER AND RIVER TWEED
ARLINGTON

THE RIVER TWEED AT CARDRONA, NEAR PEEBLES

PUBLIC LIBRARY.

" An assistant and successor appointed to the old schoolmaster on account of his age." He had evidently reformed.

On 30th October 1702 the minister of Drumelzier, Patrick Russell, is deposed on confession of immorality. On 8th November 1711 the sentence of deposition is taken off by the Synod, and Mr. Russell, after exercising his ministry in London for some years, builds a centre for Scottish Presbyterians in London, resulting in the erection of the Chapel in Crown Court, Covent Garden, completed in 1719. His successful ministry in London lasted for thirty-six years. He was pious, humble and sincere and much respected. Edward Irving ministered to this congregation at a later date.

1814 : Drumelzier schoolmaster's salary raised from 300 to 400 merks—£22 : 4 : 5. Fees 2/6 per quarter for English, 3/- if writing is added ; 4/- for arithmetic, and 5/- if Latin added. 1730 : £4 Scots collected, upon Petition by College of Physicians, to General Assembly for voluntary contributions in all the parishes in Scotland towards erecting a hospital for maintenance of poor diseased people, the Physicians being willing to give the best of their skill, freely for their relief. Here was the beginning of Edinburgh Royal Infirmary. 1737 : Collection made annually to new Royal Infirmary or Surgeons' Hospital, as it was called. 1784 : Collection made towards cost of translating Old Testament into Gaelic. 1791 : Drumelzier and Glenholm jointly bought a tent for use at Sacrament seasons ; formerly one borrowed from Broughton. The General Assembly on 21st September 1746 " desires that the Sacrament of the Lord's Supper be celebrated in every church, not once, but twice every year." 1838 : The General Assembly maintained the spiritual jurisdiction of the Church to be independent of all State control, by a majority of 183 to 142.

At the Secession of 1843, when 451 ministers seceded from the Church and 752 continued within it, the ministers of Drumelzier, Tweedsmuir and Kirkurd " went out." The next minister of Drumelzier was the Rev. John Taylor, minister of Lachine, Montreal, whose ministry extended for 22 years, followed by Robert Meiklem, 7 years, John Hume Tod, 3 years, William Milne, 23 years, Munro Somerville, 16 years, N. G. Kesting, 10 years, and the appointment of Gilmour Neill in 1928, which concludes Dr. Gunn's survey. Mr. James Veitch the present beadle and local factotum (1945) has pulled Drumelzier Kirk bell that summoned the parishioners to worship for over fifty years. Church attendances to-day are as poor in rural districts as in towns. "A finer type of men, more honest, more independent, more hard-working than rural workers it would be hard to find anywhere ; but they are no longer great church-goers," states the present minister of Drumelzier, Rev. G. D. Sempill (*Scotsman*, 3rd November 1945). The village hall was erected in 1923.

The "trials" of a minister before appointment to a parish in the mid-seventeenth century were no casual affair. Before appointing David Thomson to Dawyck (1656) his "trials" had included "several sermons before ministers, texts to handle, theses to defend and exercise with the Presbytery. He had now to deliver a popular sermon : to discourse on the Babylonian Captivity ; to expound the 110th Psalm in Hebrew ; to expound passages in the Greek New Testament *ad aperturam libri* ; to answer catechetical questions in divinity ; and give the meaning of difficult passages in Scripture. The Presbytery was satisfied in them all."

The manse and glebe were conveyed to him by deliverance of earth and stone in presence of witnesses.

Foaming white were the sna' bree waters of the Powsail Burn when I took to the glen that stretches up into the hills from Drumelzier. Turbulent, tumbling, tossing, the sound of the waters was loud in the glen, reverberating among the higher hills of the Drumelzier mass—Pykestone Hill, Long Grain Knowe, Glenstivon Dod and Drumelzier Law. The Powsail is at all times companionable, and the glen is unequalled in its charm of wild seclusion, its panorama of solemn grandeur, its natural beauty. In sunshine the waters of this "burn of the willows" shine and sparkle like clusters of precious stones—it is the most beautiful burn in Tweeddale.

In former days Powsail drove three mills, was the companion of the village school, the post-office, the registrar, the blacksmith and the joiner, and, after saluting the manse and the kirk, joined the silvery Tweed ten miles west of Peebles.

In all the interests of the village Powsail had a part. The children learned much from it, and doubtless its message crept into the dominie's lessons and the minister's sermons. Then there were weavers, tailors, masons and smiths, but all have gone from the village now, as well as the former sweet names of the burn—"Metsyllopburn" in 1511, and "The Water of Cossalays" in 1320. In 1675 the parish kirk had 120 communicants as compared with Dawyck 60, Broughton 150, Tweedsmuir 240, Stobo 360, Manor 260, Kilbucho 200, Glenholm 300, Newlands 340, Linton 320 and Traquair 360. How much more populous were the country parishes then than now !

Both the traditional meanings of Drumelzier are eloquent— " the bright or glancing ridge " and " the ridge of Meldred," the latter built upon the traditional account of the death of Merlin at the hands of certain shepherds of Meldred, a princeling of the district, and one of the earliest owners of the lands.

Meldred's name is the first associated with the district, and connected with it is the story of a strange mystic figure, Merlin, Merlin Caledonius or Merlin the Wild, not the Merlin of the Arthurian legends, who, losing his friend Gwenddoleu in battle at Caledon Forest (573), took to the Drumelzier hills where he roamed sore at heart and despairing, yet fascinated by the spirit world in the hills in which he consciously dwelt, pondering the old Druidic Nature-worship, now undergoing contact with the new light of Christianity, and speculating upon the future life of his friend.

Among many traditions and legends connected with the bard is one that he met St. Kentigern, who, as we shall see in subsequent references, had an intimate connection with this upper district of Tweeddale, and gave him his blessing, and the Cymric poet became his partial convert.

But as Merlin took his way among the hills he was set upon by Meldred's attendants with stones and staves, and, stumbling in his going, he fell from the high bank of the Tweed upon a sharp stake used by fishermen, which pierced him through the body, so that he died, and his grave is by the burnside east of Drumelzier Kirk where Powsail joins Tweed.

The name Drumedler (Drumelzier) appears in an interesting document, the " Divise de Stobbo " or " The Marches of Stobo," to which previous reference has been made, dated about 1200, preserved in the Chartulary of the Bishopric of Glasgow (Professor Veitch, *History and Poetry of the Scottish Border*, vol. i, p. 253), which would appear to settle the etymology of Drumelzier as Drum Medler or ridge of Medler or Meldred.

If certain places retain the spirit and atmosphere of former associations, then the spirit of Merlin, poet and priest and " the fosterer of song among the streams," dwells amidst the Drumelzier hills, and along the valley of the Powsail, " a mysterious spirit world," as Professor Veitch describes it, " that Merlin felt was about and around him." John Buchan also treats of Merlin in " The Literature of Tweeddale " (*History of Peeblesshire*).

Here it was that he wandered in the woods of Caledon in the late sixth century. His gentle, pious, Nature-worshipping spirit fills the moorlands and glens. It breaks in upon the unconscious mind ; no one returns unaffected from a walk or a pilgrimage up the glen. Merlin's prophecy is fulfilled in that his spirit meets with all who would come here. No place is more suitable for meditation than the valley of this beautiful water ; and no mountain more all-surveying than The Scrape, to which we shall now make our way.

The woodlands ring with bird-song, crying snipe and twitter-ing linnets are on the moors, the odour of spring is in the scent of muirburn. The floor of the glen is a bieldy place with its stells, drystane dykes and boulders, and its line of beech and birch, lime and sycamore, beloved of bees, their buds swelling with the urge of spring and soon to be burgeoning ; but ash buds still are black, though March has long since fled. Deep calls unto deep in the notes of the burn, where the gathered volume pours over shelving rocks into stony depths and rises in foam to join the onward rush, varying in tone from that of the speaking voice to the sound of thunder in the deeper falls.

Out on the hills scattered rowan trees set against a brown heathery background have a blue-grey aspect in the mist-coloured atmosphere, and the shooters' path winds invitingly up to the butts and over the hills.

There is no sunshine to-day to make sparkle and shine the sprays of fountain bubbles dancing on the stream, no light to grace the glamour of spring-time greenery, no greenwood elves or burnside fairies ; it is a grey day on the hills.

In this Land of Merlin, the Scrape Burn joins the Powsail a short distance up the glen, a merry dancing stream that boasts of trout in deep pools under heathery banks, shingly stretches and foaming cascades. Wild duck rise from the reeds, the drake's rich colours glowing vividly. Grouse are active, Black-faced ewes wait their time, sheep bleat and plovers cry.

Spring is here in the varied colours of the hillsides, in the echoing notes of whaups and peewits, but snow lies in the corries, and high up by the burnside rowan trees rock-rooted are blenched and bare, showing wounds of winter warfare in branches slashed and bruised, and forked fragments poised on upright limbs. Still and lifeless they appear to-day, swept by the spray that leaps upon them in passing, kissing ferns and wild-flowers hidden in the banks.

Two infant ash trees set high upon the brown hillside are as tiny clouds of ashen grey—wandering fairy spirits that safeguard the glen. Under The Scrape the burn is jubilant, cascades are numerous, the waters speak in a sound of beating tomtoms. The burn is in a friendly mood to-day, a great companion. A Highland solitude is in these wintry southern uplands, but still the burn calls us. Where does it rise ? Let us follow. The broad valley contracts to a torrent-riven cleugh. Water is pour-ing from holes in the clayey hillside. These are outlets of the tunnelling made by moles, so the hillside is drained with the aid of the little fellow who loves to make his own monument. Deeper becomes the gully. Snow lies in banks at the 2,000-foot contour line. Here an avalanche has slipped and covers the burn ; a deep corrie is snow-filled to the brim 50 feet deep. Birds are few in those snowy wastes above The Scrape. Sud-denly a whaup sends his memory-haunting call across the silence, and with the call the mists descended, and everything is blotted out. There was still the burn for guide. Nearer the source, in Posso Moss, above the Craigs, the burn has many underground channels through which it croons. Springs bubble up every-where : to-day the place is waterlogged. Peaty hags drip water on the shingly beds. Out of the mist comes the querulous crying of a solitary gull, disturbed in a feast of mountain hare ; a plover calls : grouse threaten in defiant tones—" Go-back ! Go-back ! Go-back ! " Momentarily the mist cleared, revealing indistinctly what is really one of the finest panoramic views from this point of the Drumelzier hills.

I have often found joy in this wonderful prospect from the heights above Dawyck Woods, and had borne in upon me how good it is to preserve alive that sense of wonder and of apprecia-tion of the divine beauty and mystery of Nature, because there is always the dread lest the day would come, as it frequently does come, when this sense would lose its acuteness, become dulled, blunted through familiarity, and the passing years :

> The foot less prompt to meet the morning dew,
> The heart less bounding at emotion new.
>
> (ARNOLD)

Much can be done to counteract this, not only out of doors in contemplative observation, but under the influence of poetic minds, for though " we may refuse what poetry has to give ; yet under its influence serenity returns to the troubled mind, the world crumbles, loveliness shines like flowers after rain, and the further reality is once more charged with mystery " (Walter de la Mare). In this connection we may not, of course, escape the riddle as to the correct interpretation of Nature, of which there would appear to be two schools of thought among the poets. The one headed by Coleridge holding that Nature is an inanimate thing, a clod, and that the poet's interpretation of it is merely the interpretation of his own soul—the subjective view : " We receive but what we give, and in our life alone does Nature live." The other led by Wordsworth holding that Nature is a " living Presence " external to man, and in no way the creation of his own mind, a bodily image through which the Sovereign Mind holds intercourse with man—the objective view. It may be, however, that the truth is in neither of these views. The philosopher would tell us that Nature is not a clod ; neither is she a living thing, except to a percipient ; that we only know a subject-determined object, and an object-determined subject. Of what an object is without a percipient, and *vice versa*, we may be utterly ignorant. When the synthesis between percipient and object is perfect, we have beauty, which, when the object is Nature, means the " poetic interpretation of Nature " such as we have in the treatise of Principal Campbell Shairp, and in the mind of Wordsworth, as expressed in *The Prelude*. And what delight for thinking minds there is in the thoughts on Nature scattered through that divine philosopher Thomas Traherne's *Centuries of Meditation*.

After these reflections on this difficult subject let us continue our walk. " The Scrape " is a round-backed mountain " scraped " bare (2,347 feet) on the border of Manor and Drumelzier parishes, consisting of grey wacke, veined with quartz, dominating the landscape around Stobo and Dawyck, and equidistant between Posso in Manor valley and Drumelzier on Tweed. In a Charter of 1315 of the Barony of Meneris (Manor) by King Robert the Bruce, " The Scrape " is named " Crapislaw." Crossing The Scrape is the same old Drove road that comes over the Pentlands through the Cauldstaneslap (Chapter XX), thence by Linton, Newlands, Lyne, Stobo, over The Scrape and Dollar Law, to

Cramalt in Megget, Winterhope and Birkhill, and so to Eskdale and the markets of the South.

It is variously named, the "Rievers," "Raiders," "Moss-troopers," also the "Thieves" Road, after these plundering banditti who frequented it. In Tweeddale it is frequently called the "Hielandman's" Road, from the Highland drovers, shepherds, pedlars, cadgers and wayfarers who used it. Looking down upon it from some of the neighbouring heights, we can trace it for long stretches, in wavy lines, far-spreading, silent, free, with several branches and deviations that were invaluable for escape to drovers when trouble was anticipated. Along the east side of The Scrape above Posso, and over the west side of Dollar Law, the old track can be easily followed. "The spur of Scrape was called by the country people the Deid Wife, for there an Irish woman, the wife of one of Montrose's followers, had been killed by the folk of the place after the rout at Philiphaugh" (*Burnet of Barns*, p. 51). Hence "the Deid Wife's Grave" above Lour, on the old track.

As to the name Dollar Law, "A facetious old herd" says Captain Armstrong (1775), a local historian, "gave me this strange etymology : that the country folks, in pursuit of some English depredators, overtook them on Dollar Law, and being defeated, were heard to mourn their hapless fate, 'Dool! for evermair.'" So it came to be called "Dolefu' Law," now Dollar Law.

Keen as the north wind can blow on the old Drove road through the Cauldstaneslap, it is keener by far on the exposed ridges of these Tweeddale Heights where wind and rain and hail blow with nipping force, to meet which we needs must "stiffen the sinews, summon up the blood" and join battle in a spirit of like freedom and austerity, or else cowardly turn our backs to the storm.

> Come ; and strong within us stir the Viking blood,
> Bracing brain and sinew ; blow, thou wind of God.
>
> (KINGSLEY)

But the chief thrill as we tramp along this interesting old road on the high hill-tops, lies in the fact that it was used hundreds of years ago by drovers and cattlemen going to and from the English markets, and by Border raiders and blackmailers and a great host of travellers who used no other road to Yarrow and Ettrick, Eskdale and Liddesdale. Still it retains the marks of its ancient usage ; still it is used by shepherds bringing sheep over from Cramalt and Winterhope in Meggetdale ; still it is ours to-day for pure recreation and delight.

Kings and queens also travelled the old Drove road. " The King might come the Cadger's road." The Jameses knew it well. They were as well known in Tweeddale as the present Royal Family is on Deeside. James IV travelled it from Linton Roderick (West Linton) to Cramalt for the hunting, which was enjoyed by many monarchs up to the time of Mary Queen of Scots, who along with Darnley was in Megget in August 1566, but they got no hunting on that occasion—the raiders had driven off the deer ! A Royal Court was held at Rodono with a view to preserving the sport in Megget. Pitscottie says that James V and 12,000 nobles and gentlemen of Scotland, including the Earls of Huntly, Argyle and Athole, who brought their deerhounds with them, killed eighteen score of harts in Meggetland (1530). In the time of Lesly, the historian, the Henderland district was then covered with woods that afforded shelter to the largest stags in Scotland ; but hardly a tree grows there now.

In these hunts the shooting of deer was forbidden by Scottish statutes and Royal orders. The deer were driven into lateral valleys where the hunters had taken up position with their Irish greyhounds, and at the appropriate moment the hounds were unleashed and the sportsmen exercised their skill with bow and arrow. Great gatherings lasting several days were accommodated in tents, and the Chamberlain of James V enters £3 for transporting pavilions from Peebles to Cramalt. The food was on the lavish scale common in those times, cooked in the open —pots and kettles boiled, spits kept turning and winding with variety of cheer : venison, beef, mutton, goats, kids, hares, fresh salmon, pigeons, capons, chickens, partridges, muir-coots, heath-cocks, capercailzie, ptarmigan, and there was ale, claret, sack and potent " aquavitae." These expeditions, that sometimes included jousting and sports in presence of gentle ladies and illustrious visitors, were imposing and delightful gatherings much favoured by our Scottish kings and queens accompanied by large retinues —nobles and earls, knights and squires, huntsmen, grooms and attendants in great numbers.

James V in his campaign against the rievers, fatal to Scott of Tushielaw (" The King of Theivis ") and Johnie Armstrong of Gilnockie, followed the Thieves Road up the Powsail Burn and over Craigierig in Meggetdale. "The Royal Raid," one of Wilson's *Tales of the Borders*, gives a traditional account of the capture by the young King, of Cokburne of Henderland, the noted rebel, and of his execution. Like other Border lairds he was engaged in English intrigues and had brought Englishmen to aid him in quarrels with his neighbours—he had brought certain Englishmen to Glenholm for some treasonable purpose —and his partners in guilt were Stewart of Traquair and Veitch of Dawyck, who gave sureties for their good conduct. Both Cokburne and Scott were taken to Edinburgh and tried, but Armstrong was hanged without trial on the spot where he met the King (Pitcairn's *Criminal Trials*). Cokburne and Armstrong are commemorated in ballads. Nor do we forget that it was the Thieves Road with its branches down the side of the Powsail that, on 15th December 1591, Watt Scott of Harden and 200 accomplices, servants and tenants of Sir Walter Scott of Branxholme, travelled to Drumelzier, and stole from the Tweedies 4,000 sheep, 200 cows and oxen, 40 horses and mares, goods valued at £2,000, "togidder with the haill insicht and moveablis of their tennentis houssis." But Sir John Edmestoun of that ilk, cautioner for Branxholme's transgressions, was ordered by the Privy Council to pay the full amount of the damage. Long before those days, however, a thousand years earlier, here amidst the silence of the Tweeddale hills, in that far-off age when Paganism first met Christianity, Merlin singing his wild songs, in the morning of the world, saw weird sights, strange forms o' morn, shapes in the weather-gleam that silent moved along the rim of the dim world that engirds the hills, and had his first vision of Beauty undefaced and Truth undimmed. His is the spirit that pervades this land to-day, if only we may apprehend something of its mystical and spiritual glamour.

To see the dawn glow through on a better world, and better men and women in it, who would not a pilgrim be, in this Land of Merlin, that lies adjacent to Scotstoun, the ancient home of the Scotts of Buccleuch and Soonhope, the Border cradle of the Kers.

VI

THE KER FAMILY : SCOTTS
OF BUCCLEUCH

SCOTSTOUN, SKIRLING, BROUGHTON HEIGHTS

THE first Ker in Scotland is found in Tweeddale before the year 1200, in the reign of William the Lion.

He is " John Ker, the Hunter, at Swhynhope," and his signature testifies that he gave witness regarding the bounds of Stobo Manor. Probably he was a Briton, deriving his name from Caer, a fort ; and the fort situation still remains in Soonhope.

Two centuries before then, the name is found in the Norse Saga, narrating the valiant deeds and voyages of " Kari " the Icelander. No link has been found between the Border race of Kers and any Norman ancestor. The first record of the name in England is that of " Robertus de Kari " and " Johannes Kir " in thirteenth-century handwriting in the Liber Vitae of Durham.

Kar, Ker, Kerr, Kerre, Car, Carr, Carre, Cor, are Celtic and Gaelic forms of the same name found in Scotland, Ireland, Cornwall and Brittany. Car is not the anglicised form of Ker, but the Border pronunciation (Car or Cor) of Ker, just as Elliot may be pronounced " Allat," and my own maternal Border ancestry of Pender pronounced " Pandar " or " Pondor." Some hold that the root of Kar or Ker is to be found in the Sanskrit, the word being traced in all languages having that common origin.

The Ker clan spread quickly, for by the middle of the fourteenth century (David II), when John Ker of the Forest of Selkirk acquired the lands of Altonburn (1357), there were Kers holding lands in many parts of the Borders, and later we find them related by marriage with the other dominant races : Buccleuch, Home, Douglas, Polwarth. There are, of course, many families of the name in Scotland, who are not descended from the original families— the Kers of Cessford and Ferniehirst.

Cessford Castle (now a ruin), the ancient baronial residence of the family, beautifully situated on a tributary of Kale Water, near Morebattle, was a place of great strength and consequence. Ferniehirst Castle, near Jedburgh, is now a Youth Hostel.

We have only to read the *Minstrelsy* of the Scottish Borderland to learn how powerful the Ker clan became, their influence extending from Preston-Grange in Lothian to the English Border, and the part they played in the three centuries of Border raid and foray, and then to read the titles held by two of the chief representatives of the clan, to realise their achievements—that of Roxburghe and Lothian—Sir George Victor Robert John Innes-Ker, ninth Duke of Roxburghe, is Marquis of Bowmont and Cessford, Earl of Roxburghe, Earl of Kelso, Viscount Broxmouth, Baron Roxburghe and Baron Ker of Cessford and Caverton, in Scotland ; while Philip Henry Kerr, C.H., eleventh Marquis of Lothian, British Ambassador to Washington, who died in December 1940 and whose ashes lie in the vault of the Lothian aisle, Jedburgh Abbey, was Earl of Ancrum and Earl of Lothian, Viscount of Brien, Baron Kerr of Newbattle, Baron Jedburgh and Baron Ker of Kersheugh, and head of the once rival houses of Cessford and Ferniehirst, chief of the name in Scotland, holding three of the Ker Peerages, Lothian, Ancrum and Jedburgh. He presented Newbattle Abbey to the Scottish Universities as an educational centre, and Blickling Hall, Norfolk, to the English National Trust.

The Roxburghe family was ennobled by James VI in 1600 and was later raised to the Dukedom for the part the fifth Earl played in bringing about the Union in 1707. Even Lockhart of Carnwarth, no friendly critic, could not but speak well of him, for he said he was " the best accomplished young man of quality in Europe, and had such a charming way of expressing his thoughts that he pleased even those against whom he spoke." His creation was the last addition to the Peerage in Scotland.

Let us leave the genealogies and turn to the part the Ker clan played in Scottish history and Border warfare and raid. With the Douglases, Homes and Scotts they were among the most powerful in the East and Middle Marches. Each of the mighty chiefs was almost a king in miniature, surrounded by his own officers and supported on all occasions by a train of knights, squires and inferior chiefs, strong of arm and dauntless of heart.

It might be said that it was a Ker feud that led up to the battle of Flodden. With the death of Henry VII came strained relations between England and Scotland (1509). Sir Robert Ker of

Caverton had held the office of Warden of the Middle Marches during the reign. He was also Ambassador from King James to King Henry VII in 1492, and Master of the King's Artillery. Disliked by the more lawless among the Borders, seeing it was his duty, as a Crown Officer, to maintain law and good order, to punish those guilty of March treason and felony, and to uphold the ancient rules and customs of the Marches, he was murdered while at a March meeting across the Border, by three Englishmen : Lilburn, Starked and Heron. The Scots King appealed to Henry for redress, who complied with the just demand. Starked and Heron made their escape, but Heron of Ford, brother of the foresaid Heron, was seized in place of his brother, and delivered with Lilburn to the Scots. Lilburn died in prison. " Dand " Ker, son of the murdered man, determined upon revenge, and two of his retainers slew Starked in England, and brought his head to public gaze at the Cross of Edinburgh. At this Henry VIII was grieved, while the continued escape from justice of Heron was offensive to the Scottish King James. The tension grew ; then came Flodden, that left a sadness in Scottish hearts that endured for three hundred years.

On 24th July 1526 Sir Andrew Ker of Cessford, with the Earl of Angus, Lord Home and other Border chiefs, while escorting the young King James V to Edinburgh, was attacked near Melrose by Sir Walter Scott of Branxholm and 600 spears of Liddesdale and Annandale, whose object was to free the King from the hands of the Douglases. In the combat the Scotts were driven back, but in their pursuit Sir Andrew Ker was killed by a spear-thrust from one of Sir Walter's followers, Eliot. The result was a deadly feud between the names of Scott and Ker that continued for a century, and cost much blood upon the Marches. An effort was made to end the feud, and in 1529 a Bond of Alliance and Feud Staunching was entered into between the Scotts and Kers. This indenture appears in *The Minstrelsy of the Scottish Border*, vol. i. But either it never took effect or the feud was renewed shortly afterwards, for it culminated in the murder by Sir Walter Ker of Cessford of Sir Walter Scott of Buccleuch, in the High Street of Edinburgh, in 1552. The mother of this Sir Walter Scott perished in the burning of Catslack Tower in an incursion of the English under Lord Grey, 19th October 1548, an incursion instigated by the Kers.

And so the feuds went on, involving the whole sept, and

DARLINGTON
PUBLIC LIBRARY

DARLINGTON
PUBLIC LIBRARY

FERNIEHIRST CASTLE—THE N

(Now a

AL STRONGHOLD OF THE KERS

(ᵒuth Hostel)

DARLINGTON
PUBLIC LIBRARY

DARLINGTON PUBLIC LIBRARY

handed down from father to son as a sacred duty, which time itself could not set aside :

> Can piety the discord heal,
>   Or stanch the death-feud's enmity ?
> Can Christian lore, can patriot zeal,
>   Can love of blessed charity ?
> No ! vainly to each holy shrine,
>   In mutual pilgrimage, they drew ;
> Implored, in vain, the grace divine,
>   For Chiefs their own red falchions slew :
> While Cessford owns the rule of Carr,
>   While Ettrick boasts the line of Scott,
> The slaughter'd chiefs, the mortal jar,
> The havoc of the feudal war,
>   Shall never, never be forgot !
>
> (*Lay of the Last Minstrel*, Canto I)

Yet who was it but a Ker of Cessford that accompanied the " Bold Buccleuch " when he appeared before Elizabeth after the storming of Carlisle Castle and the rescue of " Kinmont Willie."

And at the funeral of the great Border chief Walter, first Earl of Buccleuch, 11th June 1634, " the armes of Ker of Pherney-hirst, first grandame on the mother's syde " and " the armes of Ker of Cessford, first grandsyre on the mother's syde " were carried by members of the Scott clan.

Among other members of the clan may be mentioned Haby Ker, who had his own " hanging-tree," frequently in use, at Holydean, Bowden ; Ker of Faldonside, implicated in the murder of Rizzio, and the Ruthven Raid (1582) ; Ker of Kersland, associated with The Cameronians in 1706 ; old general Lord Mark Ker who, on receiving two of Cope's Generals fleeing to Berwick after Prestonpans, exclaimed, " Good God ! I have seen some battles, heard of many, but never before received the first news of defeat from the mouth of the Generals themselves ! " Ker of Ferniehirst was a member of the Queen's Parliament in 1571, and though a noted Border riever, was made Provost of Edinburgh. The great Camden said of this man : " A stout and able warrior, of immovable fidelity to the Queen of Scots, and the King her son ; having been once or twice turned out of all his lands and fortunes, banished the sight of his country and children, which yet he endured patiently, and after so many crosses falling upon him together, persisted unshaken, and always like himself."

The tradition that the clan were left-handed (Carr-handed, carry-handed) like the 700 chosen men of the tribe of Benjamin who could sling stones at an hair-breadth and not miss, is without foundation. It would of course make them awkward and undesirable opponents in an encounter with swords, as narrated in the Ettrick Shepherd's ballad " The Raid of the Kers " :

> For they were all left-handed men,
> And fight against them there was nane ;

but the sequel shows that two leaders of the raid, Mark Ker and Tam o' Mossburnford, were slain, and

> Of one and fifty buirdly Kers
> The very prime men of the clan,
> They were only seventeen return'd
> And they were wounded every man.

While the Armstrongs were hung, the families succeeding to them in Border influence, Kers and Scotts, grew in power and wealth, becoming ducal houses, serving King and Country with unselfish devotion and standing for all that is best and noblest in our land of freedom. Border chieftains became the soldiers, statesmen, ambassadors and judges of a great Empire. Law and order reigned in the Borderland after the Union of the Crowns in 1606 and the Union of the Kingdoms in 1707 and the establishment of the modern sheriffdoms, and the Eastern Marches where the Kers with the Homes and Douglases had ruled and fought against English aggression, maintaining Scottish Independence and Freedom, became the most fertile and best-cultivated part of Scotland.

" The cradle of the Scotts of Buccleuch was not in Ettrick Forest,"[1] says Dr. Taylor, the authority on Scotland's historic families, " but at Scotstoun and Kirkurd," among the hills of Tweeddale, and marching with the upland parishes of Stobo and Broughton. It was from this part of the Scottish Border that there came the ancestors of those Scotts who played a noted part in Scottish History in the Borderland. Of such were Sir Walter

---

[1] From here to the end of Chapter VI was printed in *The Scotsman* of 31st August 1935 on the occasion of the public announcement of the engagement of Lady Alice Scott to the Duke of Gloucester.

Scott, who was killed at the battle of Homildon Hill in 1402, Sir Walter Scott, the first Lord of Buccleuch, who succeeded his father in 1426, and was much involved in Border raiding, and Sir Walter Scott, known as "Wicked Wat," who fought at Flodden in 1513. He led a troubled existence, and took part in many a Border foray. He quarrelled with the Queen Dowager of James IV, strove to release the young James V from the Douglas faction and was exiled under a penalty of £10,000 Scots. This was remitted, and he was made Principal Cup-bearer (1527). He was Keeper of Newark Castle (1543), fought at Pinkie (1547), became Warden of the Middle Marches (1550) and of Liddesdale (1551), and in 1552 was attacked by the Kers in the High Street of Edinburgh, and killed.

Then there was Sir Walter Scott, the "Bold Buccleuch," a typical Borderer who took part in all the Border raids of his time, and in 1596, at the head of eighty horsemen, stormed Carlisle Castle and rescued "Kinmont Willie" (Willie Armstrong). Queen Elizabeth demanded that the "Bold Buccleuch" should be delivered up to her when she heard of this. He proceeded to London, made a favourable impression upon Her Majesty, and was asked how he dared undertake an enterprise so desperate and presumptuous. To which he replied, "What is it, Your Majesty, that a man dares not do?" And the Queen turning to a Lord-in-Waiting, said, "With ten thousand such men, our brother in Scotland might shake the fiercest throne in Europe." He is the hero of the ballads "Jamie Telfer" and "Kinmont Willie," into which Scott put a good deal of original work. He became a Lord of Parliament in 1606 with the title of Lord Scott of Buccleuch, and his only son was the first Earl.

The present holder of the title is the seventh Duke of Buccleuch and ninth Duke of Queensberry, and the lands in Kirkurd which they still hold are their oldest possessions.

The name Kirkurd does not appear until 1310; prior to that date the name was Orde or Urde, signifying an eminence or height. The Orde appears in the "Divise de Stobbo" of 1200, Orde being the high-lying district towards the head of Stobo Hopes. Between 1208 and 1214 a son of William the Lion was Overlord of the Manor of Orde; and as showing that Edward II visited the place in 1310 on his way to Biggar, his Account-Book shows a payment to his farrier at that place.

The Scotts of Scotstoun owned part of Orde in the thirteenth century. In the genealogical table prepared by Sir Walter Scott, the novelist, of his ancestors, it is said that the forefathers of Uchtred Scott in the days of David I are believed to have possessed the Barony of Scotstoun from the days of Kenneth III. It is among the earliest known settlements of the Scotts in Scotland. Walter Scott of Satchells, author of the first history of the family (1686), says :

> It was called Scotstoun Hall when Buccleuch in it did dwell,
> Unto this time it is called Scotstoun still.

Tobias Smollett, the novelist, visited Scotstoun in 1755 when his mother and sister, Mrs. Telfer, were in residence there. His nephew, Alexander Telfer, Younger, of Scotstoun, was said to be the original of Jerry Melford in *Humphry Clinker* (Dr. Chambers), published in the year of Sir Walter Scott's birth (1771).

Not far southward from Scotstoun lies the picturesque village of Skirling, named Scrawline in the days of Robert the Bruce, where in olden times four fairs were held annually. The June Fair or Market was one of the largest in Scotland for horses and cattle, and continued for centuries, until 1864, when the fairs were transferred to Biggar. A local history—*Biggar and the House of Fleming*—narrates how amidst the throng that attended were cattle-dealers, horse-coupers, ballad-singers, pickpockets, prick-the-garters and hawkers of curry-combs. Recruiting parties marched up and down, with fifes and drums playing, merchants did great business at their stands, and gingerbread neds pursued their vocation with assiduity and clamour. In 1775 Skirling was a large and populous village with two inns. There are no inns now. It is a quiet country place with a village green charmingly embowered in chestnut trees ; and if the smiddy and the wheel-wright's business is not in such demand as formerly, Skirling has found a new industry, and in the increasing tide of small-holdings and poultry farms, the superlative quality of poultry frames and hen-houses produced at Skirling has earned for them a reputation far renowned. Nor do we neglect to notice, as we linger in this sweet village, the carved birds in natural colours set on wooden rods in cottage gardens, and the chastely-wrought iron-work that adorns the village kirk. Over all there is a restful spirit, a sense of repose, that breathes of the honour and respect, shared by all the countryside, for the beloved laird and the good Lady Carmichael. Baron Carmichael of Skirling was in turn Governor of Victoria, Australia, Governor of Madras and Governor of Bengal, a man of many activities whose wide sympathies and kindly humour endeared him to everyone.

But the most fascinating point about the countryside is that overlooking Scotstoun, the " cradle of the Scotts " ; midway between Scotstoun and Skirling, rises the Pyket Stane, one of the best vantage-points in the Southern Uplands from which flows Broughton Water, later joining Biggar Water, a tributary of Tweed.

Fair prospects and far views, diversified in glowing colours and graceful contours, are numerous from the heights of these Uplands. The Broughton Heights rise to the east or left side of the main high-road from Blyth Bridge (south of Romanno Toll and Mountain Cross) to Broughton, and are easily distinguished by the great hole or chasm in the hillside known as " Hell's Cleuch." One way of approach to the Heights is by an old grass-grown road along the hillside behind Kirkurd church. The kirk is tucked away among woodlands of Scots pine and larch, sycamore and yew, through which gleam the yellow walls, the stained-glass windows, the tapered bell tower.

The road bears traces of wheeled traffic, and was probably an old Drove road to Skirling Fair. Up and up it goes among reeds and rushes, along the steep side of Hell's Cleuch, sometimes on one side of the ridge, where the view is of Stobo, Hopehead, Scotstoun, Castle Craig, Romanno Heights, Kingside Edge and the higher Moorfoots ; now on the other side, looking out to the blue hills that form the ramparts of the Tweed valley and the Borderland. The higher we go, the more extensive the prospect till at last we reach the Pyket Stane, a rude collection of stones to distinguish the united marches of Stobo, Broughton and Kirkurd, and to the east, Penvalla. The origin of the name Pyket is unknown. A pike may be a sharp-pointed hill or summit, and the stones doubtless mark the highest point, but the Geddeses held land in Kirkurd for many generations, and as Geddes is the plural of Ged, i.e. a pike, and the family arms consist of three pikes (fish, however, not weapons), it may be that the Pyket Stane has a connection with the name of this former proprietor.

Given a clear atmosphere, and a good spy-glass, there seems no limit to the extensive view that can be obtained from this 1,872-foot vantage-point. Almost every peak of the Pentland range from Caerketton to Dunsyre is visible. Quothquan Law is dwarfed by Tinto that stands majestically guarding the vale of Biggar. Crosscryne, Coulter Fell, Dollar Law and Broad Law come into view, as well as Eildon's triple crown, and the blue dome-like summits of the Cheviots in Northumberland—a glorious countryside. Gleaming in the sunlight we see the infant Clyde at Symington, and the Tarth from the Pentland Hills forms a straight line from Dolphinton to Netherurd. Northwards the whole country beyond the Forth with its magical mountain ranges and peaks forms a panorama of keen interest to hill-climbers and mountaineers, who find joy in identifying the contour of familiar peaks.

Other viewpoints may thrill us with emotion. White Coomb may heighten the sense of Yarrow's haunting mystery, and show to us the "sleeping mastiffs," although the name "White Coomb" may at first puzzle us, seeing that a coomb is a hollow in a hillside, but all our doubts will be set at rest if we view the hill from the Moffat Water side, and there we shall see a weathered hollow which when filled with deep snow presents the exact appearance of a white coomb ! Broad Law may satisfy us with the spaciousness not only of its summit but with the eastward range of hill-tops and the wild scene around Glenrath. Hart Fell may charm us with its placid southward view, and every landscape may fade into illimitable distance till the power of the eye be unavailing, and we seek the azure blue of heaven for rest. But the Pyket Stane, rising above the surging sea of hills and valleys beautiful in diversity of outline and colour, commands one of the most extensive and unrivalled views in the south of Scotland, a fitting giant to arise out of the "Cradle of the Scotts."

VII

MANOR VALLEY : PROFESSOR VEITCH

"Tranquillity ! Thou better name
Than all the family of fame."
(COLERIDGE, " Ode to Tranquillity ")

IN olden times Lyne and Megget were one parish, and the minister travelled to Megget to hold services there, leaving Lyne at six in the morning, and returning the same evening, a distance of twenty-six miles.

The route by which he walked or rode was by way of the Manor valley, through the Tweeddale hills over Hind Crag and the watershed and down into Meggetvale, a route much frequented by travellers, and important enough to be marked by milestones, some of which lichen-clad and weather-stained, still remain, telling the distance from the county town. And this is the route still followed to-day by many who visit the hostels at Manor, Chapelhope and Broadmeadows.

Through this valley flows Manor Water, which, after a course of ten miles through high mountains and pastoral valleys, by farmstead, cottage and ruined tower, joins Tweed at Manor Bridge. Its source is among deep, converging, glacier-cut gullies that fall away from a hill ridge of over 2,500 feet, extending for ten miles from Broad Law to Dun Rig. Out of a spring in the soft mossy hillside gushes the lusty infant, which rapidly descends, from the brow of Shielhope Head, to the floor of the valley at Manorhope or Manorhead, about a thousand feet in little over a mile :

> . . . The hollow urn . . . gives forth a sound
> Of hidden waters from its depths remote,
> As if the Spirit of the hills had there
> Withdrawn within himself to hold lone musing
> Deep murmuring o'er the secrets of the glens.

The northward view comprises one of the most shapely and well-proportioned valleys in Tweeddale flanked by the high hills of Dollar Law, Posso Crags and Scrape on the one side, and by the heights of Blackhouse, Glenrath and Hundleshope on the other, a continuous chain of hills for six miles on both sides of the valley, the farthest barrier being Tweed and the fortress-crowned bastion of Cademuir.

Down many a sky-arched, hill-enfolded glen flow turbulent tributaries of the parent Manor, not the least fearsome being the Ugly Grain (" *Ugly*," Scandinavian, fearsome ; " *Grain*," Norse, " the branch of a stream ") that issues from the mist-crowned heights of Dolefu' Law, a wild water that rivals Gameshope in its winter gambols, with great rocks and boulders strewing its course and forming in times of spate an almost continuous waterfall of a thousand feet.

Other affluents are Dollarburn and Kirkhope or Newholm-hope, the latter associated with the site of ancient St. Gordian's Kirk, marked by a Scottish cross erected by Sir John Murray Naesmyth of Posso ; and near the former a granite cairn sacred to the memory of the historian of Tweeddale, " Raised, in his favourite valley, by a few friends, in affectionate remembrance of John Veitch, 1900," typical of the man in its rugged strength and simplicity, and in its surroundings of musical waters and spirit voices of silent hill and lonely pine.

It was while Scott at the age of twenty-six, on his way to the English Lakes, was visiting Dr. Adam Ferguson at Hallyards, Manor, the first stage of his tour, that he met David Ritchie, the original of his " Black Dwarf," who, seizing him by the wrist with one of his iron hands, enquired of him, " Man, ha'e ye ony poo'er ? " The cottage at Woodhouse attracts many visitors. On the occasion of the visit to Hallyards Scott seems to have attended Manor Kirk, and cut his initials on the book-board of the pew. And we remember it was in Dr. Ferguson's Edinburgh house—Sciennes Hill House—that Burns and Scott met : the latter was just fifteen. He wrote to Lockhart that there were several gentlemen of literary reputation present :

Of course, we youngsters sat silent, looked and listened. The only thing I remember which was remarkable in Burns' manner was the effect produced upon him by a print of Bunbury's, representing a soldier lying dead on the snow, his dog sitting in misery on the one side, on the other his widow, with a child in her arms. These lines were written beneath :

> Cold on Canadian hills, or Minden's plain,
> Perhaps that parent wept her soldier slain ;

Bent o'er her babe, her eye dissolved in dew ;
The big drops, mingling with the milk he drew,
Gave the sad presage of his future years,
The child of misery baptised in tears.

Burns seemed much affected by the print, or rather the ideas which it suggested to his mind. He actually shed tears. He asked whose the lines were, and it chanced that nobody but myself remembered that they occur in a half-forgotten poem of Langhorne. I whispered my information to a friend present, who mentioned it to Burns, who rewarded me with a look and a word, which, though of mere civility, I then received, and still recollect, with very great pleasure.

This print, along with a copy of the painting of the meeting of the two great Scotsmen, may be examined in the gallery of Peebles Museum.

Probably no valley of similar size in all the Southern Uplands lures with such winsomeness or is so rich in ancient lore as that of Manor with its archaeological and ecclesiastical remains—the chapel of Maineure is first mentioned in 1186 : whether it was at Kirkhope is uncertain—and its homes of old Scottish families, Inglis and Lowis of Manor, Baird and Naesmyth of Posso, Burnet of Barns and many others. King Robert III gave the Barony to Sir William Inglis in 1396 for accepting the challenge and defeating in combat a braggart English knight, Thomas de Struthers, who was marauding on the Marches.

No fitter description of the scene exists than that by its own historian, who held that nothing could be more perfect in valley scenery than that of the Head of the Manor :

It impresses and subdues by mountain and crag ; it touches eye and heart with a symmetry of opposing yet alternating and harmonious lines of hills, and a winsome grace peculiarly its own. In itself it is proportioned, restrained and complete as a Greek Temple, supremely perfect and lovable ; yet it adds to its apparent completeness a mysterious power of suggestion through the grandeur of its head and its far-reaching hopes and glens, passing away up and into recesses beyond the vision and here and there descried as terminated only in heights where the mountain line bars the sky beyond.

The glen is a favourite one with walkers visiting the hostel in Manor (formerly at Langhaugh, now at Barns, associated with John Buchan's absorbing novel, *John Burnet of Barns*) and thence by the bridle-track over Bitch Craig and Foul Bridge, where ravens croak and wild birds cry, on to Megget Valley, Glengaber, Henderland and Dryhope Tower, and so to the Gordon Arms, Tibbie Shiels or Broadmeadows in Yarrow. A pleasant three days may be spent in crossing from Peebles, either by Gipsy Glen and Douglas Burn or by Manor and Megget, to Chapelhope, using the second day for a ramble around Loch Skene, and thence to Shortwoodend, Moffatdale, and the third day for the walk over Hart Fell to Fruid and Tweedsmuir, and so to Broughton, from whence there is conveyance to Edinburgh. The Tower and houses at Langhaugh were in existence in 1560, when they are mentioned as being the subject of a dispute. It was high up on the steep slope of Horsehope Craig, behind Langhaugh, that an interesting group of bronze objects was found in 1864, which may be seen in Peebles Museum (*Proc. Soc. Ant.* vol. xxii), where there is a splendid collection of rocks, minerals and fossils stimulative of interest in local geology. Vol. xxiii, pp. 140-42, contains a note of cup-marked stones in Peeblesshire, including one " built into the wall of the public road, a little north of Castlehill, Manor, on the west side of the road ; cups are five in number, nearly equal in size, sharply cut, and in good preservation." For an account of the local glaciology, see Excursion led by Professor Geikie (*Innerleithen Alpine Club*). The old iron brazier for the fifteenth-century Barns Tower beacon-fire is also preserved in Peebles Museum. The " yett " with horizontal and vertical bars interlaced is one of the oldest of this style in Scotland, although the fourteenth-century Rosslyn Castle and Rosslyn Chapel crypt have similar interlaced gratings, forming a strong defence against intrusion. The part of these old peel towers where the warders kept watch and where the defence was carried on was called the bartizan, being the narrow passage between the roof and the battlements. Barns, however, does not have any bartizan, but Newark and Kirkhope have a bartizan all round, while that at Neidpath is confined to the east and west sides. The accommodation in such towers was very limited, the hall on the first floor at Barns being only 17½ by 14 feet, and the furnishings depended on the period and the wealth and rank of the owner. Jamie Telfer had

> . . . naething in his house
> But ae auld sword
> That hardly now wud fell a mouse.

The etymology of Barns is from the Anglo-Saxon *berern*, a barley store.

Few knew Manor Glen better or have written in higher praise of it than John Veitch, the Peebles boy, who, born of humble parents at the Biggiesknowe, on 24th October 1829, and giving his life to the study of Philosophy, became Professor of Logic and Metaphysics at St. Andrews University at the age of thirty-one, and four years later was elected to a similar Chair in Glasgow University, receiving the Freedom of his native burgh, and building his house, "The Loaning," 700 feet above the sea, in sight of his "own familiar hills."

No one has caught so well the spirit of the hills and glens of the Southern Uplands, and in portraying it in many prose and poetical works has so fully reflected his own personality and character. A lifelong walker and ardent Nature-lover, the call of the hills was in him a hunger of the spirit, in the satisfaction of which he found peace and realised eternal values. On every hill and by every stream in the Border country he walked and sang and gloried ; it was his supreme delight, often transfiguring his countenance as, with awe and light upon it, he paused on some hill-top. Readers for amusement will find little appeal in his books, but for the few who meditate, his appeal is strong. All the Border books were written after he was forty years of age : *Hillside Rhymes* (1872), *The Tweed and Other Poems* (1875), *The History and Poetry of the Scottish Border* (1877), *The Feeling for Nature in Scottish Poetry* (1887), *Merlin and Other Poems* (1889) and *Border Essays* (1896), published two years after his death.

> Thus would I touch each living soul
> To know and feel as I have known,
> On sun-smit height, in lonely glen,
> The vision from the Eternal throne !

In his description of Manor Glen he refers to its mysterious power of suggestion. There is much of this in his poetry. The beauty of the soft-rounded rolling hills, their multi-coloured slopes, rocky escarpments, green cleughs and dancing burns is one of suggestion as much as of actual vision. Nature that ministers delight to the eye, furnishes interest to the understanding, beauty and suggestiveness to the imagination, calm and restoration to the heart. Hills speak to the soul by their vastness and repose, of the Infinity of Spirit, of man's spirit, of the Eternal Spirit.

Long is the apprenticeship required for this intimate communion with Nature. In Nature there is just as much or as little as the soul of each can bring to it. The earlier our friendship begins, the easier intimacy grows and develops. An eye observant and sensitive to beauty must act with a heart fully alive to all that is most affecting in human life and destiny.

When the eye rests on the ranging landscape and the heart responds to its beauty, the emotion which is evoked is as true and rational as is the action of any law of Nature.

"There are few," says the Professor, "who reach a supreme satisfaction in the wilds, who delight in them merely for what they are, and who find in them, as there may be found, the near presence of a Personal yet Supreme Power, whose communion is never wanting to the solitary lover and worshipper of Nature."

Every time we feel the presence of the Transcendent Power in things there is a freshening of the springs of life, the silences calm and refresh us, the sublime stirs within us thoughts noble and majestic. Nature answers out of the depths of an indwelling spirit. Those things must be said to-day ; there is need for the seer-poet to proclaim through his individual vision what is the universal reality, and common heritage of all. The pleasures of body, mind, spirit and imagination can be enjoyed by the hill- and Nature-lover who reacts to Nature's appeal, and the ultimate aim and effect of all his country walking may be no less than that of soul-development.

What sort of man was this Professor of Philosophy who became poet and historian of this fascinating Land of Romance ? No one would claim him as a genius, an eminent philosopher or a great poet : with all his gifts of intellect, he was more than these, for he was a great personality who by his character influenced men and students, and by his writings contributed much to the historical and literary lore of Scotland's Borderland. His critics, however friendly, could not acclaim him a great poet. The poems are "you," they said, and that was enough. His face won respect and trust, reflecting the deep serious mind, the reverent soul, the tender heart great in its simplicity and power of affection.

It was of the severe impassive type, with square ample brow, deeply lined : deep-set eyes overhung by dark bushy eyebrows tinged with grey, a heavy firm jaw and firmly set mouth, a typical Scottish face in its squareness and outline.

Such was the description of one of his students, who also wrote :

His morning prayer was a thing to hear. It was to him a stern necessary duty to be lovingly and reverently discharged. He settled to it with imposing seriousness : his face fell into severe set lines, with stern wrinkles on his brow. He waited till a quiet hush came over the class, and then he began his prayer in the deepest, gravest tone, with reverent vibrations running through it. The words are grave and sad ; he shakes his head mournfully the while ; the great strong voice becomes low and quiet. For the nonce the reckless young student was sobered into sympathy. The remembrance of such a scene, of the grey-headed Professor coming to his God like a little child, brings a dim mist over the eye.

His personality was a dominant and outstanding feature of his humanity. The way by which he attained to this habitation of Divine environment was by Nature. In and through Nature he experienced a Presence, Something above and beyond, yet in, both Nature and man. " The true lover of Nature," he wrote, " is above low and earthly impulses ; he is at least in the Vestibule of the Temple, and not far from the Kingdom of God."

No matter where his lot was cast, or where long periods of his life were spent, in Edinburgh, St. Andrews, Glasgow, where he laboured in his studies and professorships, his thoughts ever returned to the hills of Tweeddale, where he found rest, strength, spiritual refreshment and restoration. He was unique, he was original, he was himself. He aped no one, borrowed from no one, his was an independent mind and spirit. And the reason for it all was just that in the presence of Nature, with all that that meant to him in his experiences of life among the Uplands, he preserved his sense of wonder and felt an all-pervading spirit of purity and strength that brought something to him, that gave him himself, till in time he became one with Nature and Nature's Spirit.

> 'Tis God,
> Diffused through all that doth
> Make all one whole.
>
> (COLERIDGE)

To all who love the hills and feel bound to them by ties like these, the Tweeddale Hills and Southern Uplands are interpreted in the writings of this man, who was a philosopher and a poet, with spiritual and religious values.

Ever in these writings is that deeper note of the existence of God, the God of Nature and the Father of all, found also in the writings of his " true and noble friend " John Campbell Shairp, his companion on many Tweeddale walks, who lived for a season at Castlehill, in Manor Valley, and who was Professor of Poetry, Oxford, and Principal of the United College, St. Andrews. Of him Veitch wrote : " a man more soul to soul, heart to heart, with me, I have not met in this world."

" That a spirit so poetical . . . so reverential, and even mystical, should have been linked in one personality with an intellect so masterfully acute, was the problem as it was the fascination of his character . . . he lived in the atmosphere of the Unseen " ; so wrote R. M. Wenley in the Introduction to Veitch's *Dualism and Monism.*

The Presence in Nature was to him the most vital thing in all his life. Spiritual intuition was in him the central fire. Manor Water was " the sweetest stream of all the South." The Well Bush in Manor Valley " the centre of my life." The Grampians were all very well, sombre and imposing : " One is the better for seeing them," he wrote, " for they enhance the feeling of delicacy inspired by the Border Hills, but they lack the buffs and browns and greens of our Tweed and Yarrow Hills." In Manor

> Life's deeds and words here fade and pale,
> Thou dreamland of my living years !
>
> .   .   .   .
>
> The memories of the higher self
> All that the grave can never claim—
> All that the immortal cares to keep—
> This thou alone for me canst name.
>
> .   .   .
>
> Thus do I yearn to thee, dear Vale,
> So live I as the life in thee—
> Hours, days, years are gone—are nought—
> In thee I find Eternity !
>
> .   .   .
>
> Let fickle fame go by me,
> Mean forms of earthly good,
> If God my mountains leave me
> And my mountain solitude.

Nature, of course, is but the hem of His garment, and healing is not from the garment, but from Him. No one realised this better than Professor Veitch, and from it he received a strength beyond his own ; it transfused and transfigured him as a man above his fellows and gave him that personality or soul that attracted all who knew him and learned of him. It made him, as it makes all hill-men, independent in mind and thought, and in a large measure, of human companionship. Not that he entertained any dislike of his fellow creatures, far from it, but other orders of creation soothed, instructed and elevated his spirit far more than they could ever hope to do.

He loved to roam the hills alone ; because it was a sacrament to him—this communion in the silences with the Highest, interpreted through Nature on the high hills. Deep answered unto deep : Spirit spoke to spirit ; and life arranged itself in clear perspective, and became not a life seeking fame, power or friends, but a state for soul-development and expansion in a framework of humility, courage and high endeavour. Strength and happiness are the attributes of the man of wisdom who is a poet in soul and a religionist at heart.

VIII

A DAY ON BROAD LAW

ROB ROY confessed, "Were I to lose sight of my native hills, my heart would sink and my arm would wither like fern i' the winter's blast." So it is that the hills to many become as steadfast friends in whose companionship they find liberty of thought, serenity of mind, fellowship of spirit. It matters little whether the hills be highland or lowland ; their appeal to the Nature-lover is universal.

In the Southern Uplands of Scotland the highest hill is Broad Law (2,764 feet), belonging to the Hart Fell group—"the Broad Law of Hairstane" as it was commonly called, according to Captain Armstrong, in 1775. There are many ways of approach. We may take our way by the Manor valley, and by the Hope of St. Gordian's Kirk reach the high ridge of the Long Grain Knowe, and skirting Dollar Law and Cramalt Craig, arrive on Broad Law above Polmood Craigs.

Professor Veitch favoured the climb by Herstane opposite the Crook Inn, and so up the Dark Glen, Glen Heurie, the spirit of the place interpreted in the wild rushing sound of the foaming waters ; and he wrote of the aged mountain ash that flourished there, defying the storm and telling of other days :

> The huntings, the night raids ;
> Of Hawkshaw and Polmood,
> Fruid, Stanhope, Cardon,
> Drumelzier and Dawyck,
> Each a stalwart Baron.

But the usual approach is by Talla, where Edinburgh's water-supply is gathered up in the valley, fed by the Talla Water, and the roaring Gameshope—Gameshope that casts out the flood as a needless thing, and relies on her own unfailing springs—and surrounded by the great, round-shouldered hills of Muckle Side, Muckle Knowe, Erie Hill and Garelet Dod.

Arrived at the head of Talla, Tal Ard in early days, we begin the ascent of Talla Linns—the "Witches' Linn"—where the great Conventicle described by Sir Walter Scott in *The Heart of Mid-*

lothian took place in 1682. One gets full value for the climb, for there is no descent when the top is reached, but a pleasant pause at the bridge over Talla Water, and a view westward over the Cascades and the spreading waters of the loch to Tweedsmuir —Tweed Moor as it was once called, indicating the wild character of the district.

At the Megget Stane, a short distance farther on, we leave the road and take to the heather for the well-known landmark "The Porridge Cairn," and so to Broad Law by way of the boundary fence of Peeblesshire. From Megget Stane to the Porridge Cairn is a steady upward climb by the shepherds' track, with unfolding views as the hills emerge out of the horizon. The cairn is surrounded by an outcrop spread evenly around like a plateful of porridge—a plateful of rocks ! And there is no better preliminary to a day on the hills than a good plateful of porridge !

The prospect lends aid to the imagination as we view the peaceful Vale of Megget rich in historic lore ; once the famous hunting-ground of early Scottish kings and queens and the home of noted Border rievers, where at the end of the eighteenth century ten thousand sheep were grazed, and among the farms such names as Henderland, Cramalt, Syart, Shielhope, Winter-hope and Meggethead. Here descendants of the Ettrick Shepherd laboured for generations in the same faithful spirit and proud of the history and traditions of the Vale. In the dim blue distance we survey the varied tumble of hills surrounding Moffatdale, the nearer hills dappled in cloud shadows and sunshine. "I like these quiet hills," says Dr. Chalmers, speaking of the "sober Uplands" of Tweeddale, "hills all bare like these are what I call the statuary of Landscape." And Sir Walter wrote : "I like the very nakedness of the land ; it has something bold, stern and solitary about it. When I have been for some time in the rich scenery about Edinburgh, which is like an ornamental garden, I begin to wish myself back again among my own honest grey hills." Cries of whaups and flapping peewits fill the air, and there is balm in the music of mountain streams that comes and goes on the wings of the wind. From Porridge Cairn to Broad Law there is a long flat approach of about two miles until we come to the summit. If that of the former may be likened to a plate of porridge, the summit of Broad Law is in shape round and flat like a scone girdle.

The great mass of Broad Law can hardly be called a beautiful hill, since variety in form and colour more than size comprise mountain beauty ; height produces awe, line gives dignity, a sense of nobility or grace in form, colour gives richness and beauty raises emotion. But Broad Law has nothing particular in form or colour to acclaim it. It is an honest, friendly hill. Armstrong said the summit might admit of a circuit horse-race of two miles, without the smallest inequality of surface ; that the view from this attic plain is very extensive, and is " much frequented by the curious and sportsmen."

Here on the summit there is calm and peace ; a hush, a gentle wind in the ears, a lark is singing, an insect buzzes, a beetle emerges from a crevice to sun itself, and a roving, solitary wild bee goes bumbling past, burly and jovial, " freeborn wanderer of thy mountain air "—and he incites our thought to philosophic and poetic reflection—whence and whither ! life's origin, purpose and destiny. Not many hills provide amusement and recreation for a whole day, but a summer's day can be spent profitably on Broad Law, if conditions are pleasant. Deep glens and cleughs on every side call for exploration and stir the sense of wonder, which is " the seed of knowledge." Here can be seen the fierce attrition of winter storms in deep-cut gullies and moraines, bogs, mosses, fair pasture-lands and mountain flora. The Rig of Glen Heurie is of stately beauty, the sides rising stream-lined from the valley, and along the centre of the broad back is a clear stretch of vivid green, bordered on each side with heather and moss, Nature's happy combination of colour and contour.

Beyond the Hearthstane or Herstane valley the white buildings of the Crook Inn appear, an inn that has been in existence for over three hundred years, and has pleasant associations with Professors Veitch and Shairp, Wilson, Knight and Blackie, Dr. John Brown, Russell, Andrew Lang and other literati of their day, who roamed the Tweeddale hills, drew inspiration from the far views and the lonely places, and explored the mysterious cleughs and hopes by Polmood, Stanhope, Drumelzier and Dawyck.

Herstane takes its name from two standing stones by the burn, probably old boundary stones. The estate formed part of the Barony of Oliver Castle. In the famous litigation about Polmood (1780–1814), Margaret Tweedie, " the guid wife of Herstanes," is referred to as the niece of Robert Hunter, the owner of the wonderful dog Algiers, of which we read in Chapter I. It was at Polmood—after having travelled from Lochiel's country by Glen Lyon, Breadalbane, Balquhidder, Carnwath and Kilbucho —that John Murray of Broughton was captured after the 'Forty-five, in the house of his half-sister Veronica, daughter of Sir David Murray of Stanhope, and wife of Robert Hunter. He bought back the ancestral estate of Broughton about the time of his marriage, soon after 1738 (*Mem. of John Murray*).

Here all the Southern Uplands are spread before us. North-wards the hills of Fife and the Grampians. Eastwards the Moor-foots, the Lammermuirs, the Eildons and the Merse. South and east, the blue aerial ridges of the Cheviots, the old boundary line between the rival Kingdoms ; and south and west, ridge after ridge stretches away to the Solway. All around is a wild tumble of hills, with rounded hill-tops, and innumerable ridges linking them one to another. Here we stand on the great backbone of these southern hills stretching from Scrape, Pykestone and Dollar Law forming the watershed between Tweed and Manor, to Lochcraig and Loch Skene, White Coomb and Hart Fell, all over 2,000 feet above sea level—the " Arctic Alpine " centre of the Uplands of Southern Scotland. Indeed the general average height of the county is probably greater than that of any other, the whole area being an irregular mass of hills intersected by narrow valleys. As Professor Veitch has well expressed it : " These hill-tops follow each other in wavy outline. One rises, flows, falls, passes softly into another. This again rises, flows and passes into another beyond itself ; and thus the eye reposes on the long soft lines of a sea of hills, whose tops move, and yet do not move, for they carry our vision along their undulating flow, themselves motionless, lying like an earth-ocean in the deep, quiet calm of their statuesque beauty."

In these high hills with the strange wild names—Glenrath, Hundleshope and Blackhouse—are hidden lonely glens and burns visited only by the shepherd, and the solitary walker in search of that spiritual fellowship of which the Professor is Tweeddale's chief exponent. Here it is that the Nature-lover may find that for which his heart cries out.

True, the love of Nature followed till it becomes a passion, brings, like the mystic's transcendental life, its own hardship, mis-understanding, loneliness, so that there is experienced as much of sorrow as of joy, an ebb and flow of both. Character is strength-ened, and there may be withdrawal of affection from the world, yet who would not say that victory over self and the world is worth all the striving and the wrestling and persistent endeavour towards that last hope of likeness to the Divine. And if the way seem hard, there is courage in that mastering thought of Meredith, supreme singer of Nature and the open air : " Believe at the outset that life is joy ; only let joy be read spiritually ; in other words not as a thing to claim, but as a thing to share in."

Many have found in the still green beauty of these pastoral hills and dales visions of Fairyland and the Elysian fields, and what Christopher North said of Hogg, the Shepherd of Ettrick, applies equally to the wilds of Tweeddale which were also his home : " When he speaks of Fairyland his language becomes aerial as the very voice of the Fairy people, serenest images rise up with the music of the verse, and we almost believe in the beings of those unlocalised realms of peace, of which he sings like a native minstrel."

He it was who made this land in Border life and feeling charming and attractive as a heaven of imagination, and set the bells of Elfland ringing. Beside many a green glade and dancing water, shot through with merry sunshine, we may see the little green folk at play, and hear amidst the evening silence :

> Spirits talk along the hill.
> Came voices floating down the air,
> From viewless shades that lingered there :
> The woods were fraught with mystery ;
> Voices of men they could not be.
>
> (" Queen's Wake ")

Robert Louis Stevenson as a boy knew the hills and glens and streams of Tweeddale, and in 1882 he stayed at Stobo Manse, and wrote his amusing letter to Henley about his imaginary friends :

Old Mr. Pegfurth Bannatyne is here staying at a country inn. His whole baggage is a pair of socks and a book in a fishing-basket ; and he borrows even a rod from the landlord. He walked here over the hills from Sanquhar, " singin'," he says, " like a mavis." I naturally asked him about Hazlitt. " He wouldnae take his drink," he said, " a queer, queer fellow." But did not seem further communicative. He says he has become " releegious," but still swears like a trooper. I asked him if he had no headquarters. " No likely," said he. He says he is writing his memoirs, which will be interesting. He once met Borrow ; they boxed ; " and Geordie," says the old man chuckling, " gave me the damnedest hiding." Of Wordsworth he remarked, " He wasnae sound in the faith, sir, and a milk-blooded, blue-spectacled

NEWBATTLE ABBEY

SWARE BRIDGE

DARLING ...
PUBLIC LIBRARY.

bitch forbye. But his pomes are grand—there's no denying that."
I asked him what his book was. "I havenae mind," said he—that was
his only book ! On turning it out, I found it was one of my own,
and on showing it to him, he remembered it at once. "O aye," he
said, "I mind now. It's pretty bad ; ye'll have to do better than
that, chieldy," and chuckled, chuckled. He is a strange old figure to
be sure. He cannot endure Pirbright Smith—"a mere æsthatic," he
said. "Pooh ! " "Fishin' and releegion—these are my aysthatics,"
he wound up.

To Edmund Gosse he wrote :

. . . From Stobo you can conquer Peebles and Selkirk, or to give
them their old decent names, Tweeddale and Ettrick. Think of
having been called Tweeddale, and being called PEEBLES ! Did I ever
tell you my skit on my own travel books ? We understand that
Mr. Stevenson has in the press another volume of unconventional
travels : " Personal Adventures in Peeblesshire." *Je le trouve méchante.*[1]

His projected travel-book did not, however, materialise ; but
" Heathercat " has a Tweeddale background, culled from " all
my weary reading as a boy." Sydney Colvin suggested that
" Upper Tweeddale with the country stretching thence towards
the wells of Clyde " was not far away from his memory when
in Samoa he was writing *Weir of Hermiston*. " My imagination
continually inhabits that cold old huddle of grey hills," he wrote
to J. M. Barrie. He knew the lonely and subtle peace of Tweeddale hills and valleys. He was enamoured of the name " The
Cauldstaneslap," which occurs thirty times in *Weir of Hermiston*,
although I doubt whether he ever really walked through the
Slap, seeing that he refers to the Cairn hills, over 1,800 feet,
as " hillocks " ! which is their appearance as viewed from
a distance. " The Slap opened like a doorway between two
rounded hillocks," he writes, " and through this ran the short
cut to Hermiston." And it was Kirstie Elliott, the Fair Lass o'
Cauldstaneslap, who soothed to Archie Weir, in the Slap, the
story of her ancestors :

> O ! they rade in the rain, in the days that are gane,
> In the rain, and the wind, and the lave ;
> They shoutit in the ha' and they routit on the hill,
> But they're a' quaitit noo in the grave,
> Auld auld Elliotts, clay cauld Elliotts, dour bauld
> Elliotts of auld !

[1] *Letters*, 1900, vol. i, pp. 241–44.

And when they parted in the Slap Archie felt as if something went along with her out of the deepest of his heart.

Lord Braxfield was a Tweeddale laird, the Laird of Broughton, who had monetary transactions with the Presbyterian Kirk Session of Stobo in 1779. He purchased Broughton for £14,200 in 1774, and in 1783 became proprietor of the whole parish. Broughton estate was owned by the Murrays of Stanhope for many years and was sold by " Secretary " Murray to James Dickson of Ednam, a London Merchant, from whose nephew, Captain William Dickson, Braxfield bought the property when exposed for sale in the Exchange Coffee-house in Edinburgh. His daughter Katherine married the oldest son of Clanranald of the 'Forty-five (John Macdonald). He spoke the broadest Scots on the Bench, and witnesses, both Highland and Lowland, frequently could not understand what he said :

JUDGE (*to prisoner at the Bar*) : Hae ye ony Counsel, my man ?
PRISONER : No.
JUDGE : Do ye want to hae ony appointit ?
PRISONER : No ; I only want an interpreter to make me understand what your Lordship says.

Walter Scott dedicated his thesis for admission to the Faculty of Advocates to Lord Braxfield.

Whether R. L. S. had Upper Tweeddale in mind when he wrote *Weir of Hermiston*, as suggested, we shall never know. The description might well fit this part of the country :

The road to Hermiston runs for a great part of the way up the valley of a stream, a favourite with anglers and with midges, full of falls and pools, and shaded by willows and natural woods of birch. Here and there, but at great distances, a byway branches off, and a gaunt farm-house may be descried above in a fold of the hill ; but the more part of the time, the road would be quite empty of passage and the hills of habitation.

There are quiet habitations :

. . . the whole colony, kirk and manse, garden and graveyard, finds harbourage in a grove of rowans, and is all the year round in a great silence broken only by the drone of bees, the tinkle of the burn and the bell on Sundays. . . . All beyond and about is the great field of the hills ; the plover, the curlew and the lark cry there ; the wind blows as it blows in a ship's rigging, hard and cold and pure ; and the hill-tops huddle one behind another like a herd of cattle into the sunset.

None will dispute the atmosphere and spirit of this delectable countryside in Lord Tweedsmuir's *John Burnet of Barns* and *Scholar Gipsies*, those early books which most of us love so well, while in *The Watcher by the Threshold* there is subtle imaginative writing of the eeriness of the peat-hags, the lonely places and the dwellings of the little Brown Men of the Moors : and in *The Herd of Farawa* and *Fisher Jamie*, " who lo'ed nae music, kenned nae tunes, except the sang o' Tweed in spate, or Talla loupin' ower its Linns," there are true pictures of rural life in this hilly pastoral land that lies stretched before us, and is viewed so comprehensively from the summit of the Broad Law of Hairstane.

IX

OLD WAYSIDE INNS

FAMOUS HOSTELRIES IN THE SOUTHERN UPLANDS

"Sweet is old wine in bottles, ale in barrels."
(BYRON, *Don Juan*)

MOST of the old inns and alehouses on the Edinburgh–Moffat road have now disappeared. In some cases the house, now reconstructed, remains; in others, only the locations remain. Many disappeared in Peeblesshire when the tolls were abolished after 1st January 1866, and the toll-houses sold. Toll-bars stood at Tweedshaws, Bield, Rachan, Harestanes, Romanno and Leadburn.

On the fifty-miles stretch of road there existed in early days inns or alehouses at the following places : Tweedshaws, Tweedhopefoot, The Bield, The Crook, Broughton, Harestanes, Blyth Bridge, Newlands, Noblehouse, Leadburn, Howgate ; and also at Carlops and The Brig'us, West Linton, when the road went by Blyth Muir and Blyth to Knock-knowes (Blythbridge), where it joined the Broughton road.

A historian, writing in 1715, narrates that at " Tweed's Shaws or Tweed's Slush there was lately built a little Alehouse, mean but comfortable, by the road side from Edinburgh to Carlisle by West Linton, Broughton, Moffat and Dumfries," near the source of Tweed at Tweed's Well, 1,300 feet above sea level. It was in this alehouse that one of Prince Charlie's Highlanders, on the way south, left behind him an officer's silver-mounted sword and Highland dirk, which is in possession of the descendants of the family by whom the soldiers were entertained. This house disappeared when the present road was made about 1830, and a new inn was built, a little to the westward of the former one, with walls three feet thick, containing spacious stabling and sleeping accommodation. It has now been reconstructed as a dwelling-house. The innkeeper at the time of the tragic snowstorm (1st February 1831) was Dan Kirke. It was he who directed the search party where to look for the lost guard and driver of the mail-coach (Chapter XII).

A little over a mile away stood the " Old Inn and Alehouse " at Tweedhopefoot, where lived early in the eighteenth century Jamie Welsch, ironically named " The Bairn of Tweedhopefoot," known for his great bulk and strength, of whom tradition asserts that he once carried on his back a load of meal, 16 stones, all the way from Peebles, 24 miles, and rested only twice ! Some say the load was 20 stones, that he rested only once, and that, on coming to Drumelzier Ford, he was asked by his companion how they were to get across, and he replied, " Jump on to the tap o' the meal, an' A'll cairy ye ower."

It was while Welsch of Tweedhopefoot and his companion, John Hunter, both Covenanters, were fleeing from the pursuing dragoons over Erickstane Brae to the Beef Tub that Hunter was shot. Welsch escaped to his aunt's house at Carterhope in Fruid, but the persecutors were in pursuit. They entered the farm-house, saw the apparently sleeping man by the fireside, while his aunt called out to him, giving him a slap on the shoulder, " Get up, ye lazy lout ; gang oot, and haud the sodjers' horses." His life was saved. Hunter lies buried in Tweedsmuir (1685 : tombstone erected 1727), the only martyr's grave in the church-yards of the Border.

The next inn was The Bield. Originally it was the post-office, and the postman went his round perched high on his old-fashioned single-horse gig. This inn marked the second stage on the Edinburgh–Moffat road, the chief turnpike authorised by Act of 1753. It was said to be difficult to maintain, especially in the southern portion, and was in bad repair, owing to the heavy lead traffic from Leadhills, notwithstanding that the tolls were higher than any in the Lothians. Burns and Thomas Campbell, the poet (*Pleasures of Hope*) friend of Hamilton Paul, the witty Broughton minister, author of the song " Jeanie o' the Crook," frequented The Bield. The story is told that one night Campbell was awakened by the maid's request, " Please, sir, could ye tak' a neebor into yer bed ? " " With all my heart," replied the dreaming poet. " Thank ye, sir, for the Moffat carrier's just come in a' wat, and there's no a single ither place." Up came the reeking carrier man ; exit the dainty little maid.

The notorious Claverhouse spent a night there, when as Sheriff of Galloway he was travelling from Edinburgh to his headquarters at Kenmure Castle. The Covenanters held their great Conventicle at Talla Linns (1682), but the innkeeper kept his own counsel. Later Claverhouse learned of the fact, when the Rev. Francis Scott told him that the Covenanters had come from Clydesdale, crossing Tweed by the stepping-stones connecting the manse with The Bield, and stated diplomatically "they did no prejudice in his house further than meat and drink." Claverhouse stationed a dragoon in the inn.

The present house dates from 1726. The timber and iron-work of the old tower which existed in 1696 was used in the building of it by James Tweedie. Here was born in 1819 that gifted divine, Rev. John Ker, whose published sermons ran into sixteen editions, and whose *Psalms in History and Biography* is a religious classic. At a later date the mail changed horses at The Crook, where "post-chaises and horses" were also to be had ; and Crook became the post-office. In 1841 the mail-coach passed daily, and the road was in excellent repair (*New Statistical Account*). This item is significant, because ten years previously the mail-coach travelled so slowly owing to bad roads that a visitor staying at The Crook wagered with the driver that, given an hour's start, he would cover the distance to Edinburgh (36 miles) on foot in less time than the coach. While the driver was loosing his horses the walker arrived ! (*Peeblesshire Advertiser*, 3rd June 1831.) Christopher North walked from Penrith to Kendal, because he was unable to obtain a seat in the mail-coach, and reached Kendal before the coach ! Christopher was of course a prince of walkers—to attend a public dinner in Edinburgh he walked from Kelso, and walked 70 miles to be present at a Burns' celebration ! In his prime no distance was too great for him.

In 1846 "The Enterprise" coach ran to and from Dumfries daily in summer, by West Linton, Biggar, Abington and Thorn-hill, leaving Princes Street, Edinburgh, at 8 A.M.

Captain Armstrong in his *Companion to the Map of Tweeddale* (1775), remarks that "a small cot house, within a few yards of the Crook Inn, and the farm of Herstane opposite to it, gave rise to the vulgar apophthegm that Tweed runs between the crook and the hearthstane."

The "Cruik of Tweddell" is the name given to the inn in the account of the rescue of Sir Patrick Porteous of Hawkshaw, who being at the horn for debt in 1621, was being conveyed by a messenger from Hawkshaw to the Tolbooth of Edinburgh, but they broke their journey at the house of James Geddes in " Cruik of Tweddell," and Sir Patrick was immediately rescued by his neighbours. On another occasion Lord Yester, the Sheriff, sent an officer to poind his cattle at Hawkshaw ; the cattle were being driven to Peebles when Sir Patrick overtook the officer, threatened him with death, and drove the cattle home (*Reg. Privy Council*). Notwithstanding all which he was made a burgess of Peebles (1634) ; appeared before Tweedsmuir Kirk Session for following Montrose ; and had a daughter, Elizabeth, married to James Williamson of Hutcheonfield, and another, Janet, married Walter Scott of Gamescleuch, from whom descended the Napiers of Merchiston. Gamescleuch's brother, Sir Robert Scott of Thirl-stane, took part in the rescue of Kinmont Willie, and was killed in a duel in 1600 by John Scott, son of Walter Scott of Tushielaw (*Scots Peerage*, vi, p. 430).

In the days of Episcopacy, the Crook Inn became a Presby-terian meeting-house, and on 5th September 1688 James Thom-sone, minister of Tweedsmuir, was ordained there. Prior to 1643 it was in Upper Drumelzier parish, which extended from Merlin's grave to the source of Tweed, a distance of twenty miles. It is now in Tweedsmuir parish.

A hunted hill-man was hid in a peat-stack by the landlady until the dragoons had refreshed themselves and departed. Chambers in his *Traditionary Tales* tells the story of how a prisoner —one of Prince Charlie's men, being taken to the South for trial in 1746—guarded by a detachment of military, made his escape in the mist by breaking from his guard, and fixing his head be-tween his knees and holding his feet in his hands formed his body into a rounded form, rolled heels over head into the Devil's Beef Tub, and so regained freedom, the soldiers being unable to follow. In due course he returned to The Crook, hid in a peat-stack, and escaped after the guard, who had returned to The Crook at night, departed next day. Scott introduces the story into *Redgauntlet*, and describes the place—" it looks as if four hills were laying their heads together to shut out the daylight . . . a d——d deep black, blackguard-looking abyss of a hole it is, and goes straight down from the roadside." Scott halted for a night at The Crook on his fateful journey to the English Lakes in 1797.

Jeanie Hutchison, the daughter of another landlord, was made famous in her day by the Broughton minister we have mentioned, in a popular song sung to the tune " Jock o' Hazeldean." Jeanie lies in Tweedsmuir Kirkyard under a tombstone inscribed " Here lies Jeanie o' The Crook."

The Crook Inn, which was in existence before the year 1600, has pleasant associations of many celebrated literary men of the nineteenth century who roamed the Tweeddale mountains and drew inspiration from Nature's bounty, and when evening came dined and supped to the accompaniment of merry wit and jocund song. Many happy days were spent at The Crook when the jovial Christopher North was in his prime !

Ah, those post-prandial gatherings of congenial souls around the fire, when the joys of the day on the hills are recounted—the pleasures of the table, followed by the pleasures of the pipe, the toddy-tumbler—for Christopher was no teetotaller—and the feast of memory ! Strange influences are at work when men lift up their eyes to the hills ! And often there is silent thought of those who company with us no more, so finely expressed by John Buchan :

> Some slender nook of memory spare
> For our old happy moorland days.
> I sit alone, and musing fills
> My breast with pain that shall not die,
> Till once again o'er greener hills
> We roam together, you and I.
>
> (" Fratri Dilectissimo ")

Or Wordsworth's reflections upon the passing of Scott and the Ettrick Shepherd with whom he had companied in the vale of Yarrow :

> When first, descending from the moorlands,
> I saw the Stream of Yarrow glide
> Along a bare and open valley,
> The Ettrick Shepherd was my guide.
>
> When last along its banks I wandered,
> Through groves that had begun to shed
> Their golden leaves upon the pathways,
> My steps the Border-minstrel led.
>
> The mighty Minstrel breathes no longer,
> Mid mouldering ruins low he lies ;
> And death upon the braes of Yarrow,
> Has closed the Shepherd-poet's eyes.

.   .   .   .   .

Like clouds that rake the mountain-summits
Or waves that own no curbing hand,
How fast has brother followed brother,
From sunshine to the sunless land !

Of course in the case of inns, as of much else, circumstances alter cases. Sir Thomas Dick Lauder (*Scottish Rivers*) described The Crook as " one of the coldest-looking, most cheerless places of reception for travellers that he ever chanced to behold— isolated and staring in the midst of the great glen of Tweed, closed in by high sloping hills on all sides." There may have been justification for his state of mind—it was a cold, raw November night ; and a wheel had just come off his post-chaise ! William Black in his *Strange Adventures of a Phaeton* makes his travellers spend a night at The Crook Inn, to dine on ham and eggs and whisky !—probably more satisfying than the Scotsman's proverbial haggis and whisky, the Englishman's oysters and Chablis or the Irishman's potatoes and potheen ! All the Tweeddale inns have their own traditions. It was in the Cross Keys Inn, Peebles, in the lifetime of Miss Ritchie (" Meg Dods " in *St. Ronan's Well*) that the Tweeddale Presbytery always dined, and their comfort was her special care. Her death occurred one afternoon while the members were at dinner, and almost her last words were, " Are the ministers a' richt ? " They immediately broke up the Club for the day. She died in 1841 (Williamson's *Glimpses of Peebles*, 1895).

" In Meg Dods Scott has drawn one of the best hostesses in literature," writes John Buchan in his incomparable *Sir Walter Scott*. ". . . Meg talks perhaps the best Scots in the novels, with the rhythmical lilt which is the chief beauty of the vernacular speech " :

" My gude name ! if ony body touched my gude name, I would neither fash council nor commissary—I wad be down amang them, like a jer-falcon amang a wheen wild-geese, and the best amang them that dared to say ony thing of Meg Dods but what was honest and civil, I wad sune see if her cockernonnie was made of her ain hair or other folk's. *My* gude name, indeed ! "

And many a tale has been told in the inn. Here is a poaching story concerning a stretch of the Tweed not far from The Crook, introduced with a warning by that prince of anglers—Izaak Walton :

71

If thou be a severe, sour-complexioned man, then
I here disallow thee to be a competent judge.

While walking up one of the glens in Tweeddale, not far from
The Crook Inn, I met Tammas, an elderly native, from whom
in days of yore I had learned much local antiquarian lore, so we
sat down on the heathery hillside for a crack. He had been
reading *St. Ronan's Well*, and spoke in high commendation of
Sir Walter's skill in describing Tweed fishers : " Man," he said,
" it's grand, just listen," and he read Mistress Dods' eulogy of
fishermen :

They were pawky auld carles, that kend whilk side their bread
was buttered upon. Ye never kend of ony o' them ganging to the
spring as they behoved to ca' the stinking well yonder.—Na, na—
they were up in the morning—had their parritch, wi' maybe a
thimblefull of brandy, and then awa' up into the hills, eat their bit
cauld meat on the heather, and came hame at e'en wi' the creel full
of caller trouts, and had them to their dinner, and their quiet cogue
of ale, and their drap punch, and were set singing their catches and
glees, as they ca'ed them, till ten o'clock, and then to bed, wi' God
bless ye.—And what for no ?

Ever since he was a laddie, Tammas had been getherin' lear.
" Ay be learning something new, it's the secret o' longevity,"
he would say to me, and I believed that this rule was born of his
own life experience ; but in the course of time I found the saying
" I grow old learning something new every day " was over
2,500 years old, being attributed to Solon, who lived 638–558 B.C.,
accounted one of the Seven Sages of Greece and the wisest of
them all, a great statesman and founder of Athenian democracy,
so Tammas was in noble company. " To be wholly devoted to
some intellectual exercise is to have succeeded in life," wrote
R. L. S. Tammas had succeeded. He liked to talk about what
last he had learned. " Man," he once said, " it's no the eagle
that's the symbolical bird of our race, it's the parrot ! " And he
knew the poets also. " Here," he said, " is when Brown Trout
fishing should close :

> " When corn's fa'n to the shearer clips
> An' broon the tatie shaws,
> The rose trees hangin' red wi' hips,
> The hawthorns red wi' haws,
> The breckans rustin' in the beil,
> The summer flow'rets gane,

> I think that ilka angler chiel
> Should lea' the troots alane.
>
> When hushed are a' the woodland sangs,
> An' silent is the lark,
> When ilka tree wi' russet hangs
> An' days are short an' dark,
> Lay past your rods, an' lures an' creels,
> An' wait for Spring again,
> Till then I think a' angler chiels
> Should leave the troots alane."

And Tammas had something to say on cooking trout—" Medium-sized are best," he said ; " and see how bonnie the skin is when they're newly caught, with a fine fresh smell. Handle them carefully," he urged, " wash quickly, dry with a soft cloth, keep the head on : and here's the real Scots way to cook them—' Dry them carefully ; dip them in fine oatmeal ; and fry them in smoking hot fat, till they're brown and firm ; and serve them with fried parsley and cut lemon.' There now !—remember. Ah ! "

On my remarking that the fisher got much comfort and real enjoyment out of his days on the water, and that there was a time, long since vanished, when he was never heard to complain, Tammas reminded me of a quotation by John Buchan, of a lad who asks a canny old fisher—" Whaur hae ye been ? " " Mony miles, laddie, ower the Kips sae green." " Fishin' Leithen Water ? " " Nay, laddie, nay. Just a wee burnie, rinnin' doon a brae ; fishin' a wee burnie nae bigger than a sheugh." Asked if he gat mony troots, he replied :

> " I gat enough—
> Enough to buy my baccy, snuff and pickle tea,
> And lea' me tippence for a gill, and that's enough for me."

But what Tammas had at the back of his mind that day, and what he really wanted to tell me was a poaching story he had heard, and so with glee and many a chuckle he continued :

" There were three of them ; they had done quite well ; and three silvery salmon averaging twenty-five pounds apiece lay on the grass at their feet, when suddenly the water bailiff appeared on the scene. Like a flash the lads were up, and off, and over the hillside, leaving the bailiff in possession of the fish. But what was he to do with them ; how was he to carry them ?

Taking off his waist-belt he strung them through the gills, and dragged them in the direction of a near-by shepherd's cottage, where he asked the good wife if she could give him a bag in which to carry the fish. 'Aye,' she replied, 'I'll gie ye a bag, in exchange for ane o' the saumon.' 'Right,' was the bailiff's laconic reply, 'choose which you will have.' She pointed to the middle one. 'Na, na,' said the bailiff, 'that's the biggest and the best; guess again!' 'Then deil a bag ye'll get then,' said the good wife, and banged the door on the bailiff's face. Dumb-foundered, the bailiff took up the fish again, and dragged them to a sandhole by the water's edge, where he hid them with bracken, still strung on his waist-belt, and betook himself to The Crook in search of a bag, and much-needed refreshment. Here he met a crony from Biggar, and in the course of conversation the whole story of the capture was told. Now the crony was fond of salmon, and, at a certain stage in the conversation, he was promised one of the fish in exchange for a drive home in the Biggar man's gig. Several others joined in the talk, including the good lady of The Crook, and the fun grew fast and furious. Yes, she had long promised a salmon to a friend, and here was the very opportunity she had been looking for—a salmon from the bailiff; no questions asked, and no fear of a fine. So she, also, was promised a salmon, and a ride in the crony's gig to Broughton Station. In due course the lady of The Crook, the bailiff and the crony mounted the gig, and arriving at the spot on the river-bank where the fish had been hid, the bailiff got down and proceeded to the sandhole. But, alas! he failed to find the fish. The crony and The Crook landlady, unable to understand the matter, joined in the search, but all to no purpose. The fish had disappeared. The bailiff was sure of the spot where he had deposited them; the lady grew suspicious; and the crony was much in anger, thinking that the bailiff had played him a trick, and thereupon refused to drive him home. The lady of The Crook had now no need for the drive to the station, and as the crony, loudly vociferating, was about to depart, a long derisive laugh rang out from the hillside opposite, and three tousy heads appeared above the heather.

"The poachers had kept an eye upon the bailiff, watched him hide the fish, and enter The Crook, and in the interval had stolen down to the water's edge and recovered the salmon, waist-belt and all. The bailiff was sore distressed, forfairn and forfoughten. To cross the river, and give chase, was out of the question. Once again the poachers had triumphed, and for long afterwards they chuckled at how they had outwitted the water bailiff, and brought discomfiture to him and to his friends."

And after Tammas had told me his story, he went on his way again. His zest for life was an inspiration, and I found myself repeating :

> Success to every gentleman that lives in old Mercia,
> Success to every poacher that wants to sell a hare,
> Bad luck to every gamekeeper that will not sell his deer.
> O 'tis my delight of a shiny night, in the season of the year !

Part of the old Crook Inn is incorporated in the present modern popular inn, which still retains its lively associations with the past.

The farm-house at Calzeat, pronounced Callate, beside Broughton Parish Church, was an inn in the beginning of last century with the sign :

> Call late or call sune
> Ye'll get drink till your money's dune.

The Rev. Hamilton Paul is said to have adjourned the service in his church, at which only seven persons were present, on account of the stormy weather, to the comfortable inn parlour, taking the Pulpit Bible with him, and ordering refreshments " for the good of the house." A native of Ayrshire, he was an early biographer of Burns—*The Poems and Songs of Burns with Life*, etc., 1819. His sermons " exhibited extensive learning and singular originality of thought " ; and he was accounted the best story-teller of his day, having a joke for every occasion, a bon-mot for every adventure, " while the ease of his manner, the variety and extent of his information, the readiness and point of his wit, attracted men of taste and learning from different quarters." In 1834 the Edinburgh mail-coach passed through Broughton at one o'clock in the morning ; and the coach from Moffat at midday. The 17th of July 1617 must have been a memorable day in the village, for when sending back to England James VI's carriage and baggage after his Scottish visit, the county had to provide fifty horses " to lift His Majesty's carriage and carry the same to Dumfries." Inhabitants failing to supply horses were liable to a fine of £20 for each horse, and imprisonment for a year and a day (*Privy Council Reg.* xi, pp. 184-86). Broughton was the first stage for the cavalcade journeying from Holyrood.

Inn signs are now almost a rarity in Scotland, and do not
ppear at any time to have been so common as across the Border,
where the Red Lion, the King's Head and the Open Arms suggest
" ease at mine inn," good-will, good fare and interesting local
talk, for after all the inn and not the churchyard is the place to
find the history of the parish. The oldest inn sign was the Bush,
symbolical of Bacchus. For all interested in the names of these
southern inns, there is always the itch to go inn-hunting to find
the " Trip to Jerusalem," the " Pure Drop Inn," the " Crooked
House " and the " Beehive Inn " with the sign

> Within this hive, we're all alive,
> Good liquor makes us funny :
> If you are dry, come in and try—
> The flavour of our honey.

The inn at Cant's Walls, near Newlands Kirk and Romanno
Hotel—of which even the exact site cannot now be identified,
is celebrated by the genial Tweeddale physician Pennecuik, where
the lairds of the surrounding lands met, to lull the cares of life to
rest in a cup of nappy ale, and listen to the lively witticisms of
each other. It was the scene of many jollifications, and in his
poem inviting a friend to join him in the country, he writes :

> When our limbs are weary and our sport is done,
> We'll trudge to Cant's Walls by the setting sun,
> And there some hours we'll quaff a cup of ale
> And smoke our pipes, backed with a wanton tale.

The hostess was Lady Effy, whose mirth-inspiring ale was brewed
at West Linton with " Rumblin' Tam " spring water ; and is
referred to in " The Gentle Shepherd " (1725) :

> I'll whistle Pate an' Roger frae the height,
> I'll yoke my sled, an' send to the neist town,
> An' bring a draught o' Ale baith stout an' brown.

Ale in 1652 sold at 1 penny-farthing sterling for 2 quarts or
16 pennies Scots per pint (Chambers's *Peeblesshire*, 1864). Four
gallons were taken to Peebles Cross by command of the Magistrates to celebrate the revival of the Beltane Fair horse-race in
1661. Three ale-cups were broken, entered by the Treasurer at
6 shillings !

In *Ancient Scotland from 1149–1370* Fraser-Tytler writes :
" From the multitudes of Brewhouses, from the Royal manu-

factories of ale down to those in the towns, burghs, baronies and villages it is evident that this beverage must have been consumed in great quantities " ; and probably good bread and cheese and ale were as much enjoyed by travellers in those days as they are by hungry wayfarers to-day. No doubt the Picts brewed Heather Ale on the Pentland Hills.

It is interesting to note in passing that Dr. Pennecuik wrote his *Description of Tweeddale* (1715) following upon the *Description of Linlithgowshire*, 1710, by Sir Robert Sibbald, M.D. (1641–1722), founder of the Royal College of Physicians, 1681, and first Professor of Medicine, Edinburgh University (1685), appointed Geographer for the Kingdom of Scotland by Charles II, and commanded to publish the *Natural History and the Geographic Description Thereof* in 1682 (Sibbald MSS., Nat. Lib.). His *Tweeddale* is still an interesting book of reference, although he had little appreciation of the beauty of Tweeddale, but at that time appreciation of scenic beauty hardly existed. Yet he had a sense of humour, as we see in his *Panegyric upon the Royal Army in Scotland*, and he concluded his book with the lines :

> So farewell Tweeddale, I'm no more thy debtor ;
> Let him that censures this describe thee better.

Perhaps he would have agreed with Walter Bagehot, who said that the reason why so few good books are written is that so few people who can write know anything ! And then he adds : " Having done with Tweeddale ; for the further satisfaction of the curious, especially our learned and worthy Physicians, and Apothecary Chirurgeons in Edinburgh, who most of them, I believe, may be strangers to the Shire I have now described, here follows an Alphabetical Catalogue of several Plants that I have observed to grow wild in Tweeddale, besides the common, which I found more rare in my search through the other places of the Kingdom." Then follows the list of plants. He was joint founder with Sir Andrew Balfour of the Botanic Gardens in Edinburgh, 1667. The 1815 edition of the *Description*, which includes the poems, is the best, as it contains Notes by Robert D. C. Brown, Laird of Newhall, Carlops. The doctor lived at Romanno House, not far from Cant's Walls, and knew how to enjoy his leisure hours :

> I love the net, I please the fishing hook,
> In angling by the pretty, murmuring brook.

To curl on the ice, does greatly please,
Being a manly Scottish exercise ;
It clears the brains, stirs up the native heat,
And gives a gallant appetite for meat.
In winter, now and then I plant a tree,
Remarking what the annual growth may be ;
Order my hedges, and repair my ditches,
Which gives delight, although not sudden riches.
So, when of these sweet solitudes I tire,
We have our trysts and meetings in the shire.

He married the heiress to the property in 1676, Margaret Murray of the noted family Murray of Romanno, Halmyre, Stanhope and Cardon. Romanno under varying forms, Rothmaneic being the earliest, was originally a wide district, and formed the nucleus of Newlands Parish, the monks of both Holyrood and Newbattle being interested in parts of it. " Newlands " indicates that " the founding of the church was contemporaneous with the opening up of the lands " and Newlands came to be the designation of the whole district under the vicar's jurisdiction (Renwick's *Historical Notes*). In this parish Noblehouse, on the main Edinburgh–Moffat–Dumfries road, was a prominent stage inn for travellers, being the first stage from Edinburgh. County records of 1636 make reference to it. In 1768 George Dalziel, previously innkeeper at West Linton, became landlord at Noblehouse. He was the first farmer to sow turnips in the open field and cultivate potatoes on a large scale. George Williamson, the innkeeper in 1848, bequeathed a present of his hearse for the use of the Newlands parishioners. Innkeepers of stage-coach days were personages of importance.

The most picturesque company who ever dined at Noblehouse must have been the Tweeddale Shooting Club, founded in 1790, and now one of the oldest sporting and dining clubs in Scotland. Professor Veitch, in his Centenary Memorial [1] of the Club, tells how it had its origin in a shooting party on Glendean banks at the head of Quair Water, who were dressed in " a coat of grass-green colour with a dark green velvet cape, and a silver button with the letter T engraved upon it, a white vest and black satin breeches." In 1797 it was ordered that members who should attend any of the regular dinners without wearing the uniform coat should be fined two bottles of claret, and in 1804 the penalty

[1] Prepared by the late Professor Veitch, and privately printed for the Tweeddale Shooting Club in 1890.

THE LEITHEN WATER AND MOORFOOT HILLS

DARLINGTON
PUBLIC LIBRARY.

TALLA RESERVOIR

DAWICK HOUSE

DARLINGTON
PUBLIC LIBRARY.

THE CROOK INN

for appearing at the Annual Ball otherwise than in uniform was fixed at one Scots pint of claret. Exact compliance with those rules was enforced, for in 1813 the Sheriff of the County paid a fine of one guinea for not having a green velvet collar on his coat.

Early in its history the Club dined in Miss Ritchie's inn in Peebles ; later, the festive board was spread in the Tontine Hotel, opened in 1808, financed by means of a Tontine proprietary, and considered a great undertaking in its day, when arrangements were made for the Annual Ball " to the Ladies of the County and their friends." The main consideration, which has been amply justified, seems to have been that the county required a central hotel, with a ballroom ; but the ballroom does not appear to have at first conformed to the required standard of decoration, for in 1809 we read, " the Ladies very spiritedly subscribed £150 to paint the Ball-room." " Six dozen of port and claret glasses and four decanters, inscribed with the letter ' T ' were the exclusive property of the Club, as well as a cellar in the Tontine well stocked with wines." The founders of the Club were Lord Elibank, Sir James Naesmyth of Posso, Sir George Montgomery of Macbiehill, Walter Williamson of Cardrona, Robert Brown of Newhall, Aeneas Mackay of Scotstoun, Captain R. N. Campbell of Hallyards, William Montgomery, Younger of Stanhope and James Wolfe Murray, Advocate, Sheriff of the County. It may be interesting to add that in addition to having had a Shooting Club since 1790, Peebles had also a " Silver Arrow " which has been shot for by the Royal Company of Archers (King's Bodyguard for Scotland) since 1628 in the reign of Charles I, which is the date of the oldest medal appended to the arrow, which consists of a stalk of silver, with a flattened and barbed point, fifteen inches long, attached to which, by small silver rings and chains, are a number of medals with names and coats of arms of the winners, presented by James Williamson, Provost of Peebles, of whom there is record that he was the Commissioner sent by the Burgh of Peebles to the famous General Assembly in Glasgow in 1638. The arrow may be a few years older than the date of the first medal, although it may not be so ancient as the Musselburgh Arrow, instituted by the Town Council of Musselburgh for the encouragement of archery, first competed for in 1603 and won by J. Johnston of Elphinstone. The last competition was held on Musselburgh racecourse in May

1946 when the archers turned out in full uniform with their pipe band. Since 1676 the shoot has been confined to members of the Royal Company. The Burgh Accounts of 1628, and subsequent thereto, show that the shooting competitions at Peebles were not unaccompanied by refreshments. The Silver Arrow is now preserved in the Archers' Hall, Buccleuch Street, Edinburgh, along with other muniments, and is still periodically shot for, on which occasions the Council present the Royal Company with a riddle of claret or port. A list of the medal winners (1628–1921) is contained in *The History of Peeblesshire*, vol. ii, p. 203). Among the other muniments in Archers' Hall there is one of considerable interest to Tweeddale. Prior to 1643 The Carlops was acquired by Alexander Burnet, Advocate, son of William Burnet of Barns —"The Hoolet of Barns." Then came Archibald Burnet in 1707. The Burnets were Jacobites, and in the 'Fifteen Rising there was a Company called "Barns' Company." Archibald was admitted to the Royal Company of Archers in 1708, and the portrait of him in the Archers' uniform by Richard Waitt, Edinburgh, painted in 1715, is the earliest known representation of the uniform of a private of the King's Bodyguard for Scotland. This picture formed part of the Newhall (Carlops) Collection, in which it was entered as " a whole length of the Old Pretender in the Archers' uniform," and for a long time it was thought to be a picture of the Chevalier de St. George, but the last laird, Dr. Horatio Robert Forbes Brown (1854–1926),[1] stated " there is little doubt that this is a portrait of Archibald Burnet." It was subsequently purchased by the late Sir Henry Cook, W.S., who presented it to the Royal Company, and it was added to the gallery of portraits in the Hall, where I inspected it in company with Sir Henry, who was much interested in the subject.

The date when the Shooting Club dined at Noblehouse was 1804. The old inn is now a farm-house : but Leadburn, standing 900 feet above sea level, with bracing air and far-stretching views of the Tweeddale hills, still flourishes, a homely, comfortable place retaining the old-fashioned atmosphere of the country inn. Before the railway to West Linton was built in 1864, a coach left Leadburn's " well-known inn," to take passengers to West Linton, Romanno Bridge and Broughton. It has been in existence since the seventeenth century.

William Black called it a cut-throat-looking place in his novel,

[1] *Pentland Days and Country Ways*, ch. viii, " Pentland Poets."

a dingy dilapidated building standing at the parting of two roads. " It looked like one of those remote and gloomy inns in the annals of romance." Nevertheless the travellers obtained both food and stimulant that enabled them to complete in comfort the last stage of the journey from London to Edinburgh.

In John Buchan's romance *John Burnet of Barns*, with its vivid picture of life in Tweeddale in former days, this inn is described as standing in the middle of a black peat bog in a forsaken country-side, but the landlord was an active, civil man, and the laird obtained an excellent dinner—a brace of wild fowl, and a piece of salted beef, " washed down with a very tolerable wine." It was here that he was joined by Nicol Plenderleith, his loyal and devoted servant. He is advised by a footpad at Leadburn " to haud doon by the Brochton and Newlands ways, for a' the way atween Leidburn and Peebles is hotchin' wi' sodjers."

In addition to the inns in the county town in 1856—Tontine, Commercial, Crown and Cross Keys—the following inns existed in the county :

Innerleithen	Traquair Arms	James Riddle
,,	Inn	Alex. Brodie
Broughton		J. Masterton
Crook		John Ecclesfield
West Linton	Haystoune Arms	Robert Brown
Carlops		James Veitch
Romanno Bridge		Mrs. E. Hope
Harestanes		James Hogg

Many a wayfarer walking over the hills and finding himself hungry and thirsty has blessed the inn, travelling the miles nearing its approach in a spirit of reverence and respect in anticipation of the satisfaction of all he stands in need of for the moment, rest and food and refreshment, and he calls upon Him to bless the place where thus he will find sheltering and nurture, a type of Mother Nature by whose side he has been walking all the day, in whose presence there is for him orderly happiness and good-fellowship.

But there are those who do not look upon it in this way, and do not recognise its sanctity and the office of its beneficence. Into the quiet old house they rush, arriving it may be by train or car, and must talk and call loudly, disturbing the quiet and restful peacefulness of the place, startling it would seem even the ancient walls with the shock of modern selfishness and vanity. The personality of an inn often meets one at the door, and immediately, if the inn be a good one, there is mental assent to the atmosphere of the old house that with charity, the wisdom of the years and the memory of other days, smiles benignantly upon all who approach her in the proper spirit, and with like understanding.

Let the inn be old and quaint, and ever so small, only let it be clean, spotlessly clean, with a personality all its own ; and let the homely meal, of which the savoury aroma has filled the house, be served daintily on spotless linen, for the walkers just arrived. Let the bedroom be well aired, and the windows open, that one may see the hills and the stars, that the smell of the earth and the grass and the flowers may enter to greet us with the rising sun, and the call of bird and fowl ; and let the sheets be dry, perfectly dry, and not of linen, and our rest sweet and satisfying, to furnish us with peace and energy for the day's travel. Much of the success of a walking tour depends upon our experience of the inn.

Let me conclude this chapter with the recollection of one who was in many respects an ideal innkeeper—" Mother " Veitch of the Carlops Inn, who passed on nearly thirty years ago. She knew what was required when you dropped down from the hills, wet and hungry and thirsty, and up would blaze the welcome fire, forth would come the dry socks and shoes, and soon the savour of ham and eggs would be streaming from the kitchen. It was this kindly interest she took in her visitors, this sympathy and warm-heartedness, that endeared her to many. " Hae ye cam ower the hill ? " she would enquire. " Aye, but ye've had a graun' day for it " : or if it was wet and stormy— " Mercy me, man, ye're no wise tae cam ower the hill on a day like this—off wi' yer coat ! " While she was thus ever happy in providing for the bodily and temporal wants of all who sought the hospitality of the inn, life for her did not consist of meat and drink only. She was equally encompassed with thoughts of things eternal. She spoke frequently of the more intimate relationships of the human soul with the Most High, and she would say, " There's mony a chance for pittin' in a word in a place like this, ye ken," so that often when least expected someone would hear " instruction's warning voice " ! " Ye see a' kinds o' folk here," she would say. " I mind a great big proud man was here aince, and he was boastin' about hoo wealthy he was, and what a lot o' money he had, and I asked him what guid a' his money wad dae him when he came to die. Aye, he was very quiet efter that. On another occasion there was a large party who had come out to spend the day, and they were ' singing and dancing like mad folk,' and one of them was swearing and saying ' by Christ.' I took him aside, and spoke to him, and said he wasna tae use the sacred name in that way. ' Do ye no ken,' I said, ' there's nae other name under heaven, given amang men, whereby ye can be saved ? ' and he was very quiet efter that, there was nae mair swearin', I can tell ye." In her young days she was fond of dancing, and all her long life of over four-score years she had been fond of singing, especially Scots songs, and only a few months before she passed away, when she heard that a friend who could sing a Scots song well was in the house, she insisted on his singing her some songs—and no one could sing them better than Harry Gamley—her bedroom door being kept open for the purpose. She wanted to sing " The Auld Scots Sangs " in return, and was much distressed at her failing memory when she found she had forgotten the words ! She dearly loved a " crack," and she had many stories. Her story of " The Man from the Talla " was characteristic—it ran as follows : " I mind o' a poor fella that came along the road there ae day—it was when they were makin' the Talla reservoir—he was just a bundle o' rags ; and he said, ' Mam, will ye gie me a gless o' beer ? I'm awfu' faur doon, I've walked frae Talla (over 25 miles) an' I'm gaun tae Edinburgh.' Weel, I gied him a gless, and efter he had drunk it he took oot his wee black stump o' a clay pipe, and then fumbled in his pockets for a match, and said, ' Where the hell's ma matches ? ' ' Come, come,' I said, ' there's nae sweirin' here.' ' Whit for no ? ' he replied, ' that's whaur I'm gaun tae.' ' But ye needna gaun there unless ye want tae,' I said. ' Ye dinna want tae gaun there, d'ye ? ' ' Dae ye think there's ony ither place for the like's o' me ? ' he asked, and I said, ' What does the Testament say—Come unto me, him that cometh I will in no wise cast out ; how often do ye read that in the Book ; will ye no take Him at His word, He wants ye tae come ? ' ' Aye ? ' he said enquiringly. ' Is that true ? but hoo am I tae dae it ? ' and he seemed to be thinking. Weel, I had been sharpening a pencil, and I had it in my hand, and I said to him, ' If I wis tae offer ye that pencil, wad ye take it ?' 'Sure'n a wid,' he said. 'And why wad ye take it ?' 'Because ye're offerin' it tae me.' 'Well,' I said, 'that's just what the Saviour does—He's gien ye the invitation, tak' Him at His word, and believe Him.' The poor fella stood still for a minute, then said to me, 'Will ye let me shake hands wi' ye, mam ?' an' I took his hand, as black as coal, and as hard as horn, and then he said, 'God bless ye, mam,' an' he went alang the road there, and I heard him ay saying, 'God bless ye, mam.' I never saw him again, but I think there was a different licht in his e'e when he went oot than when he cam' in."

Mrs. Veitch in her white lace cap, with the curls peeping out, often looking like the good Queen Victoria herself, was frequently to be seen at the inn door looking along the road, and sometimes she got strange news. She had lived all her life in The Carlops, through the days when the village had a mill and toll bar, and when the carts from the Leadhills passed with their load into Edinburgh, to be sent to Glasgow by the Canal, when the carrier was a familiar figure, and there were more horse-drawn machines, gigs and four-in-hands than motor-cars on the road. Rich and poor, high and low, all sorts and conditions of folk visited the Carlops Inn, and the motherly Mrs. Veitch was entrusted with many a secret, just because she had a mother's heart, and understood. She had many subjects of conversation, including Education, Politics and Religion. She was a strong advocate of the Sunday school, and the teaching of the Bible in the day schools. "If folks would read their Bibles more, they wouldna be sae feared to die." When she was a girl at the Sunday school, she could repeat the whole of the 119th Psalm. "I mind they used tae hear me say it at nights. 'O, Mary, Mary, I'm wearit hearin' ye gaun through a' that Psalm,' I think I hear them saying. Well, I've never forgotten it. Ye never forget what ye learn when ye're young." And as the evening shadows began to fall, and it was time to go, she would accompany you to the inn door, under the sign of Allan Ramsay, and her parting words were never forgotten—" Aye ; it's best tae let the darkness grow on ye." She was an ideal hostess this Lady of the Inn ; who served well her day and generation, and all who knew her as " Mother Veitch " cherish a memory that will for ever be rich and fragrant.

X

UP FRUID AND HART FELL : "THE CROWN OF SCOTLAND"

"The lark sent down her revelry ;
The blackbird and the speckled thrush
Good-morrow gave from brake and bush ;
In answer coo'd the cushat dove
Her notes of peace, and rest, and love."
(Lady of the Lake, Canto III, st. 2)

S U C H were the sounds that greeted us as one summer morning
we set out from Tweedsmuir for Fruid and the high tops
of Hart Fell.

Ever fresh and ever delightful is the winding valley of the
Water of Fruid that rises in wild lonely moorland on the Dumfriesshire border-line far up under the Rig of Hart Fell, one of the
three highest peaks that form the watershed between Tweeddale
and Moffatdale, the others being White Coomb and Lochcraig-
head.

Northwards from the watershed stretch broad-backed ridges
that maintain a high general level until at last they sink into the
lower hills that with steep faces descend into Tweed valley.
Between the ridges lie deep glens and winding straths, through
which flow Fruid Water, Talla Water and the Gameshope Burn,
that comes from Gameshope Loch, the highest sheet of water in
the south of Scotland, 1,750–2,000 feet above sea level.

"Water," it may be mentioned, is the term used in Southern
Scotland to indicate a small river, larger than a "burn," and
midway between the English "rivulet" and "river." Tweed,
Clyde and Annan all rise near each other, and each flows in a
different direction. Fruid, over six miles in length, is the longest
water, while Talla and Gameshope are the wildest and most
picturesque, having cut their way through masses of moraine left
by ancient glaciers. Gameshope Glen with its heaps of symmetri-
cal boulders and antediluvian aspect is as a giants' playground,
while Talla Glen, with frowning precipitous heights, was, as

Professor Geikie records, the rock basin of an ancient loch, and is now a modern reservoir for the city of Edinburgh. This source of supply will require to be increased for a Greater Edinburgh, and it is to come from the valley of the Water of Fruid—the "impulsive stream" which in its upper reaches lives up to its name—a pleasant, pastoral vale, wide and open to the cleansing winds and to the sunshine, through which flows Fruid singing all the way to join the shining Tweed, in its one-hundred-miles journey to the sea at Berwick, but some day, like Talla, destined to become imprisoned in pipes and cisterns of darkness.

Before climbing an unknown hill it is well to have a chat with those who live in the neighbourhood, preferably shepherds or keepers, because they know as no other the ground over which they travel daily, and their advice is always valuable. At Nether Fruid we got full directions. Under the shadow of Garelet Dod once stood the ancient castle of Fruid, the first and last seat of the noble family of the Frasers, who also built Oliver Castle, " grim guardian of the Upper Tweed." This ancient family, the first and greatest feudal barons who had place or power in Tweeddale, is said to have come originally from France, settled in Scotland in the days of Charlemagne, and bore the " fraises," the strawberry leaves of nobility, on their shields from the time of the Crusades. The hill behind the castle is to this day called Strawberry Hill.

In far-off times there was also a castle at the entrance to the glen, which may have been a Tweedie stronghold, so that often the hills must have resounded to the noise of armed men, but no trace of those old castles now exists, except that the foundations of Oliver Castle are still extant. Doubtless they played their part in Border story, when a signal lighted on Fruid could be answered down Tweed valley by beacon on Hawkshaw, Oliver, Polmood, Kingledores, Stanhope, Mossfennan, Wrae, Drumelzier, Tinnies, Dreva, Lour, Dawyck, Stobo . . . and so on to Berwick. These fortresses served as defence against the incursions of English marauders. Built in the shape of circular towers, they usually consisted of three storeys, the lowest one on the ground floor being vaulted and appropriated to the reception of horses and cattle in times of danger. Oliver estate is one of the few in Tweeddale to be still held by a descendant (Lawrence Tweedie-Stodart) of the earliest known vassals.

Famous among the Frasers was Sir Simon, " Lord of Tweeddale," a worthy Scottish patriot during the prosperous reigns of Alexander II and III (1214-85), Sheriff of Peebles, Keeper of Selkirk and Traquair Forests, Baron of the Scottish Parliament, who had to swear fealty to Edward I in 1291, who had become lord of the Kingdom of Scotland ; but Sir Simon died in the same year. He foresaw the coming storm of English aggression and the Scottish War of Independence.

Simon, his son, also took the oath, but fought against the English at the battle of Dunbar in 1296. In 1303, along with Sir John Comyn, he defeated the English army at the battle of Roslin. Friend and supporter of Wallace and Bruce, he fought in the Scottish War of Independence ; three times he saved the latter's life at Methven, but later was taken prisoner, and hanged, drawn and quartered in London, " his head smyten off and placed upon London Brig on a sper." The Oliver and Neidpath estates passed to Sir Gilbert Hay on his marriage to Sir Simon's elder daughter : the younger daughter married Sir Patrick Fleming of Biggar.

Glen Fruid has associations also of Covenanters, Border rievers, witches and giants. Many Conventicles were held in remote places in Fruid, as well as Core and Talla, and Tweedsmuir Kirk Session Record of 23rd November 1679 contains a " Memorandum of those who baptised their children disorderly at home or field conventicle " in these lonely spots.

Another story told in the glen is of a witch, Nannie Gannet, who lived at Blairshope. One day Nannie wanted to take the coach to Moffat, but when the driver saw his passenger waiting at the road-end at Riggs, he refused her entrance. At this she was wroth and, shaking her fist, cried out that evil would befall him and his coach, and that she would be in Moffat before him. She was not long on her way over the hills by the old Drove road, when a wheel came off the coach and delayed the journey to Moffat. And Nannie was waiting for its arrival in the market-place inwardly rejoicing and vigorously pouring scorn upon her detractors.

On the banks of the Fruid near Nether Menzion there once existed the grave of Marion Chisholm. It was believed that she was a vagrant who had come from the city in the time of plague, and that in wandering through the countryside she had spread the pestilence to Glencotha, Nether Menzion and Fruid, in consequence of which a number of persons died and " were buried in the ruins of their houses which their neighbours pulled down upon their dead bodies."

A short distance above the confluence of Fruid with Tweed is Hawkshaw Burn on the banks of which stood the Peel Tower of Hawkshaw, the home of the Porteouses, a family noted in Border story. This tower has also disappeared, as well as a chapel that stood on the banks of Fruid Water ; but the name " Priesthope " still survives in the Priesthope Burn flowing into Carterhope Burn. This chapel (Hawkshaw) was one of three in Upper Drumelzier Parish prior to 1643, the others being Kingle-dores, and a chapel on the lands of Menzion that occupied the site on which stands Tweedsmuir Kirk. There was a William Porteous of Hawkshaw in 1439 (*Origines*, i, pp. 206-7) ; Sir Patrick Porteous is mentioned in " The Tweeddale Raide " (Hogg's *Mountain Bard*).

If the castles and towers and chapels are now no more, if the Covenanters and witches and vagrants have disappeared, there still remains the mythical legend of Jack the Giant-killer, which may have had its origin not far from Fruid, for near Menzion Farm is a standing stone known as the Giant Stone. Tradition whispers of a giant who troubled the neighbourhood by his on-goings, and met his fate at the hands of a young archer, who from behind the stone, with his bow and arrow, killed the giant and freed the folks of Tweedside of a bully and a freebooter.

Good is the mountain air, fresh and sweet-smelling is the dewy grass in the morning hours, as we follow the track to the hill-top. " Here plays the gamesome lamb, and bleats the yearn-ing ewe." Pleasant also is the going, with all the wild life of the moorlands around us. Fruid is a land of song—snipe, linnets and larks ; and flocks of whaups, peewits and plovers are all together, yet separate. Whaups or curlews are first to spy us ; suspicious, quick of sight and hearing, rising in a flurry and sending their long birling notes echoing among the hills. In the breeding season they fly screaming about you, being then as courageous as they are timid at other times. Snow-white curlews are rare ; one was seen recently near Salen Mull (*The Scotsman*, 18th May 1946). The peewit—" *pee-e-wit ; pee-e-wit* "—also called the green-crested lapwing, teuchit and green plover, is likewise a good sentinel, and uses amusing antics to lead you away from the nest or young, its devotion to which is one of its outstanding character-istics, and a deadly feud exists between this beautiful plover and the thieving black-headed gull and the rook. It is more wary than the kindred golden plover, which has no crest, but a golden hue over the back with three toes as against the green plover's four, and an unmistakable cry in flight like " three-three " or " lou-ee, lou-ee," clear, far-reaching ; the most soft-eyed of all birds, gentler than any of its kind, with no hard darting glances. They fly rapidly, usually in companies, wheel and sweep in the air before alighting, and then keep alertly running about. They are common in Tweeddale ; so are meadow pipits, which, however, are frequently the victims of hawks, and I have heard of one which flew under a standing motor-car with the engine running, to escape pursuit by two merlins, who, unable to follow, sheared off and disappeared, while the wise pipit crept quietly back into the heather.

Hart Fell (2,651 feet), though strictly speaking a single hill, long and broad-based, is the name often applied to the group of hills, including White Coomb (2,695 feet), Broad Law (2,754 feet), Ettrick Penn (2,269 feet), Queensberry (2,285 feet), Saddle-yoke (2,412 feet) and Loch Craig (2,625 feet), forming points of radiation for most of the spurs and ranges of the Southern Uplands. " A ridge of bordering mountains," says an early traveller, " black, craigie, and of a melancholy aspect, with deep and horrid precipices, a wearisome and comfortless piece of way for travellers." But to-day it is the weird aspect that calls us to explore. Scenic beauty is the greatest attraction for modern youth visiting Scotland. The old Saxon idea of Nature and her forces as evil, of evil powers living in mountain recesses, moor-land meres and solitary places, as expressed in *Beowulf*, and through the Middle Ages, has long given place to a more under-standing and enlightened spirit. The dread and fear with which these ancients regarded wild and savage aspects of Nature is to-day superseded by a soul-felt appreciation of the beauty and sublimity, the grandeur, of Nature in her wildest and most awe-inspiring forms. Communion with Nature is won by a simple rite—that of Wordsworth's " Solitary "—". . . alone, here do I sit and watch." " Solitude can be well-fitted and set right upon very few persons," wrote the Nature-loving Abraham Cowley (1618–67). " They must have enough knowledge of the world to see the vanity of it, and enough virtue to despise vanity." To sit and watch may bring rich rewards in that flow of imagination that is the combination of reason and emotion : yet every writer knows that real creative thinking may bring to those who exercise it not only happiness and satisfaction, but also sharp suffering ; and as " G. K. C." said, " The true end of all creation is completion, and the true end of all completion is contemplation."

" If," says Aristotle, " you take away from a living being action, and still more production, what is left but contemplation ? Therefore, the activity of God which surpasses all others in blessedness, must be contemplative ; and of human activities . . . that which is most akin to the divine must be most of the nature of happiness " (*Nicomachean Ethics*). Greek culture was founded on the insight into the higher values of life, of which we may get a glimpse now and then in our moments of contemplation.

No fewer than nineteen counties can be discerned from the summit of Hart Fell, extending from the blue distance of the Cheviots to the Grampians ; from Strathclyde to the Forth. With the hill-man's pride we scan the southern prospect from west to east—there rise the hills of Galloway and The Merrick (2,764 feet), the highest hill in the south of Scotland, ten feet higher than Broad Law ; Maxwelltown Braes ; and The Criffell (1,866 feet) whose name is a variation of the Lammermuir " Mutiny Stones " legend. On this occasion, however, Old Nick was carrying English hills to Scotland when the creel fell !—near Sweetheart Abbey. Yonder is the Solway widening seawards, and over the firth the Cumberland Hills and the English Lakes, friendly Skiddaw and Saddleback, Sca Fell and Helvellyn— gleaming from atar, guardians of Wordsworth's enchanted land ; and running eastwards from the Lowthers to the Cheviots a pastoral plain with green hills and green holms. In the middle distance—Annandale, Eskdale and Liddesdale, Carter Bar and the Muckle Cheviot, and all around stretches the billowy sea of the green hills of Tweeddale and the Forest. Below us lies Blackshope ravine, dark and awesome, and guarding the parent hill is Whirly Gill, Cold Grain, Arthur's Seat, Swatte Fell and razor-edged Saddle-yoke, fit companions all for Bodesbeck and its Brownie, and other local tales of tragedy and romance.

Nor do we forget the chalybeate spring on the southern slope ; the Ordnance Survey cairn—an important triangulation point—on the summit ; " Dark Loch Skene " and its story of ancient glaciers ; a mountain lake, source of the sweet-sounding Grey Mare's Tail cascade ; and visions rise before us as we ponder upon the names of Chapelhope, and Riskinhope where Renwick, youngest and last of Scotland's martyr sons, ministered to the hunted remnant for the last time, his " fair rapt countenance with spiritual fire transfigured " ; of Birkhill, Dob's Linn, the " Covenanters' Look-out " and the old bridle-track by Penistone Knowe to Ettrick kirk—and Yarrow's story. Silent and lonely it still remains, yet vibrant with the hidden pulse of history and personality.

To the westward is Tweeds Well, 1,300 feet above sea level, where in a meadow the first fountain of Silvery Tweed rises from " its own unseen unfailing spring," bubbling up through sand and pebbles, but altered in shape from what it was when as a lad Dr. John Brown peered into its depths and saw " on a gentle swelling like a hill of pure white sand, a delicate column, rising and falling and shifting in graceful measures as if governed by a music of its own." Both Tennyson and Coleridge describe the interesting sight. Tennyson puts it concisely :

> . . . The spring, that down,
> From underneath a plume of lady-fern,
> Sang, and the sand danced at the bottom of it.

Coleridge is more colourful and uses imagination as when he turns the cone of sand into a Fairy's page, as merry and no taller, dancing alone :

> . . . Long may the spring
> Quietly as a sleeping infant's breath
> Send up cold waters to the traveller
> With soft and even pulse ! Nor ever cease
> Yon tiny cone of sand its soundless dance,
> Which at the bottom, like a Fairy's page,
> As merry and no taller, dances still
> Nor wrinkles the smooth surface of the fount.

But the strongest appeal of all comes to us from a small neighbouring hill, called the " Crown of Scotland " (1,765 feet). How did the name originate ? No one appears to be able to assist the local historian Captain Armstrong, who, writing in 1775, said " he could not conceive the reason for the name." It is a central feature in a landscape of surrounding hills, not unlike a crown in shape, and set amidst names that are significant. Here are the Rievers' Road and Resting Stone of antiquity ; Barncorse Hill, Earlshaugh, Cor Water and Tweeds Cross.

Surely some historical incident is here enshrined? Consider also
what Dr. Pennecuik (1715) says of Tweeds Cross, that it was
so called from a cross that once stood there " as was ordinary in
all the eminent places of publick roads in the Kingdom before
the Reformation," and Brown's Notes on Pennecuik's *Tweeddale*
add, " Tweeds Cross from its elevated situation, antiquity and
public resort claims a pre-eminence to every other human erection

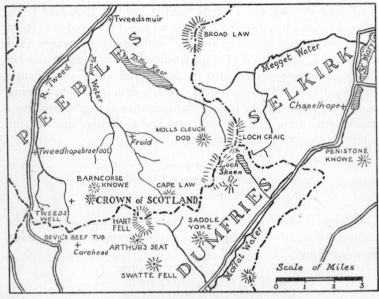

SKETCH MAP SHOWING THE LOCATION OF
" THE CROWN OF SCOTLAND "

of the kind in the south of Scotland, for here the solitary traveller
after having gained the summit of a rugged path may rest and
be thankful, contrast the distant prospect before, with the gloomy
confines he has just left, and enjoy the salutary hope of proceeding
on the descent to Moffat with more facility, where perhaps he
means to aid nature with the salubrity of the air and the medicinal
virtues of the Spa Waters."

Further, it was at the summit of Erickstane Pass near by, that
the meeting, that was to prove so momentous, took place between
James Douglas and Robert Bruce, who had proclaimed his title
to the Scottish Crown, and was on his way to Scone to be
crowned :

And ane litill fra Arikstane
The Brus with ane gret rout he met,
That rad to Scone for to be set
In kingis stole, and to be King.

(The Bruce)

The young Douglas, whose estates were forfeited, was then page to Lamberton, Bishop of St. Andrews, but obtained the permission (and also his palfrey as witness of his approval) to ride forth to join the Bruce, whose loyal supporter and friend he became—the " Good James of Douglas," who never owned allegiance to any king save to the King of Scots. May not this event have some connection with the naming of the hill ? Sir Walter Scott remembered Erickstane also. The scene of Pate-in-Peril's escape in *Redgauntlet* was Erickstane-brae.

A few centuries later, Prince Charlie's Highlanders passed along the way in search of a Crown and a Kingdom, and visited the inn at Tweedshaws. Here also was a hiding-place of Covenanters in the seventeenth century, to whom " Crown and Covenant " and " Crown of Scotland " were familiar expressions, and they may have named the hill for some reason lost in an interval of oral transition. It was at Corehead, the very base of this hill " Crown of Scotland," that the Tweeddale lad John Hunter was shot for his adherence to " Scotland's Covenanted work of Reformation." Colonel James Douglas, one of the conveners of the shire, brother of the first Duke of Queensberry, was associated in this with Claverhouse.

The name " Crown of Scotland " has a ballad ring. This is the countryside of ballads, and it may be that someone who noted the crown-like shape of the hill and loved that country, as many more have done, gave it the name for that reason. Another suggestion is that one of the old inn signs may have been " The Crown of Scotland," and that when the inns disappeared, the name was transferred to the upward road that reaches a summit at this point, with far-spreading views, and the name in time became " rationalised " on to the crown-shaped hill.

The late Rev. Dr. W. S. Crockett, who spent a lifetime in the district, stated that the oldest native in Tweedsmuir could not explain it to him long years ago, and thought it not improbable that the Bruce's coronation journey was its actual origin. To a committee dealing with place-names he gave his opinion that when Bruce and his companions rode over from Annandale into

Tweeddale they would naturally halt at the cross on the heights —a well-known wayside shrine in olden days. One of them (let us suppose it was James Douglas " the Good "), observing the crown-like eminence near by, may wittily have said, " Look over yonder, there is the Crown of Scotland ! " Others belonging to the locality and standing by may have heard his words. And so the playful simile became handed down from one generation to another. 'Tis but a pleasing fancy, yet there may be " something in it." " Three outstanding things this upland Parish has in its keeping," continues Dr. Crockett, " the source of the most famous river in Scotland, the Tweed ; the loftiest summit in the Scottish Border Shires—Broad Law, and—the ' Crown of Scotland '."

It was a Tweeddale shepherd, however, who gave me the likeliest explanation : " Had I been herding up this hillside lang years ago, and reached the top, I would have said, ' Here's the croon at last ' " (the highest point), and to this worthy man, the bounds of whose habitation was this, his native parish, it would indeed have been " The Crown of Scotland."

It was a wild, weird land in those far-off days, and many a story is told of raiders and rievers and moss-troopers who made it their hunting-ground ; of the Duke of Annandale's " Beef Tub " where stolen cattle were impounded, and of the Howe of Annandale where Kinmont Willie and his flying horsemen rode to and fro. Often in the moonlight was heard the sound of jingling spurs and bridle-bits, and the thudding of horses' hooves, for it was a land worth raiding, rich in pastures, and in flocks and herds. " The sheep of this county are but small yet very sweet and delicious . . . the greatest merchant commodity that brings money to the place," says an early writer. And sheep are still the chief commodity of these southern hills.

Hart Fell is also called Hartfiel and Hartfield by Dr. Pennecuik, because in the old hunting house at Cramalt in Meggetvale, he saw a large hart's horn upon the wall for a clock pin, " the like whereof I observed in several other country men's houses in that desert and solitary place, where hart and hynd, dae and rae have been so frequent and numerous of old."

It is time we ceased from our reverie upon the hill-top and descended to the valley, but before we go, listen to the voice of one who knew the country well—Professor John Veitch. In this very place, he tells us, in the early dawn of our history, was

THE RIVER TWEED, NEAR ITS SOURCE.

ARLINGTON
PUBLIC LIBRARY.

HARVESTING

DARLINGTON
PUBLIC LIBRARY.

SHEEP AND LAMBS, NEAR BROUGHTON

the centre of the Cymric Kingdom, and of the Gadeni tribe which occupied the upper valley of Tweed. But this land did not become " Scot-land " until the Scots gained supremacy over the Picts in the eleventh and twelfth centuries, so that it was probably long after this time that the name " Crown of Scotland " was first given. The earliest dwellers by the Tweed belonged to the Cymric branch of the Celtic, and the Cymric names belonged to the Cornish rather than the Welsh branch of the language. The Cymric names of Tweeddale streams are pleasant to the ear— Tweed, Talla, Fruid, Manor, Lyne, Tarth ; they were a Nature-loving race, with a sense of music and of poetry. Their religious worship was Druidical, observing the Beltain Festivals in May and November, and performing rites in woods and groves.

" The foundation of romance for Britain and for Europe first opened amid the Southern Uplands of the Kingdom of Strath-clyde," says the Professor, " and the breath of these Uplands gave inspiration to the literature of Europe in the twelfth century, as the ballad epics of the unknown minstrels of the Borders freshened it once again in the early part of the nineteenth century." Over these Southern Uplands the tide of war has ebbed and flowed for more than two thousand years.

Here in Tweeddale as in Yarrow and Ettrick was a last strong-hold of the Cymric nationality, their last line of defence against Saxon, Angle and Pict, but the only outward evidence that now remains of their struggle for survivance is in the forts and camps, the mounds and standing stones, and the grey cairns that mark the burying-place of their mighty ones ; but the invisible influence still remains. " My spirit shall not be wanting to all who shall come here," prophesied Merlin, of whom we have previously spoken, the Cymric bard of the sixth century, re-ferring to the wild scene now before us ; and to spend a day " up Frood " among the rolling Uplands of Tweeddale is to become conscious of a spirit, an atmosphere, in which history has been made that had incalculable effect upon the land of the Scots. " Whatever withdraws us from the power of our senses ; what-ever makes the past, the distant, or the future predominate over the present, advances us in the dignity of thinking beings. Far from me and from my friends be such frigid philosophy as may conduct us indifferent and unmoved over any ground which has been dignified by wisdom, bravery, or virtue. That man is little to be envied whose patriotism would not gain force upon the plain of Marathon, or whose piety would not grow warmer among the ruins of Iona," wrote Dr. Johnson (*Journey to the Hebrides*). Little to be envied is he whose sense of wonder and of patriotism remains unstirred, unmoved, as he surveys the very heart and Crown of Scotland, from which has come a heritage so rich in wisdom, so far-reaching in influence and power.

XI

AUTUMN IN TWEEDDALE

" Oh see ye not that bonnie road
That winds about yon fernie brae ?
Oh that's the road to fair Elfland
Where you and I this day maun gae."

(THOMAS THE RHYMER)

THE entrance to our Tweeddale glen to-day is through a
fairyland of golden light, for hedges and woodlands and
the avenue itself are fully clad in autumn colouring. Birch
and plane tree, oak and ash, lime and hawthorn are a blaze of
lemon colours, light browns and burning reds. Only the pines
and the fir plantations retain their original colours, but they
lack the olive glow, the mystic blues and mauves of earlier days.
They have already set their defences for the winter storms. And
this may be our last opportunity to see the Fires of Autumn,
for although it is stormy and squally to-day it is mild as summer,
and if after heavy rain there comes " an eager air," " a killing
frost," the trees will say good-bye to their covering, and become
once again classic in grace of outline and artistry of form.

Good it is to catch the fleeting beauty, and to store in memory
the richly glowing picture of this

Season of mists and mellow fruitfulness,
Close bosom-friend of the maturing sun.

With what wealth of colour Nature dresses herself before the
days of change ! At all times she has her distinctive glories,
and what part of the revolving seasons has not been sung by the
poets ? Nevertheless there is a peculiar charm and richness in
the pensive glories of autumn, and it may be that the Hebrew
poet had this in mind when he declared that Nature was " the
garment of Jehovah."

How splendidly the old trees carry their autumn garment,
their great arms stretching fondly over the green park, while
they repose so full of rest, not of weariness but of full growth,

dignified, noble, as if the coming change perturbs them not ; they have seen so many autumns ! Was it from them that the prophet learned, and spoke his philosophy—" in quietness and in confidence shall be your strength."

The Dell, too, is a fairyland to-day ; and cool, " cool as aspen leaves, the coolest thing in the world " (Alice Meynell, *The Spirit of Place*). Poplars are always interesting. Walter Pater wrote that it is a tree " most often despised by English people, but which French people love, having observed a certain fresh way its leaves have of dealing with the wind, making it sound, in never so slight a stirring of the air, like running water " (*Miscellaneous Studies*, " The Child in the House "). They enhance the strange beauty of the Dell. The burn too is making music, for the sluice of the mill lade is open, and there is a white cascade as the water rushes to join the parent stream, sometimes laughing, sometimes echoing like voices far away. Weeping birches are as fairy fountains of golden spray ; how Nature rejoices in this golden colour—it is her primary colour of delight! Viewed through the dancing yellow birch—the " Lady of the Woods," in which the sunlight plays, the glade becomes a bright, airy place, pulsating with radiant movement, a haunt of quiet peace. Here we may " see into the life of things, with an eye made quiet by the power of harmony and the deep power of joy."

Across the park, copse woods and bordering coverts are vocal with game birds. A proud cock pheasant, like a gilded cavalier, walks out, struts forward and returns. Partridges in a far corner are finding good eating, but every song-bird is silent. Against the green grass how splendidly handsome the black cattle look, grazing quietly in the shelter of a roundel of homely elms now colouring amber and gold. Beech trees are still green in the park, and the leaves make a swishing sound as the soft wind plays with them ; empty husks bestrew the ground ; no green thing grows under the beech. Oak leaves, of which no two are exactly alike, even on the same tree, are brownish yellow, but in the Dell they are still green, a vivid contrast to the flaming rowans that grow on the steep banks above the stream near the pines and the " lichtsome " birches :

Red thread and rowan tree
Mak' warlock, witch and fairy flee.

But perhaps the most wonderful tree in all the park is an old sycamore, with a girth below the junction of the two great trunks into which the tree divides, of over 17 feet. An abundance of foliage covers the spreading branches shutting out the sky, and entwining with a neighbouring ash which divides into three stout limbs reaching a height of 100 feet, and each tree has seen the autumns of two hundred years.

Passing the shepherd's and the forester's cottages still richly dight in lingering summer flowers, the track takes us to the burnside. Burns are of many kinds ; with some we make friends quickly ; they are the laughing, sparkling burns, that have the fairies for company : the wild torrent has no time for humans, its business is to find the quickest way to join the river, brawling and bickering it tosses rocks and boulders aside, and drives away all obstacles : there is also the slowly-moving burn that needs the sunshine to reveal its beauty, and the burn that is always singing.

DARLINGTON
PUBLIC LIBRARY.

"What is it you sing about ? " Bevis asked the brook, and the brook replied, " I do not know myself always. I am so happy, I sing, sing and never think about what it means. Sometimes I sing about the Sun, who loves me dearly and tries all day to get at me, through the leaves that hide me ; he sparkles on me everywhere he can, and does not like me to be in the shadow. Sometimes I sing to the Wind who loves me next most dearly, and will come to me everywhere in places where the sun cannot get. He plays with me whenever he can, and strokes me softly, and tells me the things he has heard in the woods and on the hills and sends down the leaves to float along, for he knows I like something to carry. Fling me in some leaves, Bevis dear " (RICHARD JEFFERIES).

But this burn has varied character, and yields its secrets slowly. Its source is up among the mosses of the high hills, several miles away ; for the most part it is a placid stream, with countless windings, and never a straight stretch in the whole course of it— it is the very soul of liberty. Sheep and lambs and all manner of creatures come down to drink at it, and grouse rise startled when you draw near. Where the high hills close in to keep it company it becomes melodious, and they carry the song upwards to the heavens. It looks best in the moonlight, and as you cross the little turf sheep bridges in the still autumn evenings, you will find a star in the water underneath.

It is the haunt of the heron : sometimes he fishes from the banks, but always facing the sun when it shines, so that there may be no shadow on the water ; often he stands in midstream, but he is quickly conscious of your presence and then he flies away. His nesting-place is over the hills in the topmost branches of the tall trees.

Farther up the glen a few rowan trees overhang the burn, and claim the loudest colour notes in all the varied scene. Sun and wind, cloud and shadow play their part upon the changing colours that are reflected in purple and gold and every gradation of autumn hue.

There is a soft beauty, an elusive charm about the hills and valleys of Tweeddale. Tweeddale does not call, it woos you with its enchantments of exquisite beauty and charm, its hidden romance, its musical waters, its happy bird-song, its homely pageants of labour on hill and field.

> The piping robins and the rustling corn,
> The shout of reapers from the busy strath,
> Birds feasting in the crimson-fruited thorn,
> Leaves flickering lyart o'er the windy path,
> The schoolboys eager quest in brambly dens,
> The rasp of mower as he whets his brand,
> The nutter's song in hazel-shadowed glens,
> Mark autumn's progress o'er a teeming land.
>
> (From " Autumn Thoughts," by Rev. Robert Meiklem,
> Minister of Drumelzier, 1866–73)

If autumn-tinted trees and landscape are a source of pleasure to the contemplative walker, the old road that winds along the hillsides appeals strongly to the imagination. " A path over a hill," wrote G. K. Chesterton in his notebook, " is one of the things that makes me think ; things beyond all poetry " : the others were " a yellow space or rift in evening sky " and " a pinnacle high in the air." I see it shining in vivid green away up the glen, a symbol surely of " going," and of going pleasantly, for its surface is good to walk upon ; and it is centuries old, and so " latent with unseen existences." Along it have gone the great Companions, and those of the Order of Walkers, the innocent and single-minded, the humble, the devout of heart, and to-day it is waiting invitingly, it is the pathway to freedom. In the Middle Ages idle people roved about the country and asked charity under the pretence of going à la Sainte Terre, to the

Holy Land, till the children exclaimed, " There goes a Sainte Terrer "—a Saunterer, a Holy Lander.

This road has no end ; in its free abandon it winds up and over the hills, through the bracken and the heather, and out to the open moor, where are purple patches of close-cropped thyme, butterwort, tormentilla, wild pansies, purple, white and yellow blaeberry, bog-myrtle. In its going it grips you with an alluring fascination ; there is a thrill in every stretch of it ; then come cleughs and glens, bustling burns, slow-moving streams, fords that the sheep have chosen, broad places where waters are shallow and the approaches low and safe for lambs to cross, up and down it goes, and so out to the bounds of our Tweeddale habitation. And yet like all hill roads it has a reason for its existence. Wheel tracks reveal that hay for storm-stayed sheep has been brought to the glen heads, and peats from the high moor moss ; sportsmen, beaters, keepers and panniered ponies use it for a brief season ; part of it is travelled by the shepherd and his dogs passing to the high bounds of his hirsel ; black-faced ewes lead white, woolly lambs along the centre of the green track beaten hard by countless hooves and finely terraced, and animals of fur and feather leave traces of their presence. In its far-spreading, friendly wandering it passes solitary dwellings among the hills, white against the blues and greens and rich dull colourings of the landscape, into which they merge so beautifully, otherwise it is little used by human beings ; and the glories of the morning and the evening skies come and go. But to the hopeful pilgrim whose heart beats to the rhythm of the universe this road goes to the sanctuary of the hills among the high tops, a house not made with hands, where is fulfilment of man's desire, and laying aside all thoughts of things temporal, in which is strain and much anxiety, he ponders in silence of heart the eternal values, and the wondrous beauty of the garment with which the earth is clothed. Here contemplation

> May plume her feathers and let grow her wings
> That in the various bustle of resort
> Were all too ruffled, and sometimes impair'd.

XII

GLENHOLM AND TWEEDSMUIR
PANORAMA: KINGLEDORES
AND KILBUCHO

AWAY up among the high hills in Glenharvie, between Glenwhappenrig and Coomb Hill, rises Holms Water, which, after a course of several miles through Glenholm, joins Tweed in Drumelzier Haugh, near the grounds of Rachan House.

Glenholm, the valley of Holms Water, with the green hills surrounding the pastoral scene, is one of the fairest in Tweeddale. Its name is correctly descriptive of the valley which in its higher reaches is a glen, while lower down it is a haugh or holm, a place for pasture, a stretch of plain by the river—so Glenholm. Its form and outline and graceful setting, with the classic Hill of Cardon, the turreted demesne of Quarter, the spring-time air so fresh and sweet, resounding to the bleating of sheep and lambs, green fields, dotted woodlands, the surging of waters, the singing of birds, all combine to make this vale, with its feeling of pastoral quiet and old romance, one of the most charming. The hills are friendly, less stern than Fruid, more rich and varied than Megget and Broad Law, more intimate than Manor. A glen that spring seems to love, and upon which she lavishes sweetness and colour. One is reminded of what John Buchan says of Tweeddale— "Though Highland in character it has valleys of a lowland rich-ness, its hills are for the most part green and gracious and a classic charm dwells in their outline which softens the stern Gothic of the Borders."

After passing Rachan Mill travelling south, the road to Glen-holm strikes off to the right, and unless attention were called to it Glenholm would pass unnoticed in all your motoring up and down the Moffat road. Glenholm of course is a Hope, not a Highway. There is no outlet, save for the walker. Its peace and remoteness, for those who seek Nature's bounty in quiet places, are real and satisfying.

First we come to the hamlet of Glenholm itself, whose story goes back to the twelfth and thirteenth centuries, and is closely connected with its ancient church, of which we shall treat later. On the hillside opposite is Quarter House, and Cardon, whose early proprietor took his name from his trade—James Bowmaker—in the fifteenth century; and after passing Glenhighton and Chapelgill we come to Glencotho with its giant gean tree in full blossom. Here the soft road ends and the track begins. Glenkirk, the old home of the Porteous family, no doubt connected with the family of Porteous of Hawkshaw, reflects the morning sun, cuckoos call from every copse, and Coulter Fell, with the blue sky over it, beckons the climber, and the pilgrim. Did not Patrick Gillies of Glenkirk, a bailie of Peebles, obtain protection and respite in license by James IV in his pilgrimage to Jerusalem in 1508–9? He fell with the King on Flodden Field, as did also the Sheriff of Peebles, John, second Lord Hay of Yester. We, too, are holy-landers, seeking the heights, and the cool, sweet-smelling air of this May morning makes all walking and climbing a mental and physical tonic and delight.

Wending our way along the hillside, we come to Holmswaterhead, and make for the shoulder of the hill that forms the first stage in the climb up the beautifully stream-lined Coulter Fell, whose face is scarred like that of Carnethy in the Pentlands. There is much temptation to pause frequently because of the wonderful views eastwards of successive ridges of round swelling hills, while southwards Hart Fell stands out distinctly. The easiest way up the Fell is by the wood beyond the shepherd's cottage at Waterhead, avoiding the steeper ascent by the shoulder. The loch below us is Motherwell's water-supply fed by Snow Gill, Ram Gill and other streams. Out of the loch flows Coulter Water that passes Birthwood sheep farm, and Coulter Allers (Alders); and near the confluence of Nisbet Burn is Cow Castle, that may have been the seat of Cu, a King of Strathclyde, who married a daughter of Kenneth Macalpine, first King of Scots and Picts in the ninth century, in this, the heart of the ancient Kingdom.

The summit circumference of the Fell (2,454 feet) is small in contrast with Broad Law, with bare short grass and moss, and the sides drop down sharply. South-eastward and westward views contrast vividly. In the former, the Tweedsmuir hills and Hart Fell range; in the latter, Tinto (2,335 feet) sits squarely looking down on Biggar, and for many miles, as far as the eye can see, there is flat pastoral country with no hill or eminence save Quothquan Law (1,097 feet). The infant Clyde gleams brightly, and farm dwellings dot the plain. Houses in West Linton are plainly visible.

Views that stir the imagination are obtainable from the summits of the range between Holms Water and Tweed. Let us choose the Worm Hill (1,776 feet) and Gathersnow Hill (2,262 feet). Worm Hill is like a pyramid, surmounted by a tower having an iron rod on top, an outstanding feature in the landscape. But its only interest is that the tower was erected by engineers engaged in the Talla Water Supply for Edinburgh—22 miles away—as an observation point for a theodolite used in ensuring a straight line in boring a tunnel of one and one-third miles through the base of the hill. The first sod of Talla was cut on 29th September 1895, and the waterworks were inaugurated on 28th September 1905, the cost being £1,250,000. An aqueduct 34 miles in length had to be constructed. The embankment to contain the immense volume of water measures 350 yards along the top water-line. About 5,500 tons of squared pitching stones were brought from Craigleith Quarry and North Queensferry, and set on the face of the embankment from the top to about 10 feet below the top water level. A railway had also to be constructed for the making of the reservoir. The land acquired by the Water Trustees around Talla amounted to about 6,118 acres or nearly ten square miles, mostly hill pasture-land. The reservoir was designed for a total capacity of 2,800 million gallons, with a maximum depth of water close to the embankment of about 80 feet. The supply for the Greater Edinburgh of the future will be increased by impounding the waters of the neighbouring glen—the Waters of Fruid. Talla Loch is about two and a half miles in length. (For an account of the other Edinburgh water reservoirs see *The Call of the Pentlands*, ch. xiii, " A Ramble round the Reservoirs.")

From the summit of Worm Hill we see Mossfennan ; and over Tweed, Hopecarton, and Stanhope identified with the Shepherd poet John Dickson. Stanhope Glen looks dark and fearsome with Dollar Law at the glen-head. A massive bronze Late Celtic armlet, and two small objects of bronze (horse-trappings) found with a Roman bronze patella, at Stanhope, in 1876, are described in vol. xv, p. 316, *Proc. Soc. Ant. Scot.* Sir Alexander Murray of Stanhope owned lands in Ardnamurchan and Sunart which were rich in mineral deposits, and the mineral strontium was first found at Strontian in this district, while lead deposits were worked for some years. Sir Alexander in 1724 was the first seriously to work the lead mines at Strontian, North Argyll. Others associated with him were Thomas, Duke of Norfolk, Sir Alexander Grant of Monymusk, General Wade and others. The York Buildings Company of London were also interested for a time. Edward Burt (*Letters from the Highlands*) was manager in 1733. The mines were abandoned in 1740, although efforts were made from time to time with the view to further development, the last effort being in 1904; but this also proved unprofitable, and only ruins and mounds of debris remain of a venture which, had the native population collaborated with those responsible, might have proved more successful, but instead they were resentful of outsiders coming in to work what they considered were their mines, and indeed General Wade was on one occasion asked for a sergeant and twenty men, with a warrant to use arms, in case of trouble ! General Wade evidently used some of the materials for his roads and bridges (*Wade in Scotland*, p. 85). Stanhope farm-house buildings and cottages, like Dawyck and Haystoun, have electric light and power obtained by harnessing the water power of the burns in the glens.

Like Oliver and The Bield the Superiority of which belonged to the Knights Templar until the Order was suppressed in 1312, Stanhope once belonged to the same Order, and perhaps to its successor the Knights of St. John of Jerusalem (Renwick's *Hist. Notes*, p. 208). To the left is Wrae Castle, a Tweedie stronghold. Wrae once provided farmers with good limestone, " also a blue slate quarry wrought with great emolument to its owner " (Pennecuik). Sir James Hall, the pioneer of experimental geology, discovered fossils in the Wrae Limestone in 1792.

Mossfennan recalls the ballad of " The Logan Lee." Three young men came courting the heiress, who replies :

> " . . . It's no to be my weel-faured face
>   That ye hae come sae far to see,
>   But it's a' for the bonny bob-tailed yowes
>   That trinle alang the Logan Lee.
>
> . . . . .
>
>   Graham o' Slipperfield on his grey mare,
>   Young Powmood wi' his greyhounds three.
>
> . . . . .

But young John Graham is a weel-faured man,
And a cunning man he seems to be ;
But a better lad, wi' less parade,
An' he'll be the Laird of the Logan Lee."

There was a Graham, owner of the Old Berg'us Inn, West Linton, on Slipperfield estate, a friend of Burns, who called to see him twice, but Graham was absent, and Burns scratched on the window-pane :

Honest Graham, aye the same,
Never to be fand at hame.

If this " honest " Graham and the " weel-faured " Graham of the ballad were the same, the reason for his absence would appear to be obvious.

Opposite the Logan Burn is the site of Linkumdoddie, where Willie Wastle dwelt on Tweed, with a wife whose face " wad fyle the Logan Water " immortalised by Burns.

Mossfennan was also the scene of a drovers' " tuilzie." Donald Macpherson, a Highland drover, and his attendants were driving four hundred black cattle to the English markets, and while Macpherson was being entertained at Mossfennan House, the cattle grazed on the laird's grass. This annoyed the laird's servants, and a fight ensued in which drovers, cattle, lairds, servants and dogs were all involved, and dirks, pistols, shearing hooks and whips were used, the cattle being hounded for several miles, some being disabled, others seized by the laird and twelve dying on the road to Carlisle. In the Court of Justiciary in 1712 the laird, William Scott, son of the supposed " Leddy o' the Logan Lee," was found guilty and fined, but was allowed to keep the cattle he carried off, and those which had been injured and left with James Tweedie at The Beild Inn.

A little to the north of Polmood there existed in olden times a fold for the security of cattle called " Chester Knowes." Glenwhappenrig is on the county boundary-line that runs from Biggar (Hartree Mill) along the tops of King Bank Head and Coulter Fell, Clyde Law and Hart Fell. It was at Glenwhappen that James Tweedie, Thane of Drumelzier, with sixteen uniformed attendants on white horses, pursued King James V when he learned that a stranger had passed his mansion without paying the wonted obedience, and demanded corporal satisfaction ; " but the King discovering himself, brought the proud Sir James on his knees for pardon, which was more readily granted than forgiven by the Thane." Such is Armstrong's traditional account as to the granting by the King to the cobbler, John Bertram, the property of Duck Pool near Rachan in consideration of his having escorted that monarch through the domain of the Thane of Drumelzier.

In 1654 Tweedie of Kingledores brought upon himself the censure of the Kirk for breaking the Sabbath day by riding to and from Edinburgh, and "staying away from the afternoon service in Tweedsmuir Kirk to speak worldly business." He was, however, "so ingenuous in confessing" that he escaped with a rebuke and "promised not to do the like again."

In 1524 John Tweedie of Drumelzier quarrelled with the second Lord Fleming about the heiress of Fruid, Katherine Fraser. The noble Lord claimed the Superiority of Fruid, and the Ward and Marriage of Katherine, who held Fruid, Moss-fennan and lands in Glenholm. He wished her to marry his son Malcolm, who became Prior of Whithorn. Lord Fleming and his other son and heir, also called Malcolm, and retainers, were hawking in Glenholm, when he met the ambitious Tweedie with fifty men ; a conflict ensued in which Lord Fleming was killed and his son captured. The son was freed on consenting to the marriage of Katherine with James Tweedie ; and his brother and two others were imprisoned in Drumelzier Castle as sureties. Katherine was duly married, but the Tweedies had to make serious restitution both in lands and money. Settlement was arrived at in 1531 when Katherine handed over to Lord Fleming all her possessions in the county except Fruid, and the actions against the Tweedies were withdrawn. Mary (born 1542), the daughter of the third Lord Fleming, was " the flower of the Queen's Maries," and married the Queen's Secretary, William Maitland of Lethington, at Stirling, 6th January 1567/8. Their daughter Margaret married Robert Ker of Cessford, Earl of Roxburghe (1570–1650).

From the high hills we survey Tweedsmuir Parish, which prior to 1643 was known as Over or Upper Drumelzier and had then a larger population than Drumelzier itself, but long before that time Stobo embraced all the hills and glens of Upper Tweed-dale, extending from the source of Tweed to its confluence with the Lyne. Tweedsmuir Parish, which celebrated its tercentenary in 1943, is the youngest of the older parishes in the shire, and the only one whose inauguration can be definitely dated.

It is an extensive sheep-farming parish in the glorious Tweed Uplands, girdled by green pastoral hills, and musical with the sound of mountain streams that flow to join the parent Tweed ; it is the largest parish in the shire of Tweeddale, having an area of 72 square miles from The Crook to Tweeds Well. John Buchan, the late Lord Tweedsmuir, spent much of his boyhood by its burns and braes. Among its wild hill streams he had his first fishing adventures ; he climbed its hills and explored its farthest glens and moors, and much of the finest doric we find in his novels is the speech of its kind and hardy folk, who in former days seldom went far from home, but by educative thought and religion so developed character as to become worthy and distinctive personalities. Shepherds changed less often in former days. In Tweedsmuir as in other glens of Tweeddale there was contentment and life was simple, kind and bien. That this distinguished man of letters and high servant of the State should have honoured the parish by choosing its name for his title was something of a romance, and proved that Tweedsmuir was very near his heart. This beautiful name is now known all over the English-speaking world, but where exactly it is may not be so well known.

Stobo Church is probably the oldest ecclesiastical structure in Tweeddale. It was founded by St. Kentigern, who had special ties with the Southern Uplands, during his second missionary journey from Glasgow (A.D. 578), and during all these centuries the same evangel has been proclaimed in this place. The ancient Cell at Stobo, one of the most interesting objects in Tweeddale, at the celebration service of the restoration of which the writer was present, in August 1929, is much older than the Norman church and its predecessor. Fifteen of the stones show primitive tool marks, curiously grouped, and the dry built stonework of the lower courses, reach back to the Celtic period.

The Christian religion came to Tweeddale early in the fifth century by St. Ninian, followed in the middle of the next century by St. Kentigern. The district was involved in the troubles arising out of the Celtic pagan reactions against Christianity, which ended with the battle of Arderydd, nine miles north of Carlisle, won by Rydderch Hael, friend of Columba, in 573, when the Uplands became part of the British Celtic Kingdom of Strathclyde, of which St. Kentigern was appointed Bishop. He was the first Christian missionary at Stobo, and there, as at

Glasgow, continued St. Ninian's work, connecting Glasgow with Stobo for all time. Stobo was a mother church, having several other chapels in Upper Tweeddale under her charge—Lyne, Broughton, Kingledores, Dawyck and Drumelzier.

The restoration of the Cell was undertaken by James Grieve, F.S.A., and was carried out with material and labour from St. Kentigern's diocese of Old Strathclyde. The waterworn stones for the walls came from the Tweed at Stanhope and Mossfennan ; the sand from Bellspool, Stobo ; the freestone forming the ribbed vaulted ceiling from St. Kentigern's province in Cumberland. The oak for the aumbry with Lindisfarne Cross, the gift of Mrs. Murray-Philipson of Stobo Castle, was grown in Stirlingshire, and is also used in the Celtic rail gifted by Mr. Grieve. Its inlaid jewels were collected in Ayrshire and polished by local workmen. The dedication panel, gifted by Mrs. Balfour of Dawyck, is made from stone obtained near St. Kentigern's Muinntir, Llanelwy, now St. Asaph's in North Wales. While the Celtic designs on the rail represent early and late examples, and the silver medallion is a replica of the oldest known Seal of Glasgow, representing St. Kentigern with the tree, the bird, the salmon, the Queen's ring and his sacred bell.

In Stobo parish also is Happrew, which was part of Sir Simon Fraser's estates, where in a fight two Scottish warriors who had fought for Scotland's independence, Sir Simon Fraser and Sir William Wallace, were ousted by three Englishmen, Latymer, Seagrave and Clifford, for bringing the news of which to Edward I the messenger Nicolas Oysel, " vallette " of Earl Ulton, was given forty shillings. This was in 1304 and subsequent to the defeat of the English armies at the battle of Roslin, which battle was the severest blow the English aggressors and occupiers of the land received till their final defeat at Bannockburn.

An interesting personality was " gud gentil Stobo," Sir John Reid, churchman and notary, commemorated in Dunbar's *Lament for the Makaris* (Poets), who was with James IV in a hawking expedition in Tweeddale, at which the King must have been most energetic, for the Treasurer's Accounts show that a few days later (3rd June 1497) 2s. was paid for half an ounce of white silk with which to sew " the Kingis sarkis," and 6d. for black silk for the collars. In 1489 the King bought a horse from Reid, and in 1492 he gave him £10 for a ring and chain, which he took from him, and the same King continued a pension of

£20 which James III conferred on " gud gentil Stobo " for writing His Majesty's letters to the Pope and other foreign correspondents. He was minister of the Church, 1474.

Of the Tory trooper-minister of Stobo Kirk, William Russell, we shall read later (Chapter XXII, " By Garval Syke and Medwin Water ").

A story is told of another Stobo minister, whose patron was that unique personality the Lord Chief Baron Montgomery. The minister was inclined to neglect his sermon preparation when he knew the patron's family would be absent ; but the Chief Baron once appearing unexpectedly, the minister was taken by surprise. Both congregation and sermon were poor, and after the service the preacher hastened to the chief to pay his respects :

" A very small attendance to-day, Saunders ! " said His Lordship.

" The weather was unfavourable," was the excuse.

" Nothing in the weather to prevent the people coming out," the Chief Baron remarked ; when the minister apologetically added, " Had I known Your Lordship was to be here, I would have been better prepared."

To which the Chief Baron rejoined with the withering reproof : " Saunders, you should remember that the Lord Almighty is always here."

Stobo slate quarry, a feature in the landscape, existed early in the seventeenth century when the heavy, dark-blue slates were used in Edinburgh, and at mansion-houses at Craigmillar (Sir John Gilmour), Newbyth (Sir John Baird) and Prestonhall (Roderick Mackenzie). " Stobo slates were transported far and near for covering the houses of the nobility and gentry." But in time they failed to compete with the light Welsh slates, and work at the quarry ceased. The " Black Dwarf's " father laboured there. A quarrymen's house adjoining was nick-named " Cheat-the-beggars " because these itinerant folks on the highway, on the opposite side of the strath, frequently mistook the building for a mansion-house, and it is still so jocularly referred to. The Dreva road from Broughton to Stobo is much favoured by all lovers of Tweeddale because of the unrivalled prospect of one of the fairest views in the county.

Tweedsmuir Church and manse were originally built in 1648. When digging for foundations on the site then known as the Quarter or Chapel Knowe, on the lands of Menzion, skeletons

STOBO KIRK

DARLINGTON
PUBLIC LIBRARY.

POLMOOD

TWEEDSMUIR AND THE INFANT TWEED

DARLINGTON
PUBLIC LIBRARY.

were found proving an ancient burial-place and site of a chapel (Presbytery Records, 1623–49). Quarter Chapel was the chief messuage of the barony of Oliver Castle which remained with the Frasers till the fourteenth century. A Crown Charter of 1606 of neighbouring lands includes in the specified feu-duty " two carriages to the Quarter Chapel " (R.M.S. No. 1706).

The present church was built in 1874. Beautiful for situation, in design and interior grace and dignity, the square tower and tall tapering spire form a significant landmark, welcomed by travellers in this land of hills. The late Rev .Dr. W. S. Crockett (minister from 1894) was well renowned for his lore of Border history and his literary activities ; his book, *The Scott Originals*, being an exhaustive treatise on the Tweeddale associations of the Waverley Novels. He was also a historian of the Church of Scotland, being general editor of the revised and enlarged edition of Hew Scott's *Fasti Ecclesiae Scoticanae*, the biographical history of the ministry of the Church of Scotland from the Reformation to contemporary times (in which the writer's own " Edward Bayley : History of St. Matthew's, Edinburgh," 1913, is entered as a contribution) ; and " to mark the completion of this work of national importance " Edinburgh University in 1928 conferred upon him the honorary degree of D.D. He died 25th June 1945, aged seventy-nine, after a ministry of fifty-one years in Tweeds-muir.

A wayside cairn and tablet (first suggested by Dr. Crockett, *The Scotsman*, 31st January 1931) stands near the summit of the road at Tweedshaws, in memory of the devotion to duty of James McGeorge, guard, and John Goodfellow, driver, of the Dumfries–Edinburgh mail-coach, who perished while fighting the snow-storm of 1st February 1831. The coach-and-four with postilion from Moffat stuck three miles from Tweedshaws. " I can carry the bags myself, and come ye or bide ye, I go on," said McGeorge to Goodfellow. " Then if ye gang, I gang," replied the latter. The mail bags were found attached to a snow-post at the sixth milestone, a mile beyond the Beef Tub, bearing blood-stains from the frost-bitten fingers that had tied them so tightly, after having been carried for some distance. The search for the men continued for several days until the Tweedshaws innkeeper, Dan Kirke, dreaming he saw a funeral passing along the old road, urged the searchers to look there, where they found the dead driver, stretched on his back, and the guard, half erect, as if asleep, " a kind o' pleasure on his face," as a shepherd who saw him remarked. Dr. John Brown in the " Enterkin " essay gives a cameo sketch of McGeorge.

Many happy days I have spent among the high hills of Tweeddale, and the sunshine of memory lights again the joy of standing on the top of Coulter Fell. Hills are not primarily to be climbed for the view—although there may be great reward in the prospect of scenes of unusual beauty where one can pause and be solaced—but for the feeling of exaltation which the process of climbing and the sense of achievement bring to us. Each season brings its own memories dear to the hill-man and the Nature-lover, and all who have the characteristic passion of the good and wise for walking. For walking means good health, and with good health and a good library life can never be dull or uninteresting ; and happy are all to whom it is vouchsafed to have

> . . . Converse with old friends, and pleasant walks,
> Familiar faces and familiar books.
>
> (CLOUGH)

And when strenuous walking days are over, and one is " no longer lord of territory "—as George Meredith expressed it to R. L. S.—then

> May I a small house and large garden have !
> And a few friends, and many books, both true
> Both wise, and both delightful too !
>
> (COWLEY)

The abiding and unchanging reality which lies at the heart of all great literature is thus stated by Sir Arthur Quiller-Couch (*Studies in Literature*, Third Series) :

All great literature—be it poetry, drama, philosophy, history, whatever we will—has the strange, inestimable quality of permanence. . . . Religions pass, poetry remains. Plato may be full of mistakes, Dante and Milton may throw their fervour into creeds now discredited. . . . But our daily life is not only the better and saner because these tremendous writers *have been* ; it is conditioned always, if we would be cultivated men, by the fact that their works *are*.

From the knife-edge of Coulter Fell Rig we pass on to King Bank Head, buttressed Chapelgill and classic Cardon in order to complete the circle to Glenholm. Beyond this range of hills to the west lies Biggar Water, the Biggar–Peebles railway, and

Tweeddale's main access from the west—the Biggar–Broughton pastoral strath—and upon the surrounding hills are situated farms with such names as Thriepland, Backshaw, Goseland, Howslack, Blindewing. Pennecuik speaks of " The Hole above Thriepland " as if it were a place-name, but it was said there once existed here a great hole caused by mining operations, or perhaps a natural hollow, which gave rise to the local rhyme :

> Glenkirk and Glencotha,
> The Mains of Kilbucho,
> Blendwin and The Raw,
> Mitchellhill and The Shaw,
> There's a Hole abune Threipland
> Wad haud them a',

said to have been spoken by a gangrel body disappointed in his efforts to secure charity !

In discovering the charm of Tweeddale we shall come across many strange place-names. Certain glens may be couthie and bien, others brave the upland storms :

" Frost-Hole "—a vanished shiel by Tairth Water near Ladyurd.
" Deid-for-Cald "—a highly situated shepherd's house at Meggethead.
" Cald-Shoulders "—" a small seat in the bosom of a hill near Tweed " between Wrae and Rachan.
" Fiend's Fell "—near Talla Linns, where eagles nested.
" Hell's Cleugh " and " The Pyket Stane " on the Broughton Heights.
" Bitch Craig " and " Foul Bridge "—above Manorhead.
" Deid Wife's Grave "—above Lour on the Thief's Road, near Stobo.
" Stand-the-lane "—on Eddleston (Athelston) Water.
" Cockieland "—" below the Kirk of Tweedsmure."
" Call-late "—a smith's house on the main road below Whitslade.

While hills are variously named according to their magnitude—law, pen, kip, coom, dod, fell, etc.

Biggar Water joins Holms Water before flowing into Tweed opposite Tennis Castle and under Dreva Craig, near Rachan House and grounds with the finest Scots pines in Tweeddale, ornamental pools and rustic bridges, fish, and fowl, and aquatic plants ; and on a side gate a modest but effective Scots admonitory notice :

Be ye ⎰ MAN SUNE GAUN SURE ⎱   or be ye ⎰ WOMAN LATE COMIN' GATE ⎱ and shut this

Merlindale House, formerly Rachan Cottage, overlooking Tweed, was built by the Tweedies and is an attractive modern residence.

Before descending to Glencotha we pick out Kilbucho and Broughton, which two parishes along with Glenholm were all combined in 1794. The old church of Kilbucho was at Mitchell-hill, and may have been founded, neither by St. Kentigern nor St. Cuthbert, but by St. Be-oc, associated with St. Llôlan, who founded Broughton Church in the seventh century. The Cell beside the ruins of the old Broughton Church has been skilfully restored also by James Grieve. In 1602 there were 200 communi-cants. Only the ruins of the old church remain, with the church-yard and manse. The last minister of Kilbucho and first of the combined parishes, William Porteous, was a clever if somewhat eccentric divine. Indeed Professor Lawson, Selkirk, regarded him as " one of the greatest men of his time in the Church of Scotland." Born in 1745, he acted for a time as tutor to Loch of Rachan's family. The Lochs who acquired Rachan from the Geddeses (eighteenth century) were descendants of Eadulf, the twelfth-century Saxon settler who gave the Tweeddale village of Eddleston its name (Chapter XIX). He was schoolmaster at West Linton, and became licensed by Biggar Presbytery in 1775. Many stories are told of him, as of his successor Hamilton Paul of the combined parishes at Broughton.

In stormy weather the minister held services in the manse kitchen, and would suddenly interrupt his sermon by telling one of his hearers nearest the fire to " steer aboot the kail pat," or ask his sister, who kept his house, to put more peats on the fire. (" He that's in the corner let his eye be on the fire "—Gaelic proverb) ; and as the discourse neared its close, " to clap the potato pat on the swee." Of one of the incumbents the following story is told—his stipend was small, his living frugal, but the glebe supported several milk cows and other cattle, and he sold his cheese and butter to the cadger who perambulated the country-side purchasing eggs, butter and fowls, and carrying the gossip of the district. The minister learned that if he sold his butter in Edinburgh he could get a better price for it than he could get from the cadger, so one day when bargaining with him he said, " I'll tell you what it is, John, if you will not give me a better price, I'll send my butter to Edinburgh." " Weel, weel," said the cadger, " do as ye like. I can gie ye nae mair for't, for ralely, whan I tak' into account my trouble an' a' ma losses, I am, in the main, nae great profiter by any bargain I can make wi' ye."

Shortly afterwards, the minister, on being appointed a commissioner to the General Assembly, resolved to take the opportunity of consulting an Edinburgh merchant. Before starting out, his housekeeper made up a pound of butter, wrapped it up carefully and put it into one of the pockets of his overcoat. He mounted his pony and took his way to the city. His progress was slow, the road by Knock-knowes and Romanno was uphill, the day was hot, but at length he reached his destination, and put up at the George Inn, Bristo Port, a well-known hostelry in its day—alluded to in *Guy Mannering*. In due course he sallied forth in search of a dealer, directing his steps to the City Weigh-house in the Lawnmarket, where dairy produce was dealt in. " Are you in the habit of purchasing good butter ! " he enquired of one. " Yes," he replied. " Well," said the minister, " I have the produce of two or three splendid cows, which I could send to you weekly by the Biggar carrier, if we could agree as to terms." " Much will depend on the quality," said the buyer. " If it is cleanly manufactured, and the pasturage rich, perhaps we might treat with you." " Nothing can excel it," said the minister, " and to convince you of this I will show you a sample." He then produced the bundle, and, placing it on the counter, began to unfold it, when to his dismay and astonishment he found that, in spite of the covering of cabbage blades and napkins, the heat had almost converted it into a liquid. " I observe," he said, " that the intensity of the heat has disturbed the solidity of my butter, but you will find from the flavour of it that the quality is most excellent " ; whereupon he lifted the parcel and presented it to the nose of the merchant, who immediately threw up his arms and drew back exclaiming, " Na, na, I'll buy your butter at nae price. If the stock is like the sample, ye had better keep it at hame, and gie it tae some of yer neighbours to creesh the wheels o' their cairts." At which the poor parson, much abashed, folded up his napkins and cabbage blades, and sorrowfully departed. Nor did his arguments fare any better with other dealers. From that period the cadger found it a matter of less difficulty to drive a bargain with the minister ; and having learned particulars of the visit to Edinburgh, the wily old fellow, with a twinkle in his eyes, gleefully made use of his further stock-in-trade as he plied his custom among the Tweeddale valleys around Kilbucho.

Broughton Place farm-house was built from the ruins of Broughton House (Little Hope), burnt in 1773, once the residence of Secretary Murray, from which, as previously mentioned, his strong-box with its secrets was removed just before the 'Forty-five and secreted by the Laird of Hundleshope ; while Burnetland, an ancient holding, and once the property of Burnet of Burnetland, afterwards of Barns, has memories of John Buchan (Lord Tweedsmuir) who visited his kinsfolk there. The village possesses an old-world charm.

After Kentigern came St. Cuthbert, the Lammermuir shepherd :

> Cuthbert on the banks of Leader
> Roamed, a Godly-minded boy,
> Watching fleecy flocks that cropped
> The braes of Lammermuir with joy :

an old rhyme about the early life of St. Cuthbert. He became prior of the original monastery of Melrose, and frequently made journeys, either on horseback or on foot, among the hills and glens of Tweeddale, and the churches of Glenholm and Drumelzier are associated with his name, as well as chapels at Kingledores and Hawkshaw, and one on Chapel Knowe, where stands Tweedsmuir Kirk. He died in 687. The hermits of Chapel, Kingledores and of Kilbucho, Cristin and Cospatrick respectively, who lived in the twelfth century, may have been the last representatives in the district of the ancient Scots Church until the rise of the parochial system. The hermit life of meditation and prayer in solitary places was highly esteemed in the early Scottish Church, and was a development of St. Columba's system. The Romish form of religion went out, and was succeeded by the Reformed faith at the Reformation in 1560.

Dr. Gunn (*Drumelzier Church*) refers to a right-of-way which can still be traced, granted to the monks of Melrose for their carts and waggons from their chapel at Kingledores to their property at Harehope in the Meldons in Eddleston Parish, through Sir Simon Fraser's " lands of Happrew in Stobo, by the road which stretches beyond the moor of Happrew, namely, from the burn which is called Merburn to the King's highway below the land of Edwylstone." Part of the wayleave passing through Mossfennan was granted prior to 1249, which indicates that the monks held land in the neighbourhood before Sir Simon Fraser's time (Renwick's *Historical Notes*, p. 302).

In the Covenanting days and the troublous times of the seventeenth century many of the landowners in Glenholm came into conflict with the Discipline enforced by the Kirk, for we read that Geddes of Rachan, Tweedie of Wrae, Crichton of Quarter and Porteous of Glenkirk were rebuked and censured for their actions. On the other hand, one of its ministers in 1690 was refused entrance to his own church, and resigned, because the Episcopal party said he " went not to that excess of severity which at that time was run into " (persecuting the Covenanters).

Persecution for witchcraft in the district was common, and on one occasion the Presbytery met at Glenholm (1640) to try several suspects having dealings with one Graham, burned at Peebles, and charged with telling people to take sick children to a south-running stream to be cured. The supposed justification for this campaign of the Church against these aged crones, hysterical women and deluded victims of jealousy and malice, was the Mosaic Law—" Thou shalt not suffer a witch to live " ; and after trial by the Presbytery the victims were handed over to the civil magistrate for execution. The necessity of preserving the existence of the Covenanted Church in the time of peril after the Restoration of Charles II drove out the practice of witch-hunting, which began about 1628 when a woman suffered the penalty of strangulation and burning on Venlaw Hill, Peebles, and continued till about 1661.

Part of Glenholm old kirk still remains with walls 3 feet thick, and inserted in the gable wall is the memorial tablet of Simon Kellie who died in 1748 after serving the parish for forty-five years. His successor, the last minister of Glenholm, died in 1805 (Bernard Haldan), after serving with zeal and fidelity for fifty-nine years. Schoolmasters taking up shop-keeping would appear to be no new departure, for Mr. Haldan in the first *Statistical Account* (1792) writes that the Glenholm schoolmaster, having had recourse to shopkeeping to implement his scant income, has created such a prejudice against the school, as it is feared that teaching will be much interrupted by the business of the shop, that the number of scholars has declined, and education sustained a regrettable loss. The Rev. Charles Findlater (Newlands, 1790–1838) says the whole emoluments of a parochial schoolmaster in Tweeddale averaged twenty guineas a year. In Glenholm it did not equal a labourer's wages and board. From *Bygone Days in Our Village* (by Jean L. Watson, Edinburgh, 1864) it would appear that in some cases schoolmasters implemented salaries by encouraging cock-fighting, each pupil keeping a bird and paying so much to participate in cock-fights in the schoolhouse, vanquished birds becoming the schoolmaster's perquisite.

In 1792 school fees at Kilbucho were—for teaching English 1s. per quarter, 1s. 3d. for English and writing, and 1s. 6d. for arithmetic.

A great Conventicle was held in 1681 on the common at the head of Glenholm, when Donald Cargill preached. From 1679 to 1685 fines were inflicted in Tweeddale in connection with the Covenanters amounting to £2,989 of which Tweedsmuir paid £1,130. And long before that time—in 1275, when Baiamund de Vicci was sent from Rome to this country to collect the tenth of all ecclesiastical benefices towards the expenses of the last of the Crusades—Glenholm, in common with all the other Tweeddale rectories, contributed one-tenth of its annual income of £40.

In the Crusade led by Louis IX of France, continued by Prince Edward (Edward I) about 1271, it is said that the bows used were made of rare Neidpath yews, *T. baccata Neidpathensis* (*Innerleithen Alpine Club*, p. 35). It may be an indication of the scarcity of Scottish timber for this purpose at a later period that the Parliament of James I in 1426 passed a law that merchants trading overseas were to bring home from each voyage harness and armour, with spear-shafts and bow-shafts.

Just as we say that certain people have "personality," so we become aware that certain places have "atmosphere": it is difficult to define. The atmosphere of Glenholm may partake of the piety and religious life that began so early in the district, and to the independence and love of freedom portrayed in its castles and peel towers, or in a combination of both in its soldier Crusaders and Covenanters, and those who asserted Scotland's right and resolution to be free, its farmers, shepherds and all who spend their days and win their livelihood in the glen—it is a gracious and kindly atmosphere, soft as the Lowland speech, and gentle as the life and love of the rural folks of the glen.

Yes, there is such a thing as atmosphere. A strange fascination may gather about a place, casting a charm upon the wayfarer ; it becomes vibrant with the spirit of the past, holding a strange hushed life deep-buried, and a spirit of unrest having secret things to tell—such an atmosphere we may feel for instance in travelling the old cross-country routes, drove roads, kirk roads and other rights-of-way. Such tracks retain their ancient associations ; they are woven into the foot-trodden path and the heather. "Where men have walked, are always left the shades of them, their spirits lingering," says Neil Munro in *The New Road*. A sense of history or personality or men or things may be retained in a place in some peculiar way, we know not how.

In places where we have walked in quiet converse with our friends, when fresh visions and new thoughts have filled the mind, these things spring there perennially, our friend walks there for ever. A human interest clings to such places ; personalities commingle. The spirit of days long past lingers there as the murmur of the sea in the empty shell. Whether it proceeds from ourselves, or is outwith ourselves, subjective or objective, may matter little, so long as our pilgrimage brings to us joy and happiness. And yet, " if there's aught of the immortal in men's souls, there's the immortal likewise in their earthly acts." And if we are at all sensitive, we shall be conscious in many a Border glen and upland of this strange mysterious " atmosphere "—this soul of things—this Charm of Tweeddale.

XIII

IN THE GLOAMIN'

THE ROBIN

"Flame-throated robin on the topmost bough
Of the leafless oak, what singest thou?"

(BRIDGES)

I T was a dull, moist November day in town. But the country is always more colourful and thrilling than the town in winter-time, and as I heard it calling, and thought of the subtle artistry of trees, the myriad colours of hedgerow, heather and bracken, rolling fields and misty hill-tops, and smelt the odour of the pines, the call was obeyed at once. I made for the high hills —by Leadburn and Broughton.

Moorland air is the best of tonics, even the thought of it invigorates ; mysterious power lies in recollection. And, after all, where can be best acquired the two essential qualities for the ideal life—Walter Pater's " serenity of spirit and contemplative insight"—save in the country—the stronghold of happiness ; and happiness lies in preserving our sense of wonder ; and where can this best be exercised if not amid the myriad attractions of the countryside ? Country sounds are all rest-bestowing.

So I came to Broughton, which is the name of a district as well as that of the village, with many corners far apart, and encircling hills widely scattered. Above Langlaw and the old Drove road to Skirling there is a ridge that for long had intrigued my fancy for it commanded a glorious panorama of hills with an outgait to the west. And the opportunity came. I met the laird and had a crack—"Just wander where you like—and come back at tea-time." . . . "It will be in the gloamin'," were the parting words. So the car was parked, the tackety boots adjusted, then off through the steading, past the pine woods, over the fields and on to the hills. It didn't take long.

Overhead, the clouds melted away, the sky cleared to fairest blue, and the sun shone. How good to feel it upon the face—

in November ! Why, this was Elysium compared with Princes Street a short time ago. How satisfying just "to stand and stare." The sunlit landscape held many points of interest. From the level plain rose Tinto, mighty sentinel of the upper Clyde Valley—the broad-based, hump-backed, cairn-crowned "hill of fire," twin brother of Coulter Fell, across the Vale of Biggar— and all the heights of Tweeddale and Broughton, while below, Biggar Water gleamed with startling brightness. From the hill-top one glimpsed, through an opening in the landscape, a perfect silhouette of the Pentland Kips that looked more Grecian than ever. In the next fold of the hills a Scots pine, a rowan, thorns and a birch stood guard over a shepherd's ruined cottage— a never-failing appeal.

But the brief sunshine of a winter afternoon was over, clouds rolled up again, and the prospect of making a circle of the hills had to be dismissed. The clouds in the south gathered thicker and darker, and then the rain came, and so pulling down the tweed cap, buttoning up the waterproof, and feeling secure against all weather, one made for the high tops again on the return tramp. Arrived upon an eminence, an interesting spectacle developed. It was snowing on the high hills across the valley, one could see the film of falling flakes, wayward, slack, till it became a white cloud under the darker heavens above, and in a short space of time Broad Law, Dollar Law, Pykestone Hill and The Scrape were capped with snow. Ten minutes later it cleared, and a deep silence fell over the countryside.

.   .   .   .   .   .

It was drawing nigh the "edge o' dark," that gloamin' hour of November nights when strange things happen, and the reality of spirit is put to the proof, when an ethereal charm envelops all the valleys, and the hill-tops and hillsides are mystic with splendour and softness. It was in such an hour when "in the ascending scale of Heaven, the stars that usher evening rose," that I stood upon the hill above Burnetland, hardly daring to breathe, so tense was the silence—and listened ; and this is what I heard in the stillness, floating up from the valley below : the creaking of a farm cart ; the clippety-clop of some "grey mare" as she carried a farmer homeward to Kilbucho ; the final cangle of a "clan o' roosty craws" ; chanticleer's good-bye to the daylight ; the mooing of cows in a byre waiting the evening meal ; and last of all, just as I entered the road from the woodland, Robin piped his last good-night—how clear and sweet it sounded upon the still night air, how perfectly it completed the gloamin' hour !

Robin closed the day singing of memory and hope. " Goodnight, brave, friendly Robin," I replied. And the light in the farm-house beckoned.

I did not forget Cock Robin : indeed I began to think more particularly about him. If there is something delightfully human in the sparrow's persistent chirruping and irrepressible cheerfulness, there is almost an attribute of the divine about Robin Redbreast, for as he looks at you, you almost feel that somehow he knows all about you. No wonder he is a general favourite, his personal beauty, sprightly movements, cheerful carol and the special familiarity he may at times attain, all unite to make him engaging. He is often our companion, keen to observe anything we are doing in garden, lane or wood, and his is often the last voice we hear in the dusk of an autumn evening. He loves the stillness of evening best, and he is often there on the rowan tree by the gate at the wood edge, and as you pass he pipes his otherworldly notes—" Safely in ; all's well ; good-night."

In winter-time I think he's given to philosophic dreaming, for I imagine his notes are inner thoughts concerning the past and the future, and his present happiness. He is closest to us when we need him most, singing when no other bird sings—" the friends who in our sunshine live, when winter comes, are flown," but Robin never leaves us. His song, though sweet, is often regarded as sad and plaintive. Perhaps ; but Robin sings because he must, and joy is at the root of all things, the genesis of creation, even the song of the bird. It is mellow, soft, limited in compass, with a pleasing expression that compels us to listen to his story, for it is evident there is something he wishes to say to us ; rapid and crowded at one moment, as if some barrier had suddenly given way, then, as suddenly pausing and scintillating at intervals bright tapering shafts of pure tone, full of articulation. Then, philosopher that he is, he stops and thinks for a moment, and hesitates, and blurts out his notes like a stammerer, but how smooth, intense, clear, silvery are the tones !

I do not know what makes him less afraid of humans than other birds, unless it is his friendly aggressiveness, in which his red waistcoat plays such an important part—emblem of his legendary part in the Divine Sacrifice ; at any rate we love him the more for it. Certainly he knows no class distinctions, the gardener's spade and the earl's bedroom he claims with equal self-possession. He is cautious ; if he sees you shake a picnic tablecloth, he does not make straight for the crumbs, but quietly, shyly, if saucily, he comes by hops from one vantage-point to another, then rests, and one glint of his dark beady eyes, and in a flash he is off with some succulent morsel. If you really wish to win his confidence, feed him with butter, fat, grease, tallow, honey ; these keep him warm in winter. The Babes in the Wood had leaves strewn over them by Robin Redbreast, suggested to the minstrel, perhaps, by the female covering her eggs when she has to leave them.

Robin has been known to nest, and to rear a brood, in queer places—in aeroplanes, in a hole caused by a musket-shot in a ship's mast, an airman's helmet, an air-raid siren ; in fact he is not particular so long as the place gives shelter—an upturned flower-pot, a battered kettle, a discarded boot, or even inside a morning-coated scarecrow.

However pleasing Robin's relations may be with humans— and Lord Grey of Fallodon so tamed them that they fed from his hand, and in the last year of his life a robin, after being fed, would sit on his hat and sing—to the trained observer of bird-land robins " are renowned for their pugnacity." So says the naturalist who has made " the most intensive study on the life history of any British bird—the robin " (David Lack). Intimidation is their daily life ; their territory may extend only a few acres during the whole of life, but they defend it persistently and heroically. But " although highly aggressive and pugnacious, the robin's behaviour can reasonably be regarded as being mostly bluff," which convinces me more than ever that Robin is a philosopher, and that when he cocks that beady eye at you he knows a thing or two.

XIV

A LITERARY SHRINE

BLACKHOUSE IN YARROW

BIRD-SONG was ringing through the woods by Tweedside as we climbed the old Drove road from the Gipsy Glen over the hills to Blackhouse in Yarrow. Wild bees hummed in the warm sunshine, and the soft moisture of the moorlands was sweet-smelling incense to the summer morn.

The place of our pilgrimage will for ever draw the lover of the Borderland and the literary artist to visit scenes where James Hogg, the Ettrick Shepherd, spent his early days learning the hillside business and getting his first glimpse of that land of Faerie of which he was to become the chief exponent, and where Scott and Leyden and Willie Laidlaw all rejoiced together. " Yarrow and Tweed to monie a tune owre Scotland rings," said Burns.

As the track winds upwards, frequent vantage-points afford ample excuse to pause and wonder at the extent of the far-spreading northward view that includes Glensax and wooded Glentress, the Moorfoots, the Meldons and the Pentlands. Westwards Tweed winds in silvery links through straths and pasturelands, with Neidpath Castle merging in the grey-green landscape. From the swinging high tree-tops above Kailzie a stormcock is pouring forth his torrent of song, greeting the morning with clarion call, courageous and buoyant, and, catching something of his adventurous spirit, we press on past fragrant larch woods towards the heights of Birkscairn, and as we travel we meditate— ah, what a gay green gown God gave the larches, more vivid and delicate than any other spring-time tree ! Each farther ascent brings fresh delight to mind and eye—sun-flecked hillsides and glens, fast-travelling shadows, skies an ocean of cobalt blue and brightness in the west. Arthur H. Clough's lines come to mind— lines which in the stern years of struggle for survival Britain's Prime Minister sent to the American President, and in so doing sent a thrill round the world :

And not by eastern windows only,
When daylight comes, comes in the light,
In front, the sun climbs slow, how slowly,
But westward, look, the land is bright.

The Drove road that travels so securely along the crest of the ridge above Glensax between walls twenty yards apart, becomes lost in the heather when we leave the boundary walls behind, but after a time sheep and shepherd tracks lead us to the summit of Stake Law. The right-of-way passes through an iron gate in a drystane dyke, and as we breast the watershed there bursts upon us the wide southward aspect. Unemotional would he or she be who would not acclaim with joy the rapture of such a forward view, for Ettrick and Yarrow are as a sea of hills rolling onwards towards the dim line of the storied Cheviots.

Our progress is now due south ; on the left rise the triple Eildons, recalling Andrew Lang's " Twilight on Tweed " :

Three crests against the saffron sky,
Beyond the purple plain,
The kind remembered melody
Of Tweed once more again,

and the grey turret-tops of " The Glen," with radiant memories of Lord Glenconner, while far below is the white-walled lodge of Glenshiel, the shieling in the glen, near the head-waters of Quair, which after flowing through the beautiful valley of Glen and the grounds of Traquair enters Tweed opposite Inner-leithen. Spacious heathery moor and pasture-land cover the next three miles of our going, including Black Cleugh and the bridle-path by which the lovers travelled on that fatal night described in the Border ballad we spoke of in the opening chapter, in which there is only the sky above and the hills around for company, with many a converging cleugh and glen through which the beating wild birds whistle and cry. But when we enter the valley of the Douglas Burn and arrive at Blackhouse farm other interests crowd in upon us.

Here is the house where Willie Laidlaw, friend and amanu-ensis of Sir Walter Scott, was born on 19th November 1780, and here came James Hogg, the shepherd lad, in 1790, to serve that kindly master, Laidlaw's father, for ten impressionable years. A strong friendship grew up between the boys. Willie had the advantage of education at Peebles Grammar School and the masterpieces of English literature which his father's library contained. Hogg had little education at all, save what he learned at his mother's knee of the lore of the countryside in song and ballad, and fairy myth and mystery, and the metrical version of the Psalms. To him vision came, and he saw learning and wisdom enthroned ; he taught himself to read and write and rhyme, and not without trial and patient labour did he attain to the accomplishment of verse, and learned in suffering what he taught in song.

The influence of Willie Laidlaw, with his fine natural abilities, upon the sensitive herd laddie stimulated and directed the immature genius. Hogg was ambitious, and responding to Willie's influence together they found the entrance gates of literature, and shared among the hills life's morning march, preening their wings in poetry and rhyme and rising in thought and feeling and imagination far above the daily darg of wool and tar, and sheep-dip.

These were happy days for Hogg, and marked the turning point in his career. The youth, impassioned of the Muse, found a harp among the hills upon which he taught the wandering winds to sing.

Professor Veitch thus speaks of the Blackhouse days :

" I like to picture Hogg at this period, as he herded on Hawkshaw Rig up the Douglas Burn, a dark heathy slope of the Blackhouse Heights. There on a summer day you would find the ruddy-faced youth with beaming light-blue eyes and a profusion of light brown hair that fell over his shoulder. . . . With the lambs quietly pasturing he sets to work, produces a sheet or two of paper folded and stitched, has an inkhorn stuck in a buttonhole of his waistcoat, with a cork and a bit of twine and a stump of a pen, and there he thinks out his verses, and commits to writing what he has already finished and polished in his mind."

One day he goes to Edinburgh Market upon his master's errand. Meeting acquaintances, he sings one of his songs in their hearing. They are interested, and the song *Donald McDonald* is printed. It is sung by Mr. Oliver (of Oliver & Boyd, publishers) at a large Masonic meeting in Edinburgh, is loudly applauded and three times encored, commended by the Commander of the Forces in Scotland, and becomes universally popular. Hogg remains at Blackhouse dreaming on the hillsides and herding his sheep on the high hill-tops. Later, by Scott's advice, *The Mountain Bard* is published, and a Treatise on Sheep, and with the remuneration he invests in a farm, but he is not successful.

Meanwhile young Laidlaw, fresh-coloured and athletic of form, joins the Selkirk Yeomanry and catches his first glimpse of Scott, the newly appointed Sheriff of the County, with his grey-blue eyes, his deep voice and Border burr. Scott visits Blackhouse. Hogg is introduced to him. On one occasion Dr. Leyden accompanies Scott, both in quest of information about old Scots ballads. After exploring the Douglas Burn and Blackhouse Tower, Laidlaw gives Scott a copy of " Auld Maitland " with which he was formerly unacquainted. The effect was electrical. Leyden in a frenzy paces the floor and claps his hands, Scott with difficulty suppresses his excitement at the new found treasure.

Scott made several visits to Blackhouse, and Lockhart says he had the best reason for believing that the kind and manly character of Dandie Dinmont, the gudeman of Charlieshope in *Guy Mannering*, the gentle and loving nature of his wife, and some at least of the most picturesque peculiarities of the *ménage* at Charlieshope, were filled up from Scott's observations of the Laidlaw family at Blackhouse.

On another occasion as Laidlaw and he were coming down the hill from the farm, Laidlaw pointed out at the junction of the Whitehope and Douglas Burns a scrunty, centuried thorn to which Scott alludes in romantic mood in the Introduction to the second canto of *Marmion* :

> Yon thorn—perchance whose prickly spears
> Have fenced him for three hundred years.

In course of time the relationship between Laidlaw and the Great Romancer grew more intimate, till Laidlaw became indispensable to Scott, beginning his residence at Kaeside, Abbotsford, in 1817 as steward and factor, and engaging in literary pursuits. Lockhart ascribes to Laidlaw the credit of suggesting to Scott to write something about Melrose, when the latter was contemplating a novel with a German setting.

" Na, na, Sir," said Laidlaw, " take my word for it, you are always best, like Helen MacGregor, when your foot is on your native heath ; and I have often thought that if you were to write and lay the scene here in the very year you were writing it, you would exceed yourself. . . ." " Hame's hame," replied Scott, smiling, " be it ever sae hamely. There's something in what you say, Willie. What suppose I were to take Captain Clutterbuck for a hero and never let the story step a yard beyond the village below us yonder ? " " The very thing I want," said Laidlaw ; " stick to Melrose in July 1823." " Well, upon my word," Scott answered, " the field would be quite wide enough—and what for no ? " (This pet phrase of Meg Dods was a Laidlawism.) And so we got *St. Ronan's Well*.

When Scott was in Italy, Laidlaw was told to look after the house, the books, the gardens, and to be " very careful of the dogs." When Scott returned, he sat bewildered for a few moments, and then looking kindly at Laidlaw he said, " Ha ! Willie Laidlaw ! O man, how often have I thought of you ! " Could human love and affection be more finely expressed ? What a comfort that old friendship was to Sir Walter. No one mourned the loss of Sir Walter more than Willie Laidlaw.

So it is that as we sit in the farm-house at Blackhouse, memories surge around us. Aye, here sat Sir Walter, and the doctor, and Hogg and Willie Laidlaw, and the laird and his generous, warm-hearted wife, and all the others, for the inside arrangement of the house has been little altered since that time. Here is the very door in and out of which the herd laddie came and went, there the box bed in which he slept, there where the candle burned as he sat writing and thinking in the winter nights. There too Blackhouse Tower with its own story, " The Douglas Tragedy," and we can hear the bleating lambs, the yearning ewes and the music of the waters, just as it was a hundred and fifty summers ago.

In the warm sunny afternoons in summer, as well as in the quiet echo-haunted evenings of spring-time, the spirit of the place steals into the heart, and we feel the pastoral melancholy and the pensive old-world memories and minstrelsies. In the gloamings when the half-light aids the fleeting shadows from glen and tower, the ballad folks come forth—Fair Margaret of Blackhouse and her brothers seven, Cockburn and his men from Megget, Tushielaw's men, Gilmanscleugh's men, Thirlestane's men and a' the lave o' them, gliding down the dusky glens to tryst aince mair on Yarrow. And Sir Walter and Willie Laidlaw and the Ettrick Shepherd are there, but the words that tell of the spirit-land and its fair inhabitants, and the land of thought, linger in the memory. The emotion of the poet and "the stillness that rests on the emerant lea" become reality, and we hear strange voices in the silence. "Kilmeny" casts the spell of her weird spirit, and "Skylark"—"emblem of happiness"—goes singing joyfully down the ages.

XV

ETTRICK SHEPHERD TALES

I. THE ONE-POUND NOTE

ON the opening of the grouse shooting in 1832, the Ettrick
Shepherd and his relative Dr. Gray, from India, were
preparing to set out from Altrive for a few days' sport
on the moors to the south of St. Mary's and the Loch of the Lowes.
Arrangements were made that they should put up at the shepherd's house at Birkhill, near the Grey Mare's Tail.

"Noo, Doctor," was the Shepherd's explanation before
starting, "ye s'all see, lad, afore forty-aught hours gang ower
our heids, that the auld shepherd's nae lame man at bringing
down muircocks, though he may na hae shot teegers and other
sichlike uncanny wild animals that ye speak o' hunting in the
East Indies." At the same time the Shepherd was busily engaged
filling his game-bag with suitable provender for hungry and
thirsty sportsmen, which his wife—"the Mistress"—had set
apart for them. Soon they were ready to start, when the Shepherd cried out, "Dear me! Dear me! But I maun tak some
siller wi' me; the guid wife o' Birkhill's bills are no lang anes,
but we maun hae something." So Mr. Hogg put into his pocket
a one-pound note of the British Linen Company, wherewith to
meet the expenses.

. . . .

The following days on the wild upland moors around Birkhill were full of all that delights the sportsman's heart. Day
after day they spent on the moors; and each day at noon they
sat down by the burnside among the hills to partake of lunch,
and have another crack about men and sheep and other things.
When the time came to return to Altrive, the Shepherd prepared
to pay the bill, but lo! when he put his hand into his pocket
to take out the note, behold, it could not be found. Every
pocket was searched and turned inside-out, but all to no purpose.

The note was gone, and the Doctor had to be called upon to pay the lawin.

Next year, the shooting season approached, and the Doctor and the Shepherd again set out for the moors on the 12th of August, thanks to the continued kindness of Mr. Hope Johnstone, or "Whup Johnstone" as the Shepherd termed him. Again they made the shepherd's cottage at Birkhill their headquarters, and enjoyed the best of sport. On the first day, as they sat down by a spring to lunch, to their amazement they discovered the note that had been lost the previous year. Yes, there it was, lying beneath a heather bush, at the very spot where they had lunched a year ago. The shepherd declared that in setting the lunch he must have pulled out the note along with the napkins or maybe the corkscrew. Nevertheless there was the missing note, quite crisp and dry and in good condition, although it must have undergone many a soaking in the winter's snow and rain, and many a scorching in the summer's heat and sunshine. The good fairies must have known to whom it belonged, and carefully guarded it from harm, and thereafter guided the Shepherd's steps to the recovery of the lost treasure. "They're keener o' fun an' frolic than aught else," he once remarked.

. . . . . .

On returning to Altrive the Shepherd told Margaret, his wife, the good news, and handed the note to her as a present.

But in a land of romantic storytellers and literary wags, the story did not stop there. Little by little it grew—"Have ye heard ! Have ye heard o' the lost bank-note ? " And so fictitious tales were added to the true story. One day the Shepherd discovered that he required a fresh supply of powder and shot and commissioned the tutor, who was engaged by him and kept the school, to arrange with the Selkirk carrier to obtain the articles. On his way down by the side of the Yarrow with the Shepherd's order, it chanced that "the Dominie," as he was familiarly called, took the pound note out of his pocket to examine it more closely, such a prize being perhaps rare with the worthy youth ; or it may be that the beautiful copperplate penmanship on the note engrossed his attention. At any rate, as he was gazing in wonder upon the note, a gust of wind whipped it out of his hand and in a second it disappeared out of sight. The Dominie ran here and ran there, every moment growing more excited, searched every corner, examined every bush and boulder, but to no purpose. Then the scholars were let loose on the trail, and searched diligently, but the note could not be found. . . .

The story did not end there! Another bit was added. Next day a schoolboy was crossing the bridge over the Yarrow opposite the Gordon Arms when he spied a salmon in the water below. He immediately ran to Wat Amos, the best leisterer in the countryside, and brought him to the river. " Aye," said Wat, " it's a saumon wi' a mark on its side," and so poising his leister in the air, he sent it with unerring aim right through the object, and brought out on the point of the prongs not a glittering fish, but the Ettrick Shepherd's one-pound note ! From the Dominie's hands it had been carried high into the air, till it found a resting-place in Yarrow and, floating down the river, had been caught in an entanglement below the bridge !

The true part of the story is that from the year 1833, when it was recovered, till 1870 it remained in Mrs. Hogg's possession under lock and key, and although often in need of the money, she could not bring herself to use the note so miraculously restored. Then it passed to Miss Hogg, who kept it till 1891, and on her death it was handed over to Mrs. Gray Garden, her sister.

Perhaps the romance of the story lies in the fact that it should have remained so long in the one family, but it is nevertheless a striking tribute to the texture and printing of a Scots banknote that it should have survived twelve months in the wild heathery moorlands of Birkhill and still have been in a serviceable condition.

II. THE WAGER

An Incident at St. Ronan's Games

Professor Wilson (Christopher North) was a noted patron of old Scottish sports. In Edinburgh he organised " The Six-foot Club " of young men, six feet in height, whom he trained to excel in all the old athletic games. It was instituted on 1st February 1826 and Lockhart described it as " a Sportive Association of Young Athletes." Sir Walter Scott became Umpire of Games, Professor Wilson, Captain, and James Hogg, Poet

Laureate. Their exercise ground was at Stockbridge, Edinburgh, on the site of Malta Terrace, not far from the Ettrick Shepherd's lodgings in Deanhaugh Street, where he wrote *The Queen's Wake* ; and the Club frequently met at the inn at Hunter's Tryst on the Pentlands. An " all-night sitting " following upon an all-day Saturday tramp of forty miles is described by R. L. S. in *St. Ive's*, and in *Picturesque Notes* he tells of a local superstition that the place was haunted by the devil in person.

At one of their convivial meetings Wilson had been boasting to Hogg about the outstanding merit of his Six-footers. Hogg offered to bring a team of shepherds and hinds from the braes of Ettrick and Yarrow that would match the Edinburgh men, and after some friendly bantering between the two worthies, a meeting was arranged to take place in Innerleithen.

Great preparations were made for the gathering, to be held in a haugh on the banks of Tweed. Country folks and county folk flocked to the games from all parts of the countryside, and the sporting *élite* of the capital came in their carriages, till the whole course was lined with conveyances of every description. The Professor arrived with his Six-foot Club in grand array. The Ettrick Shepherd marshalled his band of Foresters at the Gordon Arms in Yarrow, and with twenty pipers at the head marched to the scene of action.

Many amusing incidents are told of that day. One of the chief events was the Long Foot-race. Amongst the competitors was an elderly shepherd named Robbie Laidlaw, who came from a farm on Megget Water. He had been a champion runner in his day ; but that was long ago ; at least he had grown bald, and this gave him an elderly appearance. Robbie, like many another shepherd, was a lithe, active man, toughened and hardened by his long treks over Border hills in the historic and romantic Vale of Megget, and was ready to test his powers of wind and limb against any of the Edinburgh champions. He entered for the Long-race. When he appeared among the fifteen competitors, his bald pate marked him out as an object of scorn and derision, and the race had not gone very far when Robbie began to fall behind. This encouraged the laughter of the spectators, especially the Edinburgh contingent, who thought their Six-foot Club members unbeatable. " Go on, Bald Head," they shouted derisively from alongside the ropes.

" Is that the best man you have in the Forest, Hogg ? " cried one of the Edinburgh gentlemen seated in a carriage by the enclosure.

" That's only one of them," was Hogg's curt reply.

" What presumption the old man must have to run against so many smart young fellows ! " said the Edinburgh enthusiast.

" Give him a chance," returned Hogg.

" I tell you he'll be nowhere," was the rejoinder.

" What will you bet ? " said Hogg.

" Five to one," came the reply.

" Done," said Hogg.

The carriage folks laughed, and jeeringly bade Hogg be ready with his money.

" Bald Head " was ten yards behind ; the others were fast out-distancing him.

" Look at your man, now ! " they cried.

" He's lazy at times," said Hogg, " but he'll pull up yet ! "

The excitement was increasing, and the onlookers cheered and encouraged their favourites, and occasionally called on " Bald Head " to go on faster or he would lose sight of the others. But " Bald Head " kept his own steady pace ; then as the turning flag was neared he began to overtake the others. By the time the turn was reached he was in the middle of the rear group. In the homeward run he continued to gain gradually, taking in man after man, until he was second in the field. The opinions of the spectators underwent a change. Contempt was turned into admiration, and the air rang with " Brave old Bald Head ! " " Well done, old Bald Head ! " " Keep it up, you'll win ! " The fate of the race was undecided. The running lay between the Edinburgh champion and auld Robbie Laidlaw o' Meggetvale. Hogg's bet seemed secure, but the first place was not so secure for the Edinburgh man. As they neared home, doughty old Robbie put forth all his powers, which he had so prudently husbanded at the outset. A hundred yards from home he began to draw in on the leading man. Now he was only a foot or two behind him : then he was abreast ; and the two champions were running neck and neck—but not for long. Robbie with a desperate effort drew ahead, and kept the lead to the finish, winning the race strongly by a good half-dozen yards.

Uproarious cheers greeted the victory of the shepherd from Megget. Hogg came running up to him, and shook him vigorously by the hand. " Man, you've done grand ; I've won

DARLINGTON
PUBLIC LIBRARY

THE EILDON HILLS AND

ARLINGTON
PUBLIC LIBRARY.

WEED, FROM BEMERSYDE

DARLINGTON
PUBLIC LIBRARY.

DARLINGTON
PUBLIC LIBRARY

five pounds on you," and he put a pound note into the shepherd's hand as a reward for the feat he had so worthily accomplished. The Ettrick Shepherd's confidence was justified. " Aye, a thocht a could dae it," said Robbie elated-like, and added with his native seriousness, " An' wha widna dae their best for the honour o' the Forest ? "

III. THE WOOING

James Hogg, poet of Nature and the realm beyond, of the land of Faerie and ethereal spirits, married Margaret Phillips when he was fifty years of age. She was twenty years his junior, and the courtship lasted for ten years—from 1809 to 1819, years in which Hogg passed through many strange vicissitudes, including residence in Edinburgh and the publication of *The Queen's Wake* and other poems, songs and novels. Comely and wise, she had for the poet a true and strong affection that never wavered ; and their marriage was entirely successful. Lockhart says she was " a handsome and most estimable young woman, a good deal above Hogg's own original rank in life." There were the usual lovers' jealousies, fears and quarrels.

" You blame me for jealousy," he writes, " and for not writing seriously to you. What would you have me to say, Margaret ? I am sure if this letter be any kinder than the last one, you will not believe it. . . . But I will try to write two lines of truth for once, a thing rather uncommon with poets, you know." " When you are here," he tells her, " there is no person I like better to see ; when you are gone, there is no one whom I would so fain see again. I dare not say any more truth at present."

Then, unlike Shakespeare's parted lover, he light-heartedly continues, " I am well, never was better or merrier, sometimes rhyming, sometimes prosing, and sometimes traversing the country."

In 1812 he tells her he had been in the Scottish Highlands and in England, where " I fell acquainted with some very fine ladies, but as soon as I left them the black-eyed Nithsdale lass was always uppermost in my mind." It was not until six years later that he could write, " My mind is quite fixed and immovable. I might perhaps get a better wife, and a richer wife ; but not one I like so well, or that would suit me better."

   .   .   .   .   .

Another year passed ; he was tired of so many arrangements having to be made. " My heart recoils from it more than from anything I ever set about. Tell Walter (her brother) I'll give him twenty guineas if he will just bring you over, and set you down at my side, and make me free of all the rest of it, save taking you by the hand and making a short awkward bow to the minister, for as to pulling off gloves, you know I never wear any." The bridal dress is discussed : he wants to see her " in white muslin, with a white satin Highland bonnet, with white plumes and veil ! "

True love never did run smoothly. The Ettrick Shepherd's case was no exception. He got the idea that Miss Phillips' friends were disposed to regard him as beneath them. " If I see the least symptom of dislike among her friends, I'll be off in a moment. I think too much of myself to truckle and cringe to man that is born of woman or woman either."

A month before the marriage he is still irritated and writhing under " a manifest insult." He had sent a letter to his beloved at Dumfries Fair, delivered by three of his friends, to her father, who on receiving it put on his spectacles, set his back to the wall, opened the letter and read it through. " Now," says the Shepherd, " I do not care much for this ; I would not make any proposals to his daughter that were dishonourable, but, done as it was, before my neighbours, I could not help taking it as a manifest insult." However, this, and many another difficulty, was surmounted, and they were duly married by the Rev. Henry Duncan of Ruthwell, whose sister had married Miss Phillips' brother Walter, factor for the Earl of Mansfield. Miss Phillips' sister, Mrs. Gray, was wife of the Classical Master of Edinburgh Royal High School ; her father, Peter Phillips, was tenant of the farm of Longbridgemoor, Ruthwell, and became bankrupt.

Whatever expectation Hogg had—and it was said he expected a dowry of £1,000—he was disappointed in it. All her dowry was in her good looks, good sense and her many excellent qualities of head and heart.

His ambitious flight to Mount Benger farm proved his undoing ; lacking capital sufficient to work it properly, he left it seven years later, penniless, glad to return to Altrive. Burns,

Hogg, Willie Laidlaw all were unsuccessful as farmers. But for this, Hogg might have lived and died in good circumstances. Then came trouble from his friends. His wife was annoyed at the appearance of her husband's name in the *Noctes*, and Hogg had to remonstrate with Christopher North and Blackwood. Hogg could stand it no longer ; he would apply to Sir Walter for advice. " Shall I," he asks, " answer him in print, pursue him at law, or knock out his brains ? " but Scott's advice showed ripe judgment and sanity : " I know the advice to be quiet under injury is hard to flesh and blood. But nevertheless I give it under the firmest conviction that it is the best for your peace, happiness and credit. The public has shown their full sense of your original genius, and I think this unjust aggression and extravagant affectation of depreciating you will make no impression upon their feelings. . . . In all literary quarrels of my time, and I have seen many, I remember none in which both parties did not come off with injured peace of mind and diminished reputation. It is as if a decent man was seen boxing in the street. It is therefore my earnest advice to you to look on the whole matter with contempt, and never in one way or other take any notice of it."

．　　．　　．　　．　　．

On visiting London in 1831, he was fêted and entertained to a public dinner, but, alas ! fame in Scotland did not penetrate to London. At a dinner on 25th January 1831, nominally to celebrate " Burns Night " but really to receive Hogg (it was also his birthday), the English toastmaster, in ignorance of who the guest of the evening was, proposed " A bumper toast to the health of Mister Shepherd "—much to the amusement of the many Scotsmen present. Laughter and applause rang through the rafters of the Freemasons' Tavern, the hero joining in it as heartily as the others.

He is grown quite grey for want of sleep, he writes to his wife. " No, no," she replies, " I suspect that it is only that you have a better opportunity of seeing yourself in your grand mirrors. You know how often I told you how grey you had got ; however, we shall be glad to have you back though your hair has changed its colour."

Their married life, that made home to this worthy man and honest shepherd " the dearest spot on earth," lasted only for fifteen years : Mrs. Hogg survived her husband for thirty-five years. Their only son died in Edinburgh in 1894 at the age of seventy-three. His life was spent in banking service in India and Ceylon and in foreign travel. He was one of the gentlest and most genial of men.

IV. AN ANGLING THRILL

Sir Walter Scott, James Hogg and Professor Wilson were all virile men, with the poet's eye and heart, and a love for Nature, conscious of the power and mystery of the hills, fond of the open-air life and tanned by the sun. All had the saving virtue of humour, were good conversationalists and could tell a story or recite a ballad—men of friendship and camaraderie.

Frequently they would gather at Tibbie Shiel's, when the Ettrick Shepherd would electrify the company with picturesque descriptions of fishing adventures, and then triumphantly produce a large bull trout, whose obsequies would thereafter be celebrated in a protracted " Gaudeamus."

Christopher North and the Shepherd were boon fishing companions, and spent many happy days on St. Mary's Loch. Tibbie Shiel kept a boat, which was always at the service of the poet and the philosopher. Her son Wullie usually rowed, although on one occasion when required, he happened to be at the peat-moss on the hill, and his mother went out, waving her arms, and calling on him to come down as " Maister Hogg an' a gentleman frae Edinbro' was wantin' him."

Wullie, a tall, raw, stripling, came running to the cottage, crying as he approached, " Gi'es a piece, mither : I'm deein' wi' hunger." Soon he was devouring ravenously a huge bannock, and told to " hurry off and no keep the gentlemen waitin'." " Come along, Wullie," cried the fishers impatiently, as they sat in the boat preparing the fishing tackle. Wullie took his seat, but not an oar would he touch till his hunger was satisfied and his " piece " finished.

Meanwhile Wilson and Hogg took the oars, pushed off the cobble and began pulling out into the loch. The " piece " finished, Wullie laid hold of the oars and worked with a will.

Fishers often went into the post-office at Cappercleugh just to have a chat with Auld Nell, for she was an interesting and entertaining old character, over four-score, and gnarled and browned by the winds that blew over Bowerhope Law. She knew all the fishers, and thought that Christopher North would be the best fisher ; but in the *Noctes* North would seem to award the palm to Hogg, for he makes him reply to one of North's feats : " Poo'. That was nae day's fishin' ava man, in comparison wi' ane o' mine in St. Mary's Loch, to say naething about the countless sma' anes—twa hunder about half-a-pun', an' a hunder about a haill pun'." While another day, on the Megget, he declared he caught a cartload. There was also the occasion on which, leaving the stream with a creelful, he arrived home with three ! The story has often been told, but it's worth re-telling :

Hogg was staying at Mount Benger, and after a night's heavy rain he gauged the streams to be in capital order for fishing. So he set off on horseback to try the Megget Water. At Henderland farm, at the junction of the Megget and St. Mary's, he put up his horse, walked up the glen for a mile or two and began to fish downstream towards the loch.

The trout were taking as fast as he could pull them out, and soon he had a basketful. Deciding that there was time to get home for dinner, he mounted his horse and began the homeward journey ; but as he did so, he saw that ominous black clouds were bearing down upon him from the hills at the head of the Loch of the Lowes. Should they overtake him he was in for a drenching, so he set his horse to the gallop. It was a race with the rain clouds, and horse and rider entered into the spirit of it with enthusiasm ; and, after all, they had the start by a minute or two.

Down the side of St. Mary's they raced, past Dryhope and Craig of Douglas, the full basket bumping and shaking violently with the pace at which they travelled. Then, alas, the pin came out ! First one trout flew out, then another, and another. At last they were flying over his head and shoulders in a continuous stream. But there was not a moment to lose, the lashing rain was just behind ; so on they dashed past the Piper's Scaur and the Gordon Arms, the trout flying all around him, but he never drew bridle till he reached the stable door at Mount Benger, with three fish remaining out of his fine creelful of trout—and one of them was hanging by the teeth on the outside of the fishing basket.

XVI

" SCOTLAND YET "

HENRY SCOTT RIDDELL

IKE James Hogg and Dr. John Leyden, the distinguished Orientalist and poet, Henry Scott Riddell, the poet-preacher, the author of " Scotland Yet," was born the son of a shepherd in Scotland's Southern Uplands, and in our survey of this delectable land we cannot but pause to pay tribute to this man, and his song that has earned world-wide fame.

His early home was in the Vale of Ewes in Dumfriesshire. Later the family removed to the " oot-bye herdin' " at Langshawburn in the wilds of Eskdalemuir. Here they were visited by Hogg at the time when he began to write, and so young Henry came under the spell of Scottish pastoral poetry. At Deloraine (locally Del'orran) in Ettrick he first became a shepherd, being given a hirsel to himself long before it was usual for a lad to have such responsibility ; but his heart was in the hills—the wild green Border hills of Ettrick—and here he mused as he herded, and began to write. Two years later he came under the friendly care of William Knox, the poet of " The Lonely Hearth," who saw in him a successful Scottish song writer. The young lad wrote his songs for the single joy of hearing them sung by some neighbour lad or lass. He had no idea of having them printed or published. But visions came to him.

On the death of his father, he gave up herding and removed to Biggar, where at the age of nineteen he began the study of Greek and Latin to qualify himself for the University. These were momentous days for the young man. He met the young lady whom he afterwards married—the " Sweet Eliza " of his songs : here too he wrote " The Crook and Plaid " and " The Wild Glen sae green." Christopher North warmly praised " When the Glen is all still," and invited him to his house where he met many of the leading literary men of the day.

He attended the Universities of Edinburgh and St. Andrews,

and became a probationer of the Church of Scotland. In Edinburgh he met two composers of music who played a noted part in his life : R. A. Smith, precentor at St. George's Church, Edinburgh, whose works *The Irish Minstrel*, *Select Melodies* and *Anthems* were well known, and Peter McLeod, author of *Original National Melodies*, to which Riddell contributed a number of songs.

But perhaps the song by which Henry Scott Riddell is best known is that which he wrote at Ramsaycleughburn, Teviothead, when he was still a young man—" Scotland Yet," of which it has been said that next to " Auld Lang Syne " there is no more popular song in the Scottish tongue.

A clear bright morning had dawned after a night of storm and tempest. The wind had blown itself out. The sky was cloudless and serene. The swollen burns were making music in the glen, sparkling in the sunshine. All Nature was rejoicing ; and the young lad was wafted to heights of poetic fervour, exulting in the beauty of the scene before him and glowing with patriotic pride. The Muse was not to be denied. He wrote his poem, and reading it to his mother, he gained " the sweetest praise he ever listened to." The music was written by McLeod, and the song became world-famous, so much so indeed that a considerable sum was forthcoming as the reward of merit. But he kept it not to himself. The profits were used to build the parapet and railing around the Burns monument in Edinburgh.

The story of how he came to write that other song—one of the sweetest of Scotland's songs—" Oor Ain Folk "—is well known. He had become minister of Teviothead Church, but there was no manse, and he had to reside nine miles away. During the time of waiting while the manse provided by the Duke of Buccleuch was being built, he returned home one night after a long journey in the rain, and as his wife assisted him with his greatcoat she murmured, " Oh, I wish we were hame to oor ain folk." Riddell caught the idea immediately, and the touching lyric recalling home and the homeland, so often sung by many an exile, came from his pen :

> I wish we were hame to oor ain folk,
> Our kind and our true-hearted ain folk,
> Where the gentle are weel and the semple are leal,
> And the hames are the hames o' our ain folk.

We've met with the gay and the guid where we've come ;
We're courtly wi' mony and couthy wi' some ;
But something's still wanting we never can find,
Since the day that we left oor auld neebers behind.

He was a popular minister, and held in high esteem by his
congregation : but ill-health befell him, and he retired. After
a time his health returned. He was befriended by the Duke of
Buccleuch who with kindly generosity provided him with a
rent-free house and an annuity. He was happy once more,
blessed with peace and great contentment, busy with many
literary undertakings, and he had the satisfaction of knowing
that he had given joy to many by the songs that had thrilled the
hearts of his own countrymen. He died in 1870 at the age of
seventy-two.

It was said by Burns' widow, when he visited her in Dumfries, that of all the men she had met he bore the strongest
resemblance to her husband. What she meant to convey is not
known, whether it was his style of conversation, manner or
personal appearance, but possibly it was the general impression
she had received of his personality.

His appearance was striking : above the average in height,
strongly built, with broad shoulders, rough and angular in outline, with a large head around which hung weird locks of long,
hoary hair. His irregular features were like those of his friend
Hogg, of whom he said, they were beyond the power of art to
portray. He was an interesting personality, of truly Scottish
type, whose noble and inspiring thoughts have made Scotland
dearer not only to those of his own Borderland, but to countless
others far ayont the seas, for in many a lonely distant place you
will hear them singing, just as in memory I hear my own dear
mother's sweet voice singing :

> Gae bring my guid auld harp ance mair,
> Gae bring it free and fast :
> For I maun sing anither sang,
> Ere a' my glee be past,
> An' trow ye as I sing, my lads,
> The burden o't shall be ;
> Auld Scotland's howes an' Scotland's knowes,
> An' Scotland's hills for me ;
> I'll drink a cup tae Scotland yet,
> Wi' a' the honours three.

The heath waves wild upon her hills,
An' foaming frae the fells,
Her fountains sing o' freedom still,
As they dance down the dells.
An' well I loe the land, my lads,
That's girded by the sea ;
Then Scotland's dales, an' Scotland's vales,
An' Scotland's hills for me ;
I'll drink a cup tae Scotland yet,
Wi' a' the honours three.

The thistle wags upon the field
Where Wallace bore his blade,
That gave her foemen's dearest bluid
Tae dye her auld grey plaid.
An' looking tae the lift, my lads,
He sang this doughty glee,
Auld Scotland's right, an' Scotland's might,
An' Scotland's hills for me ;
I'll drink a cup tae Scotland yet,
Wi' a' the honours three.

They tell o' lands wi' brighter skies,
Where freedom's voice ne'er rang,
Gie me the hills where Ossian lies
And Coila's minstrel sang ;
For I've nae skill o' lands, my lads,
That kenna to be free ;
Then Scotland's right an' Scotland's might,
And Scotland's hills for me ;
We'll drink a cup tae Scotland yet,
Wi' a' the honours three.

XVII

MINCHMUIR AND TRAQUAIR

A WINTER DAY'S WALK ON THE HEIGHTS

> " Will ye gang wi' me and fare
>   To the bush aboon Traquair ?
> Ower the high Minchmuir we'll up and awa',
>   This bonny simmer noon
>   While the sun shines fair aboon,
> And the licht sklents saftly doun on holm and ha'."

Dr. JOHN BROWN's *Minchmuir* is to many a classic and a model for all time for those who would seek to describe their walks abroad. So it was that one winter day we essayed to follow in the Doctor's footsteps, with Principal Campbell Shairp's lovely Scottish pastoral " The Bush aboon Traquair," so much admired by the Doctor, and by many more since his day, never far from our thoughts.

The ascent at first, from Traquair, is steep. The track is bounded by two dykes. Then it passes through a pine plantation, and emerges on to the open hills, from which we see the view of " eye-sweet " Tweed hills and their " silver stream." Still climbing we follow a line of stone shooting butts. The view becomes more entrancing and heart-uplifting as we near the summit of the mount of the fairies, offerings to whom are left by all strangers in the Cheese Well near by, " Minchmuir's haunted Spring."

We come upon an old rusty gate standing half open, and as we pause, we glimpse a farm-house in the valley, blue smoke trailing among the trees bielding the farm buildings. But that finest of all countryside odours did not reach the hill-top. All around us are the rolling hills, the great round-backed, kindly solemn hills of Tweed, Yarrow and Ettrick ; sleeping mastiffs as the Doctor imagined they were like, too plain to be grand, too ample and beautiful to be commonplace. One of the greatest charms of our Border hills is in their beauty of outline.

Suddenly on our left the triple peaks of Eildon rise above

the morning haze, grey-green in aspect. There is a strange beauty in half-shapes and suggested forms ; the morning mists in Borderland weave strange phantasies. " When everything is visible, there is no longer anything," said Corot.

We resume our rhythmic stride, and there silhouetted against the buff-coloured clouds ahead of us is another gate. We pass through and find ourselves again engrossed in the magic aspect of the multi-coloured hillsides—all the soft tones and contrasts of Persian art are in these hillside carpets.

The track now follows a drystane dyke, and we leave the Eildons hidden from the eastward view, but as we travel farther into the hills, and pass out of the swish of the wintry wind, we are conscious of a sudden stillness that grows deeper and softer as we descend from the higher hills towards the enchanted land in Yarrow Vale. We are under the line of the wind-swept heights. Grouse rise continually with whirr and cackle, kings of the heather. Great handsome blackfaced sheep with amber eyes lift up their heads and fix upon us a keen intelligent look.

Here on this south-east slope passed " The Catrail," the seventh-century palisaded earthwork and forts, extending from Torwoodlee to Peel Fell in the Cheviots—about forty-eight miles—which Professor Veitch thinks was made by the hardly-pressed and back-driven Cymri or Britons of Strathclyde, " as a defensive boundary against their Northumbrian assailants, call them Saxon, Angle or Pict " (*History and Poetry of the Scottish Border*).

It is the same old bridle-track we travel to-day over which Montrose fled after Philiphaugh ; along which tradition says a Duchess of Buccleuch travelled in a pony-trap to attend the Tweeddale Shooting Club Ball, shortly after the Club's institution; and over which meal was brought on pack-horses to market in Peebles during the latter part of the eighteenth century (1769). In that year the Earl of Traquair requiring to build a bridge over the Quair, asked Peebles Town Council for a grant towards the expense, reminding them of this use of the track, and succeeded in getting an allowance of six guineas towards the cost.

There is a very old reference to this track in the holding of the manor of Kailzie, which shows that it was not free from robbers in 1304–5. The manor was " held of the King in chief, paying yearly nine merks at Martinmas to the King, and four shillings to the Hospital of Peebles, 12 chalders of provender when the King comes to Peebles, and if not, 4/- for each chalder ; and a third of a Knight's Service in the King's Scottish Army, and finding a man at St. James' day for eight days during Roxburgh Fair, *to keep the road through Minchmuir free from robbers*" (Bain's *Cal*. vol. ii, 1675).

The Hospital was probably that at Eshiels across Tweed, the Hospice and Chapel of SS. Leonard and Laurence where pilgrims found food and rest on their way to the annual Festivals of the Holy Rood at Peebles. At Cardrona was the " Standing Stone " (the old name for Cardrona farm), the shaft of a wayside cross pointing the way across the ford of Tweed (" The Crossford "). This was the highway from the North of England and the Borders to the Church and Monastery of the Holy Cross at Peebles.

Now we can see the winding track in front of us ; up and down it goes, then bewitchingly reappears encircling the shoulder of a farther hill. How will it wander after it rounds the corner ? Ah ! the allurement of the strange track, the joys of the unknown route, the friendliness of the beaten path. Hill paths I have always loved.

On both sides of us now are deep glens, and we are glad that our track keeps to the heights, 1,856 feet above sea level. Events happen quickly on this short winter day. We see the " sunbeams upon distant hills gliding apace," just as the Doctor saw them, showing the deeps of the swelling hills and the green rounded summits in strange yellow light. Comes a break in the clouds through which the sun streams forth. It travels with the travelling clouds over ridge and valley, up the farther hillsides and into the next cleugh, where the course of a burn gleams like a silver wand.

Nature's harmony and dignity are supreme in all seasons, and in winter-time trees, mosses and grasses have their own seasonable beauty, and the hills a bolder outline. And what air is keener or more refreshing than that of winter-time in Scotland's Southern Uplands ?

Newark Castle now strikes upon the view, reminding us of *The Lay of the Last Minstrel* and *Yarrow Revisited*. Scott and Wordsworth visited the place together. Opposite the Tower is Foulshiels, birthplace of Mungo Park, the Peebles doctor and African explorer. Misty clouds are beginning to hide the high hills, but there is the great bulk of Broad Law, and the sharp ridge of Coulter Fell, and the jumble of giants around Manor-head. The wind is strong and caller now ; we button up our coats, and set off with invigorated step. How good it is to feel the cool hill air upon the cheek, and the turf beneath one's feet ; pleasant also to feel it yield to the pressure of the foot, and how refreshing its perennial hue.

Rounding the shoulder of the hill we find stretched out before us all Yarrow Vale ; the sun reappears, the wind dies. We feast our eyes upon the far-stretching landscape and the way of our going—Philiphaugh, Yair, Fernielee, Ashiestiel, Inner-leithen. These were the views that Scott and Mungo Park, Dr. John Brown and " Christopher North," Professor Veitch and Principal Campbell Shairp and all the others knew and loved so well. It was the green, pastoral simplicity of the Tweedside landscape that appealed so strongly to Sir Walter and remained " his abiding passion," not the wilder aspects such as Gameshope and Loch Skene. There's magic in the hillsides and the tower-ing tops and the far-stretching sea of billowy hills that stirs the imagination and raises man to noble and majestic thoughts. Here man is little, God is great. He restoreth the soul ; our whole world becomes manageable again.

> Why climb the mountains ? [asks Professor Blackie]
> I love to leave my littleness behind
> In the low vale where little cares are great
> And in the mighty map of things to find
> A sober measure of my scanty state ;
> Taught by the vastness of God's pictur'd plan
> In the big world how small a thing is man !

This track over the hill-tops from Traquair to Yarrow has been made fragrant by the lives of those who loved it, whose breezy cheerfulness and high-hearted jollity, youthful spirit and care-free abandon now finds an echo in the hearts of those many walkers who tramp the hills to-day. To a different gait, it may be, from their forebears, but, having entered into their labours, from them some day no doubt will come " some usefu' plan or book " for dear auld Scotland's sake, for they are not unacquainted with the atmosphere of the glens, their " pastoral melancholy," phantasy and tragedy that inspired the ballads and minstrelsy of those Greathearts. They remember " The Dowie Dens " and the story of Tamlane, and Willie Laidlaw's matchless lyric— " Lucy's Flittin' " :

'Twas when the wan leaf frae the birk tree was fa'in',
And Martinmas dowie had wound up the year,
That Lucy row'd up her wee kist wi' her a' in,
And left her auld maister and neebours sae dear ;

.   .   .   .

She gaed by the stable where Jamie was stanin' ;
Richt sair was his kind heart the flittin' to see ;
" Fare ye weel, Lucy," quo' Jamie, and ran in ;
The gatherin' tears trickled fast frae his e'e.

And the sweet soft melody in " The Bush aboon Traquair " :

And what saw ye there
At the bush aboon Traquair ?
Or what did you hear that was worth your heed ?
I heard the cushies croon
Through the gowden afternoon,
And the Quair burn singing doon to the Vale o' the Tweed.

And the Castle of Traquair, one of the oldest Scottish residences, dating from 1132, and still inhabited. Here dwelt early Scottish kings from David I to Alexander III, at the time of whose death (1286) Scotland, from a material point of view, was more civilised and more prosperous than at any period of her existence, down to the time when she ceased to be a separate kingdom in 1707 (Innes' *Sketches*, 157, 158). It was occupied during troublous times by Edward I in 1304, and by Edward II in 1310 ; visited by Mary and Darnley in 1566, and by King George V and Queen Mary, accompanied by the Duke and Duchess of York, their present Majesties, during a stay in Edinburgh in July 1923, when they made a thorough examination of the old House. The castle took its present shape about 1695, and is unspoiled, being received by the laird, Arthur Joseph Maxwell-Stuart, nephew of the tenth Baron Herries. He died in 1942 at ninety-seven years of age. During Their Majesties' tour of the Border district it is not without significance in view of the ancient holding of Kailzie manor, that Their Majesties should also have visited Kailzie, when the laird and his lady were presented.

A feature of the surroundings of Traquair House is the closed Traquair Gates. They were closed in 1796 by Charles, seventh Earl of Traquair, who, returning from the funeral of his countess, locked the gates and threw the key into the Tweed where it approaches close to the House, commanding that the gates should not be opened again till they could receive another

Countess of Traquair, an event which never happened. There is also a popular tradition that they remain closed until restoration of the Stuarts—"a symbol of the hopeless waiting of a lost cause." There is little ground for this tradition, however. Charles, fifth Earl, was opposed to the Prince's coming to Scotland without French aid ; he took no part in the 'Forty-five, was imprisoned in the Tower, but saved his head and estates. He died in 1764 (*Scot. Hist. Soc.* vol. 27). The gates are of wrought iron, and the piers of rusticated masonry carry bears supporting shields. A double lime avenue leads to the House. There are many fine trees at Traquair, horse-chestnuts, sycamore and beech, but the most unusual for the district are five true black poplars on the north side near the river.

This house of Traquair played an important part in Scottish history. One of the most remarkable Kings Scotland ever had—William the Lion, well-known in Tweeddale—found in Traquair his favourite residence, and held a Court there in 1209. He invaded England in the time of Henry II (1174), and was made prisoner at Alnwick. He purchased his liberty by surrendering the independence of his Crown (Treaty of Falaise, Normandy), and became vassal of Henry and of his successors, kings of England, for Scotland and for all his other possessions.

For fifteen years—from then till the accession of Richard I (the Lion-hearted)—Scotland was a dependent province of the English Monarchy, and during this period there were more recorded attendances of Scottish Kings at the English Court than at any time before or afterwards. Soon after Richard's accession, Scotland was freed from this ignominious servitude (1189). From that date till Edward I advanced his pretensions at Norham in 1290—one hundred years—the Kings of England never exercised the right of a feudal Superior over Scotland. The Wars of Scottish Independence settled all that for ever, but that there is need for a resuscitation of the old Scottish spirit to-day no one will deny.

William the Lion in 1178 founded the Abbey of Arbroath, dedicated to Thomas à Becket. It was a fitting act of retributive justice that it should have been in this abbey in the reign of Robert the Bruce, in 1320, that the celebrated manifesto went forth by twenty-nine earls and nobles in a letter from the Scottish Parliament, to the Pope, requiring the English King to respect Scottish Independence, that " so long as a hundred of us are left alive, we will never in any degree be subjected to the English. It is not for glory, riches or honours that we fight, but for liberty alone, which no good man surrenders, but with his life." A copy of this document in the Signet Library (Edinburgh) shows the beautiful seals of the granters, those of the churchmen being oval in shape.

The connection of the House of Traquair with Roman Catholicism caused concern and unrest in this Scottish Borderland for centuries, and on one occasion the House was sacked and Romish articles and vestments were burned—"Inventar of Popish Trinkets, gotten in my Lord Traquair's House 1688 all solemnly burnt at the Cross of Peebles" (*Proc. Soc. Ant. Scot.* vol. ii). The ancient church of Traquair was called Kirkbryde, having been dedicated to St. Bryde.

The influence of James Hogg, the Ettrick Shepherd, can still be felt as we travel this ancient track. "Over the hills of Traquair" was the song he sang ; and it was a Traquair legend upon which he founded that wonderful tale in which he rose to his highest and best, of a sphere of ideal natural beauty and pure womanhood—"Bonny Kilmeny," of how Jane Brown was carried off by the fairies to " a land of love, and a land of light, a land of vision—an everlasting dream." She came back—" late, late in the gloamin' Kilmeny came hame ; And O her beauty was fair to see," but the glamour of the Faerie land was upon her, she could not stay :

> It wasna her hame, and she couldna remain ;
> She left this world of sorrow and pain,
> And returned to the land of thought again.

Who that returns from a tramp over this glorious Border landscape of Minchmuir can escape that " land of thought " ?

XVIII

SECRETS OF A TWEEDDALE GLEN

" The love whose smile kindles the universe,
The beauty in which all things live and move."
(SHELLEY)

AMONG the high hills and the uplands in the heart of
Tweeddale it had been a week of snow and frost. In the
city, however, there was neither frost nor snow, but
Shakespeare's description applied in very truth :

The air bites shrewdly ; it is very cold,
It is a nipping and an eager air.

To know our favourite glen in winter-time, to see its glories,
and to learn its secrets before the impending thaw sends its thunders
down the glen ; what lover of the country would not welcome
such an adventure ?

The loud noise of the waters of the burn that comes tumbling
down from the high hills six miles away, speaks of the coming
thaw. Its usual quiet murmur has become a lusty roar ; it is
dashing headlong among great boulders and roaring like a
cataract. " It boils and wheels and foams and thunders through."
It is in boisterous mood, yet soft and melodious by turns, with
many a diapason in between, as the voice of it rises and falls.
To the discerning ear the wind may play a thousand tunes upon
every kind of harp, and bear the music of the stream for our
delight. In all our going up and down the glen that day, its
voice was ever present.

Herons stand upon the banks, solemnly and gloomily, like
old men humping their grey shoulders, their coat collars turned
up, their hands in their pockets. Of what are they thinking ?
The lines of Elizabeth Shane come to mind :

If I stood on Bo Island
As gloomily as they,
And ruffled up my collar
And hid my hands away,
It might be they would join me
And I'd hear the things they say.

As I approach, they rise from the water's edge, their great wings loose-flapping, circle over the hillsides and disappear up the glen, " their long legs hanging downwards, their slim necks all stretched out."

The wind is in the south, and it is the south wind that plays with clouds and lights and makes music in the woods. In the late afternoon, the wind and the wan light have brought colour to the snowy peaks, a touch of blue and purple, pink and yellow. The snow is melting, hillsides are ribbed in black and white, and white-lined sheep-tracks score the braes, where the snow lies sprinkled on the heather. In the valley, by the burnside, the grass is vivid green; and larches and beeches, firs and pines add notes of russet-brown and olive-green. The cart road still holds ice in the wheel-tracks, and in the distance gleams like silver.

A turn in the glen brings us to a cottage. The shepherd and his laddie are busily engaged, in the fading daylight, with a two-handed saw. "Aye," he replied, " ash and beech are fine for burnin', and Scots pine is best for kindlin' : the rosin mak's it spark." Ash and beech burn green as well as dry, give a clear fire and good heat; holly logs should be burnt green; keep elm for two years and burn with coal; old dry oak is ideal; slow-growing trees, solid and heavy, burn slowly; laburnum lasts well, so does thorn and gives good heat; birch burns too fast, chestnut hardly at all; and pear, plum, cherry and old lilac give fragrant aroma, and apple burns beautifully, slowly and steadily, and will scent your room. All woods burn better if axed or wedged instead of sawn. (Delightful too is the peat fire, with its atmosphere of welcome, warmth and comfort; peat that is such a gentle burner.) And what would life in the country be without that pale-blue wood smoke—an inheritance from primaeval days—and the delicious odour of it ? The sound of the saw followed us up the glen, till we came to a boisterous hill burn rushing down a side glen, gurgling and buoyant; how jolly it seemed, fresh and sparkling from the snowy heights ! The sight of it rejoices the heart and puts a new song in the mouth.

In parts the track is ice-bound, and where it is overrun with water from the hillside it makes walking difficult, but there is a green strip on one side, and heather on the other, and we change the way of our going as fancy or expediency dictates. Roundels of trees on the hillsides, and in the valley, add to the interest of the glen. Those on the former are silhouetted against the sky with all their delicate tracery of branch and twig. What a thrill the trees give to us in winter-time ! All the wonder and the glory that is hid in summer now stands revealed. Their calm and grace, their poise and strength, as they stand in solemn conclave, sharing some secret knowledge to which we may never attain. And yet, we may walk with their spirit and share their confidence, but only when alone.

The tall red pines, sturdy chieftains of the glen, are dwarfed under the towering heights. One had fallen—a victim of a recent gale—earth and turf clinging to the matted roots. Who will say that her sister pines do not bear her sympathy ? She who has thrilled to the Sweet Unrest of Spring, and breathed her tender sigh, caught by the ear that's finely attuned ; but lost in the wind amidst tossing boughs and singing birds.

The light is beginning to fade, the air grows colder ; winter daylight is scarce in the glen ; there is little space of sky. The south wind has brought a misty vapour, and wrapped it round the snow-capped hills, giving a kaleidoscopic aspect to the cloud-land, as intermittently the tops look out and fade away. No other pilgrim wandered there, yet at every turn there is a speaking voice : deep echoes unto deep, above the sounding waters. Here under the high hills, the landscape is white, only the trees remain untouched by the white shroud. Night is approaching. An angry hissing wind beats down from the snow-filled gullies ; its icy fingers grip the throat, and counsel retreat. It ruffles the wool on the sheep, it soughs around the stell, it rustles the ivy on the porch, and, look ! it is battling with the whirling snow upon the highest peak ! The higher reaches of the burn are not for us. That will keep for another day. Darkness is falling. The high hills have slipped into the enfolding arms of night ; the wind is moisture-laden, and icy ! " An eager air " indeed— " Cold enough to give the wild ducks rheumatism," whispers a voice. So the return journey is begun. " Crunch, crunch " on the frozen snow ; " Crash, crash " on the hill-track ice. With the wind behind, going is easier. A shower of hail patters on the icy track. In the half-light the bustling burn croons a louder note, and the waters of the hillside torrents have a purple gleam amid the flecks of foam.

From the arctic conditions at the head of the glen, we pass

to the lower reaches, where the bracken has a ruddy glow, and
elfin voices murmur in the withered fronds. Through a dark-
blue window in the clouds the Evening Star appears—and then
is gone. The clouds roll on. But the glen has kept her greatest
treasure to the last. As we are about to pass into the woodland,
we pause, and turning for a last look upon the wintry scene,
there—a mile away up the glen, a rosy glow in the window of
the shepherd's cottage shone through the darkness.

> Steel surfaced to the light the river looks.
> Pale the rain-rutted roadways shine
>   In the green light,
> Behind the cedar and the pine :
>   Come, thundering night !
> Blacken broad earth with hoards of storm !
> For me yon Valley-cottage beckons warm.
>   (MEREDITH's " Autumn Even-song ")

High above towered the snow-white hills ; a conical hill of
dark pines bielded the cottage, and made a background, the
whole framed in long lines of converging hills. The picture was
complete. Darkness filled the glen ; night had sealed the secret
places. But that rich red glow filled the imagination with all
that the shepherd's cottage stands for in Scottish rural life and
character.

" Were ye no feared to come a' that way in the dark ? "
said the herd's wife to a wee lassie who had come up the glen
from a neighbouring cottage, for help in a case of illness. " No,"
she replied, " the min [moon] cam' wi' me."

The glen has many secrets, as well as glories, in winter-time.

XIX

THE CLOICH HILLS AND THE MELDONS :
EDDLESTON AND THE LEITHEN VALLEY

"The time must come, when the gentlemen of Scotland
will take an intelligent interest in the antiquities of their own
districts, and our scholars will be ashamed to know less of
the colonising and early history of Scotland than they do
of Greece or Italy."

(COSMO INNES, *Sketches of Early Scottish History*)

MANY pleasant walks lie in this part of Tweeddale, old
rights-of-way and cross-country tracks which never
fail to provide interest as well as recreation. With a
reliable map as guide it is always best to make one's own experience in exploring a new countryside, and to vary the route on
each occasion.

The Cloich Hills are grass-covered, rounded hills affording
grazing-ground for sheep and cattle, and lie between Eddleston
and Newlands, the chief hills being Weather Law, Whauplaw
Cairn and Ewe Hill. A good plan is to follow that section of
the old Highland Drove road that goes through the Cloich Hills
by Fingland and Courhope, after it has crossed the Cauldstaneslap,
to which we shall refer in the following chapter. Let us join it
near Romanno House opposite Goldie's Mill, where it begins
to climb upwards towards the hills, passes through woodlands of
oak and fragrant pine, and at a height of over 1,100 feet crosses
a small col on the north shoulder of Drum Maw. Many fine
prospects are enjoyed as we climb the old road—the long line
of the Pentlands, Linton nestling among verdant surroundings,
Dunsyre Hill, Black Mount, Coulter Fell. At the summit there
opens before us the vale of the Fingland Burn, typical of this
green pastoral country, and as we swing down the easy gradient
the attraction of these ancient ways is renewed. All is peace
save for the bleat of sheep, the cry of the wild birds and the
tinkling hill burns. Then the road fords the burn and climbs the
east side of the valley till it joins Flemington Mill Burn. Green-

mounded founds of old sheep rees (buchts or stells) and shepherd's cottage point to former habitation. A modern bit of road leads to Fingland herd's cottage, but the main Drove road crosses the Mill Burn and climbs gradually the outlying slopes of Crailzie Hill, overlooking Courhope with its pine wood, Ewe Hill rising behind and Kilrubie Hill opposite the cottage of the Courhope shepherd. If, as has been suggested by Dr. Macdonald, Kiltarlity, Kilrubie means " the cell of the red-tonsured priest," it may have had a connection with the adjoining lands of Harehope owned by the Monks of Melrose in 1200, and down to the Reformation (Renwick's *Historical Notes*, p. 52). The road goes over the hills to Upper and Nether Stewarton where it joins a road worth knowing that starts opposite Whim Lodge, and skirting Cowieslinn, which was originally called Aldenisslauer, the head of the 30-foot "loud sounding waterfall," proceeds by Earlyburn and Shiplaw to Stewarton, the Meldons and Lyne by a grass-grown track above Darnhall. Darnhall was originally a Border tower (" dern," a concealed place) first mentioned in 1531, and from 1564 the residence of the Blackbarony family and later of the Murrays of Elibank. A fine Celtic cinerary urn was found at Darnhall and is described in vol. x, *Proc. Soc. Ant. Scot.* p. 43.

The Drove road crosses Meldon road and burn, and thereafter by the east side of Hamilton Hill enters Peebles by Standalane and Rosetta. This is the commonly called " North Drove Road " from Peebles to Linton and the Cauldstaneslap. I have conversed with old inhabitants in the countryside who remember seeing the droves of black cattle, Kyloes they were called, being driven along it. What they specially recollected, they told me, was not only the big horns of the cattle as they walked along in steady rhythmic pace with heads swinging from side to side, but the sound of their horns coming in contact with the horns of beasts on either side—" nick-nack, nick-nack, nick-nack." From Peebles, going southwards, the old road crosses Tweed to the Gipsy Glen. We read that in 1777 drovers complained that the parapet of Tweed Bridge was so low (and probably the descent to the bridge so steep) that they suffered loss through sheep and lambs jumping over it. The fifteenth-century wooden bridge of 10 feet wide, was rebuilt of stone a century later, widened in 1834, and widened again to 40 feet in 1900. Burdens effeiring to parish and turnpike roads did not affect the Drove roads, and sheep and cattle passing over Peebles or Tweed Bridge were allowed for a small fee to rest on the Kingsmuir, the site now occupied by the L.M.S. railway station. The old Drove road over the Glensax hills has already been described.

The approach to Peebles from the Upper Meldon Burn may be varied by walking to Jedderfield by Upper Kidston. Before the present road was made from Peebles up Tweedside the old road went by Jedderfield and Edston Hill and down to the Tweed valley, near Captain Wolfe Murray's house at Meldonfoot. An early traveller, Daniel Defoe (1723), describes his journey in Tweeddale :

. . . In three hours riding I got to Need-path in the County of Tweed-dale, the seat of Douglas, Earl of March. The House is a large convenient Seat, situated on a precipice, and hath a commanding prospect over the Hills of Tweed-dale, which very much resemble the Downs of Sussex. They are all green, and it's hardly credible the number of sheep one sees upon them. . . . From Need-Path in a few miles I arriv'd at Peebles, the Capital of the Shire, a small town, pleasantly seated on the banks of the river Tweed, over which it hath a fair stone bridge. There is one good street, and some bye lanes, with tolerable Stone Buildings ; and continuing the course of the river, I arriv'd in a few miles at the Palace of Traquair.[1]

From Courhope in the Meldons we may prefer to cross over to Eddleston by way of Blackbarony. Originally the name of these lands appears to have been Hattoun, Haltoun or Haltoun-Murray, otherwise called Blackbarony, in contradistinction to the lands of Whitebarony on the opposite side of Eddleston Water. But when the fortalice of Darnehall became the principal messuage, and was made " regular and Beautiful," the place was called Darnhall. It has now reverted to Blackbarony. In the modern house are incorporated parts of the peel tower, and the whole has the appearance of a French château. In the seventeenth century it was the finest mansion-house in Tweeddale after Traquair. The avenue of limes is 245 yards long, and comprises 65 very large trees. For some years prior to 1939 this beautiful house with lovely and extensive grounds was run as a residential hotel.

The history of the village of Eddleston takes us back to the twelfth century, when Eddleston was called Pentejacob, and belonged to the See of Glasgow (1115) ; and in 1170 it

[1] *A Journey through Scotland.*

was called Gillemoreston, and later Eadulfstun, from a Saxon settler Eadulf who died about 1185. Its church is somewhat unique in the history of the Church of Scotland in that it was served for 160 years (1697–1856) by four generations of the Robertson family in uninterrupted succession from father to son. Dr. Patrick Robertson, who wrote the *First Statistical Account* in 1796, mentions that at this time " a good ploughman got eight guineas per annum with victuals." His name also appears among the King's Bodyguard for Scotland in 1789 as the winner of the " Silver Arrow " shot for by the Royal Company of Archers at Peebles, his medal bearing crest and motto, " Virtutis Gloria Merces " (Chapter IX, p. 79). His son, also Dr. Patrick, wrote the *Second Statistical Account* of 1829 in which he laments the fact that the pernicious habit of substituting tea for porridge and milk at breakfast is gradually gaining ground, and " as it is a luxury above the means of a labouring man, it is doubtful whether it is not a more productive source of poverty, misery and vice than the unrestrained use of ardent spirits." He counsels the legislators to reduce the tea duty. But legislators were slow to move in those days, for seventeen years later we read in *The Scotsman* (16th May 1846) : " The Tea Duties—A memorial to the Treasury, in favour of a reduction in the exorbitant duty on tea is at present in course of signature in Edinburgh. Our improved relations with China, the extent to which tea has become a sort of necessary, and the desirableness of offering a cheap substitute for intoxicating liquors, are among the many strong reasons for a reduction of the duty." Now we hear that a *Third Statistical Account* of Scotland is envisaged (1946), which should prove as interesting reading as its predecessors. Eddleston Church was rebuilt in 1829. Some of the seats in the church in 1796 bore the date 1600.

A good cross-country ramble is to leave the bus at Redscaurhead and walk westwards by Nether Kidston farm to Harehope, visiting the interesting Harehope Rings on the slope of Crailzie Hill above Harehope Woods. Harehope Fort, half a mile east of the Rings, is on the open moor, and does not occupy the usual viewpoint situation of such forts. It is " a well-preserved example of a fort with two concentric lines of defence." Climbing Crailzie Hill and proceeding up the Fingland Burn, we make our way to Romanno Hotel, West Linton or Noblehouse, and, if desired, continue to Macbiehill across Harlawmuir to Penicuik.

VIEW UPSTREAM FROM DREVA, WHERE BIGGAR WATER RUNS INTO TWEED

DARLINGTON

TRAQUAIR

DARLINGTON
PUBLIC LIBRARY

THE TWEED, NEAR DRUMELZIER

George Meikle Kemp, architect of the Scott Monument, travelled across these hills as a lad when making a weekly journey to his home at Ninemileburn when he worked as an apprentice in Andrew Noble's carpenter's shop at Redscaurhead, where there is now a memorial plaque.

The impression gained in these Cloich Hills is that of the quietude of this unfrequented countryside, the stillness of the valleys, the variety of the birds and the pleasure of identifying from some unusual standpoint such as Crailzie Hill familiar landmarks in the Southern Tweeddale Heights, and in the Moorfoots—Dundreich, the Druids Hill, near whose base is the source of the South Esk; Powbeat with its deep mysterious spring; Portmore Loch, once famous for its eels, like Loch Leven, which yielded 500 stones in 1865; and the rugged ridge ending in the sharp-pointed Lee Pen at St. Ronan's, with its witness to intensive ice planing.

Powbate spring gave rise to strange conjectures—what if the hill is full of water! what would happen should it burst and the flood roll towards Dalkeith, and carry off three farms and several kirks! So there came the popular rhyme:

> Powbate, an' ye break,
> Tak' the Moorfoot in your gate—
> Huntly-cot, a' three,
> Moorfoot and Mauldslie,
> Five kirks and an abbacie.

The five kirks—Temple, Carrington, Borthwick, Cockpen and Dalkeith; and the abbey which shows the antiquity of the rhyme, is that existing at Newbattle (R. Chambers, *Popular Rhymes of Scotland*).

Although the land lies silent to-day, stirring scenes were enacted here in the days of the Border Raiders. The Cloich Hills, the farms of Harehope, Courhope, Deanhouses and the valley of Eddleston up to Kingside Edge were all " subject to the incursions of Liddesdaill, Ewisdaille and Annandaille," and bastel houses existed at Cringletie, Darnhall, Milkieston, Stewarton and at Hopetoun Tower east of Eddleston up the Longcote Burn, a seat of baronial jurisdiction for crimes and misdeeds in the fifteenth century. Orders from the Privy Council to suppress Border thieves and repel invasion by calling out all males between sixteen and sixty fully equipped with several days' rations, to assemble at a certain place, are found in the Records. Among the Commissioners selected to quell the raiders was Sir Gideon Murray (d. 1621), founder of the Elibank family, raised to a Baronetcy, 1628, and to the Peerage, 1643. Agnes his daughter was the " Muckle-moo'd Meg " of the story connected with the captive who preferred death to marriage with an ugly wife. She married Sir William Scott of Harden (1611). It was the Border freebooter Wat o' Harden who married Mary Scott of Dryhope Tower, "the Flower of Yarrow," famous for her beauty, as he for his courage, being of that bold band that recovered Jamie Telfer's kye, and rescued Kinmont Willie. His were the spurs, now possessed by his descendants Lord Murray of Elibank, that were placed in the dish to indicate the larder was empty, and a raid called for. He lived at Oakwood Tower and Kirkhope Tower ; and it was his son Willie Scott, caught by Sir Gideon in a rieving expedition, who married Agnes Murray. Willie's third son became Laird of Raeburn and his wife was a MacDougal of Makerstoun, of a family which has some claim to be the oldest in Scotland. Sir Walter Scott was descended on his father's side from Wat o' Harden, and on his mother's side from Rev. John Rutherford of Yarrow. Sir Gideon's brother, Sir John Murray of Blackbarony (d. 1617), was popularly called "The Dyker" because he was the first in Tweeddale to enclose his estate with stone walls. He held the office " Coroner of Tweeddale." The duties of this office, which was also held by his son Sir Archibald, became merged in those of the Sheriff, and are supposed to have embraced, in the seventeenth and preceding centuries, the responsibility of apprehending prisoners, citing witnesses and jurymen, recovering Crown revenues, etc. (Renwick's *Historical Notes*, p. 47). Charles Geddes of Rachan also held the office of " Coroner or Crowner of Tweeddale " conferred upon him by James VI, on 21st February 1577–78. Cosmo Innes (*Legal Antiquities*, p. 84) says, " At one time the functions of the crowner were very high both in England and Scotland, and seem to have been co-extensive with the sheriffdom. . . . The office went early out of use in Scotland." It was Patrick, the fifth Lord Elibank, who, when Dr. Johnson defined oatmeal as " food for horses in England and for men in Scotland," rejoined, " Yes, and where will you see such horses and such men ? "

The Meldons form two summits, the Black and White

Meldon, between which runs a favourite highway from Eddleston to Lyne. Long before the days of the raiders this district must have played an important part in the life of Tweeddale because of the adjacent Roman Camp at Lyne, reports on the excavations of which are contained in the *Proceedings of the Society of Antiquaries*, vol. xxxv, 1901. The hill-top of White Meldon with a triple rath, the largest of the Tweeddale forts, a fortified camp rather than a fortress, may have been the scene of some of the last efforts of the original Britons as they retreated before the advancing Roman legions, and we can imagine the Roman sentry looking out from his camp towards the Meldon Hills held by the defiant tribesmen. " That cross-shaped earthwork on Meldon slope," says Dr. Gunn, " might well have been the place of worship of the Christian soldiery ; or at a later date might have served to indicate the lands of the Knights Templars who had holdings among the hills. The pass between the mountains—the Via Regia of the early Charters—has not only been traversed times innumerable by kings and armies, but also by the more peaceful cavalcades of the Monks of Melrose and Newbattle on journeys to their properties at Kingledores and Harehope " (Chapter XII, p. 116).

In Innes' *Scotland in the Middle Ages*, p. 146, we find that " Roads appear to have been frequent (A.D. 1000–1290), and though some are called the green road, viridis via, and by other names indicating rather a track for cattle, others, bearing the style of ' high way,' alta via, the ' king's road,' via regia, via regalis— and still more, the caulsey or calceia, must have been of more careful construction, and some of them fit for wheel-carriages. We find agricultural carriages of various names and descriptions, during the thirteenth century—plaustrum, quadriga, charete, carecta, biga—used not only for harvest and for carriage of peats from the moss, but for carrying the wool of the monastery to the seaport, and bringing in exchange salt, coals and sea-borne commodities. The Abbey of Kelso had a road for waggons, to Berwick on the one hand, and across the moorland to its cell of Lesmahagow in Clydesdale. A right-of-way was frequently bargained for, and even purchased at a considerable price " (Burton's *Hist. of Scot.* vol. ii, p. 110).

The hamlet which we now call Mountaincross between Romanno and Blythbridge (Knock-knowes) is by some said to have been called of old Monktown.

In a sixteenth-century charter there is a hill called "The Green Meldon" adjoining Hamilton Hill. The lands of Meldon and Kidston are mentioned as early as 1326; and previous to 1452 the Lauders of Hatton, Midlothian, held Kidston, probably the nucleus of the Cringletie Barony. The name Cringletie first appears in a charter of 1586 when there was confirmed to Alexander Lauder and Mary Maitland (daughter of Sir Richard Maitland of Lethington), his future spouse, "the lands and town of Cringiltie, of old called Wester Wormestoun, with tower, fortalice and manor" (*Great Seal Register*, V, No. 1031).

All this district of Tweeddale was largely interested in the old-time displays of armed might, which consisted in weapon-showings. Sir Walter Scott gives an interesting and accurate description of the wapinschaws of ancient Scotland in *Old Mortality*, with all their attendant formalities and sports, when the feudal army of the county was called out, and each Crown vassal was required to appear with such muster of men and armour as he was bound to make by his fief, and that under high statutory penalties. In every county and shrievalty these local meetings of militia took place annually, and were so named from the arms and accoutrements of the assembled force being then and there inspected by the Sheriff, who was under instructions to make such meetings agreeable to the young men, upon whom the military exercises of the morning and the sports of the evening might be supposed to have a rousing effect. There are two places in Tweeddale which still retain the respective names of Kingsmuir, and Sheriffmuir, originally derived from the scene of these periodical meetings of the Tweeddale militia, the former lying to the south of Frankscroft, Peebles, and the latter to the south side of Tweed between Lynesmill Bridge and the Beggar-path Bridge—not to be confused with the Sheriffmuir near Dunblane, where the Duke of Argyle and the Earl of Mar fought a drawn battle on 13th November 1715. A roll of one of these field armaments held on Kingsmuir on 15th June 1627 is still extant. Here are specimen entries :

Sir Archibald Murray of Darnhall, well horsed, with a collet, accompanied with 42 horsemen, with lances and swords, ten jacks [doublets of leather quilted with iron plates, being the armour of irregular cavalry of the period], and steel bonnets, within the parishes of Kilbucho and Eddleston.

David Murray of Halmire, well horsed, accompanied with 39 horsemen, and a buff coat, collet ; all the rest with lances and swords ; within the parishes of Newlands, Stobo and Drumelzier.

The duty of these larger proprietors was to appear with a body of men proportionate to the size of their estates. Lesser personages are also included :

John Sander of Foulage, present for Foulage and Melin's Land, well horsed, with coat of mail, plet sleeves, and steel bonnet, sword and lance.

Robert Porteous, for Winkston, present with a buff coat, a pair of pistols and a rapier.

These few extracts show that this wapinschaw armament, which amounted in all to 294 horsemen and 10 footmen, must have been rather a mixed one as regards weapons, dress, accoutrements. Some even came having no arms at all :

William Brown of Logan, present, well horsed, with lance and sword ; and a horseman, with nothing ; parish of Glenholm.

No doubt there would be an even greater degree of incongruity in the nature and appearance of the horses, some of the steeds being clean-limbed bits of blood from the stables of " my Lord," while others came rough from the farmer's plough.

The lairds themselves were equally diverse in character, according to the Tweeddale doctor, Pennecuik, who was a member of the Tweeddale Militia and described a meeting in 1685. The whole of the county militia was ordered to oppose Argyle when he landed in Scotland from Holland in support of Monmouth's unsuccessful attempt on the throne, but his speedy capture and death rendered their term of service brief and bloodless. Indeed after being in camp for forty days on the Kingsmuir, the poet tells us, in his best satirical vein, all the members of the loyal Tweeddale troop began to be heartily tired of their soldiering experience :

Stout Kaillie [one of the lairds] claws his shoulders, swears and damns,
" Must I not clip my sheep and spane my lambs !
I'll turn my tail on Friday without faillie,
In spite of all the troop, or deil tak' Kaillie."
And yet for all his heat, and fiery fary,
Good honest Kaillie to the last did tarry.

The upshot was that the honest men were sent home " to clip

their sheep and spane their lambs " under the superintendence of the lairds themselves.

The practice of archery was much encouraged in Scotland long before those days. In 1424 James I, on his return from captivity in England, had an Act passed providing that every person over twelve years of age should equip himself as an archer, " that bow marks be made near every paroch kirk, wharin, on holy days, men may cum and schutte at least thrice about and have usage of archerie ; and wha sa uses not the said archerie, the laird of the land or the sheriff, shall raise of him a wedder."

For further variety in the gentle pastime of walking, the eager wayfarer, young, healthy, vigorous, may enjoy walking from Moorfoot farm up the valley of Gladhouse Water, over the county boundary ridge of hills, and descend by a tributary to the valley of the Leithen Water. It is easy going thereafter all the way to Innerleithen. But from Leithen Lodge there are several miles of hard highway, and to avoid this there are two alternatives, either to leave the valley at Craighope and by way of the Dunslair Heights walk along the hills to Eshiels by Glentress, or cross over from Craighope by the gap between Makeness Kipps and Dunslair Heights, and walk to Peebles by Shieldgreen and the Soonhope Burn. For the motorist-walker, leave your car at Eddleston, proceed up the Kirk road and over the hills by Burnhead farm into the Leithen valley, then choose your route to arrive on the Peebles–Innerleithen highway, where a motor-bus will bring you back to Eddleston.

An Innerleithen tradition says that when the Scottish monarchs visited Traquair (a favourite sporting residence) their road from Edinburgh lay through the wild glen of Leithen, and there is still a bridle-path along the banks of the stream at Craighope and Woolandslee known as the King's Road (Smail's *Guide to Innerleithen and Traquair*, 1867). The way from Traquair to Newbattle Abbey would lead along Leithenhopes. This Vale of Leithen was granted by Alexander II to the Monks of Newbattle in 1241. Leithenhopes was purchased by William Grant, Lord Prestongrange (1701–64 : see Tytler's *Life of Lord Kames*), son of Sir Francis Grant of Cullen (Lord Cullen) ; subsequent holders were the Earl of Hyndford, who married Prestongrange's daughter, the heiress of the Barony of Prestongrange, which included Leithenhopes ; the Grant-Sutties and Miller-Cunninghams.

" The Road up Leithen " was made in 1794 and was used for the carriage of lime and coal to the Borders, " this line of communications shortening the distance from these commodities from 12 to 14 miles " (*Statistical Account*, 1796).

Various relics are found among the peats at divers times, of animals now extinct. There are records of horns of the Urus, *Bos primigenius*, the original wild ox of Britain, found on Porridge Knowe, one mile east of Craighope, at a height of 1,620 feet ; now in Innerleithen Library (*Scot. Nat.* 1921, p. 104). Another was found on the summit of Carlavin, Talla, at 2,000 feet (*Scot. Nat.* 1922, p. 68). The first trace from Tweeddale of a horn of the prehistoric Celtic Shorthorn, a primitive breed of half-domesticated ox and probable ancestor of our West Highland, Ayrshire and Galloway breeds, was found near the source of Manor Water at 2,000 feet, now in the Royal Scottish Museum (*Scot. Nat.* 1920, p. 65). The Celtic Shorthorns were the dominant cattle in this country for 6,000 years, terminating about A.D. 1000 (Dr. Ritchie).

Much potential wealth is locked up in peat—crude petrol, acetic acid for explosives, fibre for cardboard, briquettes for combustion ; but it plays a large part in Nature's economy as in absorbing moisture it acts as a regulating source of supply for burns and streams which otherwise would be subject to rapid overflow following heavy rains, or to long dry spells in times of drought.

Strabo wrote that " when they saw the men of Rome walking for pleasure they thought they must be mad," and many such reflections are not unknown in the present age, but walkers and Nature-lovers know better. There was a time when walking was a necessity. Our ancestors in travelling from Peebles to Edinburgh were able to cover the distance on foot in shorter time than those who rode. The road from Peebles climbed Venlaw past Smithfield and Hutcheonfield, and continued along the heights to the east of the present road (which is dated about 1770), and was so hilly and difficult as to be almost impassable by wheeled vehicles, which required four horses averaging three miles an hour. The county boundary was near Portmore, and from Craigburn the road went direct to Mosshouses, Venture Fair, Howgate, Cleikhim-in, and Auchendinny, which in the fifteenth and sixteenth centuries was known as " Auchendinny Briggs, commonly called Lourstane." The duty of the Peebles official carrier of 1732 (instituted 1685) was to " go to Edinburgh ane every week, winds and weather permitting (if he be in health)." Travellers on horseback carried pistols, and went in convoy for safety against highwaymen. Tolls existed at Eddleston and Nether Fala, and later at Milkieston, Scarcerig (an empty ruin near Scarcerig is the old Cockmuir Inn) and Craigburn, and at Tweeddaleburn on the Portmore–Gladhouse road. Tweeddale abolished all tolls in 1866, twelve years before the rest of Scotland (Roads and Bridges Act, 1878). Willie Wilson's one-horse " Caravan," which continued until 1806, covered the 22 miles in 10 hours, fare 2s. 6d. : succeeded by an old-fashioned post-chaise, " The Fly," 3 inside and 1 outside on an uneasy swinging seat, along with the driver ; 2 horses, time 5 hours, including 1 hour at Howgate. As " The Fly," described by one commentator as " a lumbering machine," went one day and returned the next, only twelve passengers could travel in a week, and seats had to be booked a week in advance. Then as the fare was 10s. 6d. each person, only the affluent could travel, and some had recourse to less legitimate means. Walking a short way out of the town, they thought to get a ride when the conveyance came along by bribing the driver with a shilling ; and by a " hangy " of this description " The Fly " was robbed of the mail-bag on one occasion. The story goes that one day after leaving Peebles, the driver took up three hangies, two of them respectable natives, the third a stranger lad dressed as a labourer. The two were set down near Edinburgh, the third continued to the head of the Cowgate. Arriving at his destination, The White Hart Inn, Grassmarket, the driver found that the mail-bag was missing. Enquiry followed. " Yes, he had taken up three hangies." The first two were found to be innocent, and suspicion rested on the third. No one knew who or where he was. Later it was discovered that, on making off with his booty up the West Bow, he was seized by some soldiers as a deserter, and lodged in the Tolbooth, but, strangely, no search was made of his person, the mail-bag remained hidden, and he remained unidentified. Next day he was removed to the Castle. Later a prison officer found a number of torn letters stuffed into the deserter's bed mattress, and imprudently burnt them. One envelope, however, survived. It was addressed to Wolfe Murray, Esq., Sheriff of Peeblesshire. This aroused suspicion, and the truth came out. The deserter was brought to trial, convicted and sent to Botany Bay ; a warning to all stage-coach drivers to be more discreet in their dealings with hangies.

Croall's stage-coach followed (1830), 3 hours, 5s. each, with two changes of horses. Winter snow-storms held up all travelling. The first locomotive reached Peebles in 1855 " and gave the small boys an opportunity of racing it along Eddleston Water, while parents looked on in wonder from their cottage doors." It was feared that the semi-liquid moss of Leadburn Moor would prove a difficulty, but upon it was laid a floor of rough planks, a thick coating of boughs of trees, and a layer of mud, on which the sleepers were laid traversely, the superfluous water being drawn off by side drains, and this process made the moor crossing secure. The train descends 300 feet in 10 miles from the summit level. Eddleston Water is always referred to by Dr. Pennecuik as the Water of Athelston—an older name was the Peebles Water " having its first and farthest spring from Kingside hill "—and it was over the high ridge at Kingside almost 1,000 feet above sea level, north-east of Leadburn, that the old highway from Edinburgh to Peebles passed. The farm of Kingside was also known as King's Seat, a reputed hunting station of James VI.

Tweeddale offers splendid scope for the walker and Nature-lover. Every height, hill and glen in its rolling landscape has its track, every glen its story, every keep its legend, and every hope and valley its shepherd's cottage where wife and weans —" bairnies fu' o' glee "—make glad the shepherd's return from the day's rounds amid these Border solitudes. It is a land where the broad rounded summits, the interconnecting ridges and sloping shoulders are the remains of an ancient undulating plain in which hundreds of streams have carved out the hopes and cleughs, the glens and straths we love so well. Lyne, Eddleston and Leithen valleys are no doubt remnants of ancient stream courses. Through the ages history has been in the making— in Border warfare, rieving, raiding, hunting and hawking and the pastoral scene. Heroic deeds and supernatural beliefs have been enshrined in ballad, song and story, told by those who dwelt in the " land of thought," caught up by the spirit of the eternal hills. Those days may be past, but the spirit of all such adventuring still inhabits the land. It remains a spirit land, latent with unseen presences, where amidst the " trivial round and common task " we find our way, it may be, by some favoured old grass-grown road to the temple in the hills in which our hearts uprise, where assurance is attained that life has a purpose related to powers and ideals of goodness, truth and beauty far transcending the limitations of life in the valley. It may even be by the memory of some such old road in the hills we find our Arcadia, where human needs are met and satisfied by the great simple things of life, love and friendship. " Happiness or unhappiness depends on the quality of the object which we love ; love towards a thing eternal and infinite feeds the mind wholly with joy, and is unmingled with any sadness " is a famous sentence of Spinoza. In the temple of the hills we are in touch with things eternal ; that is why it is such a splendid thing to be a walker.

Let us now visit that inviting part of the county of Tweeddale that is included in the Pentland Hills country.

XX

LINTON SHEEP MARKETS:
THE CAULDSTANESLAP DROVE ROAD

As one walks over the Cauldstaneslap, in the Pentlands, to West Linton, in Tweeddale, or "Linton Roderick" as is the early name (see *The Call of the Pentlands*), one's thoughts naturally turn to what took place upon this old Drove road to which we referred in Chapter V, "Drumelzier in the Land of Merlin," in days when it was the route followed by drovers coming from Lochaber and the Highlands with large herds of black cattle for the English markets.

The drover's life was a strenuous one, and there were occasions of emergency when the kilted Highlandman had to use his skean-dhu (sgian-dubh, literally black knife) for purposes other than those of its normal office, which might range from the skinning of a deer to cutting one's viands. Every journey was an adventure. Yet it was the life he loved, and he beguiled the miles whistling a pibroch or singing a Highland tune, as, with his cudgel, he urged forward the laggards of the herd. He was proud of the confidence he enjoyed, not only as guardian of the herd, but as being responsible for its disposal to the best advantage; and experience made him astute in bargaining. His wants were meagre, a few handfuls of oatmeal and some onions, renewed from time to time, and a ramshorn of whisky, of which he partook morning and night sparingly. His black cattle were valuable, and, after they were sold, he returned with his black pocket-book filled with bank-notes, and his sporran lined with gold. It was this that made the drover's life a dangerous one, and encounters took place in the Cauldstaneslap when blood was spilt and sheep and cattle stolen. This Drove road was also called "The Thieves' Road," a road frequented by Border raiders and moss-troopers; and it was necessary that the drover should have a stout heart as well as a strong arm.

The Cauldstaneslap was an eerie place, whether in the darkness of night when the north wind was tearing through the

Slap, or on a still night of fitful moonlight, when upon the wings of the wind was heard the thudding of horses' hooves and the sound of bridle bits. There are records of such raids in the books of the Privy Council. And there was no redress ; the raiders were off like the wind, and the cattle impounded in the Devil's Beef Tub. It was, however, possible to purchase immunity from their depredations by paying blackmail in the shape of a yearly tax.

Such Blackmail Contracts were in common use till 1743 and perhaps later. Under them the first parties, who might be the raiders themselves, or someone prepared to take the risk, under-took either to return the stolen cattle, horses or sheep, above six in number, or pay their value, within six months, to the second parties, whose lands were to be protected, provided notice was given to the first parties within forty-eight hours after the animals disappeared, and proof furnished that they were seen upon the usual pasture forty-eight hours prior to the intimation, with a note of their number and marks, the consideration being payment of about 4 per cent of the valued rent of the land, for each year, during the term of the Contract (sometimes seven years). All thieves caught to be brought to justice, and the Contract to be void in case of war arising in the country. Such Contracts were replete with every legal formality, even to the extent of being recorded in the Books of Council and Session.

When the drover had sold his cattle in the south, he frequently returned to West Linton and bought sheep, which he drove over the Slap to the Highlands, there to be fattened and driven back again later. Linton was the chief market in Scotland for two hundred years for the famous "Linton" breed of blackfaced, black-legged, horned and coarse-woolled sheep and 30,000 were sold at two market days in June each year in the eighteenth century.

From early times a market was held in West Linton, known as the Brighouse Market. Power to hold such markets was given to Linton when it first became a Burgh of Regality in 1631, jurisdiction being exercised by a bailie named by the Lord of Regality (the previous grant of Regality in 1383 not apparently affecting the village).

It was of new erected into a Regality by Charter of Charles II, the manor place of Drochil to be the principal messuage.

Authority to hold weekly markets and two annual fairs was granted by Letters Patent on 26th January 1664 ; also to levy tolls, customs and casualties ; and the markets continued until the middle of the nineteenth century. No such markets are now held at West Linton, but there was a time when they were the chief interest in the life of this Pentland village and the surrounding district.

Dr. Pennecuik, in his *Description of Tweeddale*, says : " Here at Bridgehouse (Brig'us Inn, now incorporated in Medwyn House, near the Golf Course) was the great sheep Mercat holden, before the Earl of Teviot removed it to Linton " ; and in the *Agricultural Survey of Peeblesshire* (1802) it is stated :

This is still the principal Sheep Market in Scotland for the Linton Breed : most of the business is now conducted at two of the five Weekly Markets, the Second Linton Market on the third Wednesday of June, and the Third Linton Market on the following Wednesday. The sheep come to market early on the Tuesday, and are generally all sold off that evening. The former being the principal market for Tweeddale holding sheep, the latter the great Market for Linton Breed, all sold by character, from Tweeddale, the Upper Ward of Clydesdale, Dumfriesshire, Selkirkshire, and the hilly parts of the three Lothians.

Shearers for the ensuing harvest were also hired at the June sheep markets.

The native Tweeddale breed, which has continued the same as far back as memory or tradition extends, are all horned, with black faces, and black legs, and coarse wool. Their shape, to which alone attention has been paid in selecting the breeders, is compact, short-coupled, short-legged, round-bodied, with a rising forehand.

The coarse wool was sold to Stirling, Hawick and Leith for export to England, to make carpets, shalloons, etc. Black-faced wool was sold " in the grease," which acted as a preservative in transport, " lanoline " being a manufactured by-product of the grease. To-day wool grease is valuable because of the shortage of animal fats (1946).

As to the origin of Blackfaced sheep so much is given as conjecture that it is quite impossible to form any definite conclusion based on reliable authenticity. All that can be ascertained is that from time immemorial Blackfaced sheep have been settled in the hill districts of the South of Scotland, and they are supposed to be the direct descendants of the aboriginal Scottish sheep, their present improvement having been brought about by a long-continued and judicious process of selection.

The Blackfaced breed are by themselves in this respect, as all the other breeds of sheep have been at some stage crossed with some other breed with a view to improving them. In fact this applies to all other domestic animals, with one exception—Highland cattle. There is a tradition that, previous to the introduction or general prevalence of sheep in the Parish of Tweedsmuir, the farmers in that parish paid their rents from the summer grazing of oxen, then generally used by Lothian farmers for winter ploughing.

The " Tweeddale holding sheep " referred to in the *Survey* would be what is known to-day as " in-by " or " Park sheep " and perhaps of the Cheviot breed or a cross thereof, probably less numerous at that time than the Blackfaced or Linton breed, which were sold " by character," that is, the sheep were not at the market on the day when they were sold, but grazing peacefully on the hills at home in the shires mentioned. The hoggs were sold off at these fairs as well as the " holding sheep " which were not usually sold by character.

Sheep were introduced into Galloway about 1603, and into the Highlands about 1750, and West Linton may have been selling sheep as early as the sixteenth century. James IV grazed 10,000 Blackfaced sheep in Ettrick Forest in 1503—a large number in those days, but small compared with present-day stocks—and exported wool to Flanders, Andrew Bell being the farmer, and John Hope and John Hall the King's shepherds. Some say it was a pedigreed flock, but pedigree breeding of sheep at that early date would probably never be thought of.

When the Cheviot breed of sheep was introduced in 1785, as likely to be the best of the fine-woolled sheep suitable for high ground, the Ettrick Shepherd was highly indignant, and resented the idea that those " white-faced gentry," as he called them, should be substituted for the blackfaced " ewie wi' the crookit horn," native to the Border hills. But the Blackfaced have held their own, and are still the best for the high hills, and are very popular, and it is estimated that in Tweeddale the proportion in favour of the Blackfaced is somewhere about three to two. With the introduction of the Cheviots came the planting of the Scots pine woods, and the building of stells for shelter, which we now know so well as features of the Tweeddale landscape.

The purpose of heather-burning (muirburn), once in nine years, is to preserve a supply of new heather, which grows from the seed, and in three to four years the young heather is ready to eat, two years if the ground be mossy. The period of burning is subject to laws and regulations, which can be very annoying and burdensome to the farmer.

Diseases of sheep still prevail, although it is hoped that Science will soon bring further relief in this respect. "Braxy," a species of inflammation (November-February), and "Loupin'-ill," a kind of paralysis, are the most common. Sheep require to be carefully watched, and a good shepherd is worth his weight in gold. Before the days of sheep-dip, smearing or salving the wool with tar and butter mixture was the antidote for vermin and weather ravages, but at Linton, tar was replaced by train oil and cocoanut oil in 1834. It is said that Sir Walter Scott, who like Burns had music in his soul but little in his voice, had but one song in his repertoire, which he sang at the Selkirkshire Pastoralists' Association Gathering—"Tarry 'oo is ill to spin !" He once asked the Ettrick Shepherd to sing "Gilmanscleugh," but Hogg stuck at the ninth verse, whereupon Scott repeated the whole of the eighty-eight stanzas without a mistake. He had a grand memory.

In Linton "hodden gray o' the guid wife's spinnin'" had ceased to exist by that year, but in 1847 a shepherd died at Kippet, in his hundredth year, all of whose clothing was home-made ; he had moved only twice, never been farther than Leith and Lanark, reared a family on £4 a year, saved £200, and lived on the interest, with a free house and milk. But nowadays . . . ! There was a time when the ploughman's " sark " was sown, grown, woven and worn on the farm where he worked.

About 50 per cent of the total Scottish wool supply is Blackface wool and endeavour is being made to find outlets at an economic price to the producer for this coarser type of wool. Prior to 1939 it was used by carpet manufacturers here and in America, and by certain European countries, principally Italy, for mattress-making, but foreign market uncertainty has led to consideration of other uses. Evidence of carpet manufacturers is that the amount they can use in carpet yarns blend is limited.

Home bedding manufacturers are making further experiments and Scottish firms are experimenting in the production of Black-face wool rugs and furnishing fabrics (Uses of Scottish Grown Wools, Report by Scottish Council on Industry, June 1946).

As showing the originally treeless nature of the hills between the sheep markets on the high ground, and Linton Village, the Doctor tells us how the children rolled down the grassy slope from top to bottom, on some sort of chair or sledge. This was the game of " Hurley Hacket " played by boys on Calton Hill in 1790 to which Sir Walter Scott refers in *The Lady of the Lake*.

As establishing the date of these Linton markets there is an interesting sidelight on the subject of the rival markets at Brig-house and House o' Muir (Glencorse) that engaged the Town Councils of Peebles and Edinburgh for fifteen years (1644–59). Peebles claimed the custom dues of the Brighouse markets, and on 2nd July 1649, when the Provost and bailies, " accompanyit with ane grit pairt of the Counsell and honest men of the Burgh," went to the " usurpet mercat of Brighous " to " desyre the buyers and sellers to answer them of the customs of the goods to be sold thereat," they succeeded in establishing their right, and the customs collected next year for five market days at Brighouseknowe amounted to £55. In 1652 collection of the dues was let to a tacksman. But trouble arose. Along with the Town Clerk and a bailie, the tacksman arrived at Linton with instructions that if there was any opposition against the collecting of the customs they were authorised to " protest and take instru-mentes conforme to the tounes right."

The opposition came from the city of Edinburgh ; and on 16th July 1653 it was resolved to send a letter to the Council " anent the troubling of the merchantes who sells and buyes goodes at Brighousknowe." Five years later the Provost goes to Edinburgh to meet the magistrates and to " hear their myndes." The result apparently was a compromise, for on 27th June 1659 Edinburgh Town Council agreed " with thes in Lintoun for the libertie of the standing of the mercate in Brighouseknowe for this year for twelve punds Scottes."

Why, it may be asked, should Edinburgh interfere with markets at Linton ? The reason was that Brighouseknowe market was a rival market competing with the House o' Muir (1612–1871), half the dues of which were paid to the city, and in

SHEEP " CLIPPIN' ", NEAR BROUGHTON

DARLINGTON
PUBLIC LIBRARY.

THE BUCCLEUCH HOUNDS, NEAR SYNTON MILL

RIVER TWEED AT STOBO

DARLINGTON
PUBLIC LIBRARY.

THE LAKE AT RACHAN

order to evade payment of these dues, dealers took possession of Brighouseknowe—" the usurpet mercat of Brighous," where there may have been no dues payable until the Peebles Council claimed them in 1649.

Brighouseknowe appears in Edinburgh Burgh Records as early as 1644. The city claimed that House o' Muir was the only lawful sheep market conform to an Act of the Estates of Parliament in Scotland, 1649. In June 1655, finding a Proclamation against forestallers of that market ineffectual, the city obtained from General Monk, an officer and twelve soldiers on horseback, to accompany a committee of the Council to Brighouseknowe, and there commanded the flockmasters to drive all their sheep to House of Muir, where, convening all before them, they were told they would not be punished that time on condition that no more markets should be held at Brighouseknowe. The Edinburgh authorities, however, found their position untenable, and both markets continued to prosper for over two centuries.

Linton was not a large village. In 1715 there were but sixty families ; sixty years later the population numbered 320, and there was difficulty in providing accommodation for the great numbers that attended the markets. Situated on the highway to Moffat and Carlisle, the Burgh of Regality was then held of the Earl of March as lord of the manor. Unfortunately the books of the Regality Court are not now in existence ; they might have shed an interesting light upon the manners and customs of the seventeenth and eighteenth centuries in this Pentland village. In 1747, when Heritable Jurisdictions were abolished, William, third Earl of March (afterwards Duke of Queensberry and known as " Old Q."), was allowed £218 : 4s. 5d. as compensation for the Regality of Linton, and £3,200 for his office as hereditary Sheriff of the County. Linton was the first stage on the turnpike from Edinburgh, with the Brig'us Inn for the accommodation of travellers.

One of the neighbouring lairds, Brown of Newhall, wrote a poem (1817) in nine cantos, entitled " Lintoun Green, or The Third Market Day of June 1685," describing the market-day scenes :

Was never seen in Lintoun Town
Since e're it had a Fair,
Sic crowds a' rinnan' up and down,
And through it sic repair,

As was that Market Day in June
Sae mony fo'k were there,
Ilk but, an' ben, aneath, aboon,
Was filled, baith late an' ear'
That merry day.

Trade increased during market time. There were no fewer than eight vintners in the village, who had an additional calling during the quiet season until the Whipman Play and Handsel Monday brought numerous visitors again to the village. Most of the farmers, drovers and prospective buyers arrived on the Monday, and every sleeping place in the village was engaged for the night. Those who could not find accommodation were content with a sitting-room or rested during the summer night in some plantation or on a seat by the wayside until four o'clock in the morning, when the markets began. Tents were erected on the market ground, and toll-keepers and customs collectors also participated in the wealth brought to the markets by the Highland drovers.

The first improved breed of sheep introduced to the Hebrides came from West Linton, writes John M. Macdonald (sometime of Whitfield), an authority on sheep and Highland ponies. West Linton was the main source of supply for stocking the Highland hills, for the Highlanders then were inexperienced with sheep, and kept no breeding stock. Each spring therefore, they came to Linton and bought wedder hoggs which, after being kept for two or three years, were sold in Perth. Later they began to breed their own stock, and their visits to the Linton Fairs ceased. The last of the markets was held about 1857, the general conditions of Scottish sheep farming having greatly changed.

The royal forest of Alyth (7,500 acres of heath land) was long valued for the pasturage of Linton sheep (*Strathmore : Past and Present*).

It is interesting to add that there still continues in Uist the remnants of the *caora beag*, the small native sheep, which stocked the hills up to the middle of the eighteenth century, when they were displaced by the Cheviot and the Linton breeds bought from farmers at the West Linton markets.

XXI

A HILL-TOP REVERIE

NATURE'S WONDERLAND

" It is a comely fashion to be glad ! "

WHAT an overflowing of heart's content there is when under the blue heavens and the sunshine we breathe the sweet freshness of the morning air on some high ridge of the Tweeddale hills and view Scotland's Southern Uplands and the far-spreading Border hills. Or sheltering from the storm wind on the high moorland we pause in a butt to take measure of the nearer landscape, and trace the winding streams making for Tweed and Clyde.

Then it is that mind and emotion fuse, and glimpses are caught of peaceful retrospection, and right perspective regained, to meet life's challenge. Precious is the joyous freedom of the open air and the far spaces, uplifting the heart, giving strength and courage and buoyancy of spirit. All things become possible in their possession, while in our heart there is a secret source of contentment and happiness.

Look where we will, all is beauty. Sun shadows race across heathery slopes ; bold headlands tower above the pine trees ; the sky-scape is a gorgeous pageant of sunlit clouds that changes every moment.

Richard Jefferies once said that the value of clouds lies in their slowness of movement and consequent effect in soothing the mind. It is then that a dream fills the mind, he says, and a dream is sometimes better than the best reality. Much depends upon one's outlook, for there are times when the swift movement of white billowy clouds, their fantastic shapes, strange evolutions and changing colour and formation may be more in keeping with our mood, creating an alertness of vision and inspiring awe that makes the reality more precious than any dream. To witness forces acting so directly and with apparent effect on so great a scale is to replace emotion with the quiet voice of wonder.

Much of the sky picture is dependent upon clouds : wind and cloud are the magic painters of earth. Earth and air combine to make the picture glorious, but for the appreciation of this one must " study to be quiet " and be ever vigilant. Only in quietness can places as well as people come to their natural maturity. " There is in stillness oft a magic power to calm the breast," said Newman, " touched by its influence, in the soul arise diviner feelings, kindred with the skies."

Pleasant also is it to see how the passing cloud brings a transient shadow, a shadow so faint and delicate, so like the shadow of a shade that one might deem an angel's wing had brought it there. Or as when spring is passing into summer we recall the days when we lay upon the hillside, and looked up.

> Ye clouds ! that far above me float and pause,
> Whose pathless march no mortal may control !
> (Coleridge)

The colours of clouds are as various as their shapes, and how delicate the gossamer mists when the sun breaks through and reveals a background of blue and pearly white. Wonderful, too, may be the gloaming hour when the western sun scatters everywhere her fiery reds and greens and opals, and the hills enrobe themselves in purple.

Certain landscapes can make captive the eye for long periods, sometimes because of their quiet beauty, or because of their kaleidoscopic change ; it is all a moving picture, and oft times a sound picture ; and if the mist seems settled on the mountaintops, it may not be for long. For, next time we look, lo ! the mists have risen, and revealed the majesty of peak and every riven scar. Sometimes the mist clings to the hillside obstinately, or whirls over the tops, or trails slowly as if caressing the topmost height, creeping over the ridges with tentacles like human fingers feeling the countours of rocks, as a blind person learns the shape of a friend's features.

This Pentland landscape in Tweeddale is rich also in copses of Scots pine, not to be misnamed Scots fir, for the Scots pine is our one native pine ; the cones are pendulous, those of the fir are erect. These enrich the scene, giving a sense of repose. The eye rests upon their olive sheen and is satisfied. Many voices belong to the towering pine that clutches earth with firm feet, and in the storm singing louder than all the floods. Music is the very life of the pine—how often is it " a harp for every wind, a voice for every sky " :

> And if some wild full-gathered harmony
> Roll its unbroken music through my line,
> Believe there murmurs, faintly though it be,
> The Spirit of the Pine.
>
> (BAYARD TAYLOR, " Metempsychosis of the Pine ")

A fascinating stretch of hill and moor lies in the western Pentlands between Craigengar and Mendick, Catstone and Dunsyre. Here are rivers and green waterheads, valleys of waving withies, white grass amidst patches of heather, gleaming in vivid detail in the sunlight and the wind. Far to the east is the grey horizon of the sea ; the ramparts of the Lammermuirs and the Moorfoots fill in the landscape that stretches to the huddled rounded tops of the Borderland ; garnished harvest fields dot the foothills and the low-lying Lothian plains, whose colours change with the painting of the seasons, while in many a wooded estate and homely park stand ancient mansion-house and castle. Tinto reminds us of Dr. " Rab " Brown's sermon in *Jeems the Doorkeeper* on " the pursuit of Truth."

The early morning sky has changed ; the wind swings into the north-west, followed by a lowering sky, and a cloud of sleety rain scuds along the hill-tops. But soon it is over and gone, the sky is washed and clean, and there follows clear shining after rain, fine effects of atmosphere, and steel-blue reflection on runnel of water and on every moorland loch and pool.

Some have found companionship in the sea, others in mountains and hills and trees, but for real company and friendship many prefer a river, a water or even a burn, where solitary musing finds a friendly accompaniment. It is by a river that confidences may be exchanged, old friendships revived, and the mind cleansed from all false and foolish things that mar the joy and peace of living :

> London streets are gold.—Ah, give me leaves aglinting
> 'Midst grey dykes and hedges in the autumn sun !
> London water's wine, poured out for all unstinting—
> God ! for the little brooks that tumble as they run !
>
> (ADA SMITH, " The Open Road ")

Seneca wrote, " Where a spring rises or a river flows, there should one build altars and offer sacrifices," and Aristotle called certain springs in his country " Cements of Society " because the young people so frequently met there and sang and conversed. A spring in the valley is an idyll, but a spring near the hill or mountain-top is a genuine lyrical touch and cherished by every walker and climber for its unfailing thrill. Hardly anyone can pass a spring without doing homage to it ; and St. Francis, thinking of valleys of Springs of Rivers, prayed—" Praised are Thou, my Lord, of Sister Water, for manifold is her use, and humble is she, and precious and pure."

The course of the hill stream is often intriguing, for the banks as well as the water make the stream, the water moulds and carves the shore, making a bay here, a long point there, alluring bushes and trees, grasses and wild flowers to its sides, and spreading out like a mirror to reflect the sky and clouds, or breaking into foam of musical laughter, or soothing into silent motion like the flow of a dream, so that we see the golden gravel at the bottom of the pool, and watch the trout in playful mood.

Every river has its own quality, and it is wise to know as many as we can. What the eye loves the memory cherishes. Those we love most are the ones we know best, whether in childhood, youth or age, and we come back to Naaman's state of mind—" Are not Abana and Pharpar, rivers of Damascus, better than all the waters of Israel ? "

Perhaps we cherish the little river better than any, the one we follow through the heather to its native haunts where it is young and free and full of fun, where it brings to you acquaintance with flies and spiders, fishes and birds, mosses and wild flowers, and where it plays with its coloured pebbles and the thyme and forget-me-nots, bubbling delightedly to itself in its cradle among the heathery moors. Nor do we forget the hidden brook " that to the sleeping woods all night singeth a quiet tune."

Two in the Pentlands have a peculiar charm. The Baddinsgill that rises amid the lonely hills around the Wolf Craigs, where it begins in a talking, chuckling sort of mood, and is quiet and boisterous by turns like a schoolboy, meanders through a hollow in the hills and passes rocks and plantations, and then, as if tired of such restraint, issues into the open and laughs outright. It is perhaps the most talkative stream in the Pentlands. The other lines the Tweeddale boundary, the Medwin Water, which comes within our view to-day. It marks a deep declivity in the far-stretching hills from the solitary Garval Syke to its confluence with the West Water near Walton Cottage. On both of these streams you may surprise herons and hawks and kingfishers. To-day Medwin is in high flood, deeply amber-coloured, beautiful in the genial sunlight.

Such pilgrimages amid Nature's Wonderland supply a cup of pure gladness, give solace and refreshment to the mind and the spirit, and an inner harmony that is a fruit of spiritual contentment, for it is not a dead mechanic world in which we live, but one informed by a vital life which moves through all material things and makes them instinct with unity and beauty. Memoried joys keep for ever their delight, and if to the Saxons Arcady be Valhalla, to the Buddhists Nirvana and to the Greeks Elysium, may it not be for all wayfarers just that mood in which we find this supreme contentment ? It is such Arcadian haunts of peace that are mirrored of the mind when distance separates, and

> When to the sessions of sweet silent thought,
> We summon up remembrance of things past.

XXII

BY GARVAL SYKE AND MEDWIN
WATER

A PENTLAND CROSSING

WINTER lingered in the lap of spring, and soft airs mingled with the icy blast as we left the station at Harburn bound for the open spaces by the Garval Syke and Medwin Water in a day's adventure in that section of the Pentland Hills that lies in Tweeddale.

Harburn ! There is an echo-haunted sound in the saying of the name, like the eerie sough in the Pentland names—the Windy Gowl, the Cauldstaneslap, the Garval Syke—and like many place-names it is aptly named, for it strikes a note of wonder and expectation consonant with going a journey, and connects us with Cromwell's Stone and the Roman Camp near Castle Gregg at Camilty.

Passing through the wind-swept moorlands interest is early stirred. Black and bare are the branches and twigs, but exquisite in artistry as they wave and dance in the wind—a robin piped, a blackbird sang, a thrush gave three hops and a run and two rooks sat close together among the high tree-tops.

As we near the Lang Whang, the landscape rises fold upon fold till the Cairn Hills and the Cauldstaneslap, Torweaving Hill and Mealowther rim the horizon, with the Kips, Scald Law and Carnethy stretching away eastwards, less clearly defined, but graceful and ethereal in the early morning mist. From this viewpoint the hills are wide and spacious, and the peaks, although not high—all being under 2,000 feet—have a stately grandeur enhanced by the intervening distance.

Many Pentland walkers have memories of the old Lang Whang before it became a motoring highway, where at certain points walking was hard and depressing, and to ride a bicycle was impossible. An air of mystery brooded over it. Ever its solitariness and silence held us with a strange fascination. It was no great distance from the city, yet it was in the wilds, where the hills were unfamiliar and the heathery moorlands unfrequented, and the creaking of the carrier's and the cadger's cart was the only sound that broke the silence. History links it with many strange events, in which Roman legions, Templars and Knights of St. John, Kings and Queens, stage-coaches, tolls and inns, rebels and rievers, ghosts and warlocks from the Pentland sykes, all played their part.

As we crossed the Lang Whang and took the farm road for the hills, a shepherd's dog barked and warned the farmer of our approach, and soon we were translated to a different world or thought with eager talk about the hills and hill-folk, old customs and rare personalities. We recalled the annual shepherds' meetings at Limehouse on Baddinsgill Burn, where strayed sheep were exchanged by Pentland herds from hill farms all around, and the jovial meetings of " brither herds " were long remembered. This gathering was first instituted over a hundred years ago. So I learned at a gamekeeper's cottage where I found the old notice-board—" Limehouse, re-erected 1882 for the Shepherds Strayed Sheep Gathering. Instituted 1827." There were limestone quarries near by, and the cottage housed the smithy where tools were sharpened, but it is now a desolate ruin. Was it some such lonely cottage near Craigengar Moss that the Ettrick Shepherd had in mind when he wrote his dramatic " Tale of the Battle of Pentland " ?

A fox-hunt had just taken place, joined in by all the keepers, shepherds and orramen in the district, for the lambing season would soon be here, and the depredations of Reynard are frequently on a large scale and every precaution must be taken. " Aye," said my friend, " five were killed in the Slap last week." And so to the accompaniment of dogs barking, and wind whistling through the trees, we took to the hill again. Fresh impressions had been made and received, to be kept bright till our next meeting, for the memories of those who live in lonely places are sensitive and their thoughts are often long.

From this point, the Scottish Rights-of-Way Society post directs the way by Midcrosswood to Henshaw Hill. Bold Craigengar with its shepherds' cairns beckons on the left, light-grey clouds concealing the summit at intervals, and behind us gleamed the blue waters of Crosswood whipped by the wind.

A map and a sense of direction are necessary for this part of the hills, for often the track is lost or mistaken in the maze of sheep-tracks and rabbit-runs, but the clump of scraggy trees on Henshaw is a useful guide. An examination of the boulder-strewn tributary of Crosswoodburn showed the water mineral-stained. Patches of oil floated on the surface and oozed from the banks, and decomposed tree-trunks protruded from deep peat hags. Farther progress brings us to the drystane dyke forming the Lanark–Midlothian boundary, and another post directed us to the Garval Syke. Here the valleys were bathed in a blue mist from heather burning, and on coming to the source of the South Medwin Water we decided to follow its course to Medwinhead. The source of this water is in a wild sequestered spot. A place to explore, and for the boyish heart how wonderful, and yet a place in which to remain still, if only for a moment, an eerie place where spirits dwell and the cries of curlews and peewits echo in the glen.

" Never was there a footpath yet that did not pass something of interest," said Richard Jefferies, and we do not travel far down the Medwin—the Tweeddale border-line—before we come upon long reeds and rushes, mosses and sand mounds, dark pools and peat bogs, high hills and heathery cleughs, and " püles whaur the trout grow great in the howes o' the hills."

Between the Pike and Millstone Rig is the Ravens' Cleugh, and the point where the cleugh burn joins the Medwin marks the meeting-place of the counties of Tweeddale, Lanark and Midlothian, so that by striding the burn, and placing one's stick on the opposite bank of the Medwin, one is in touch with three counties at once.

In the Syke three valleys meet ; here three counties join, and in the same vicinity three rivers have their source that flow to Tweed, Clyde and Forth respectively. By climbing the ravine with its red sandstone cliffs and tumbling waters one may reach the heights of Craigengar (1,700 feet) and rejoice in a view that is like the Highlands in miniature, stretching from Dunsyre and the Black Mount to Castlelaw and Caerketton, while the cleugh itself is the nearest we can get to a cañon in the Pentlands.

Medwin valley is an intriguing place. Every bend in the river brings a fresh view. Wild life is here undisturbed. Dippers followed the winding of the stream with quick arrow-like motion, settled on a rock in mid-stream, bobbed, and sang their cheery song ; note his white bib and underparts, and how he winks and rolls his glistening eyes ; his is a happy, careless melody, jubilant in winter as in spring. Larks also sang, high up in the windy sky and fitful sunshine, for sing they must, for the joy of life, exultant in hope, foretellers of summer days. Heron and wild duck rose from reedy banks and disappeared over the valley, and a kestrel was disturbed ere he had completed his deadly work. Later, we witnessed the scene of tragedy, the victim being a " cushie-doo," and a scattering of feathers and some maize from its crop were all that remained. Grouse argued and gurgled, and the gulls' cry seemed strangely plaintive so far from the sea and shore. For a time interest centred most in the frantic scuttling of white hares, and their lightning race over wet grass and up steep hillsides, recalling Wordsworth's lines :

> And with her feet she from the plashy earth
> Raises a mist, that, glittering in the sun,
> Runs with her all the way. . . .

The Arctic hare is a relic of the Arctic fauna, coming to Scotland after the Ice Age, changing its coat to white in winter. Mountain hares were set free and established themselves on the Pentlands about 1867. After being extinct in the Scottish Lowlands they were reintroduced in Manor in 1834 and again in 1865, and are now almost a pest in the Southern Uplands.

All day long the wind carried the scent of heather burning which, like peat and wood-fire smoke, is as the balm of Gilead to the Nature-loving walker ; and the cries of hill and sea birds, the voice of many waters and the wholesome smell of Mother Earth. Here on the banks of Medwin Water one was close to Nature's heart.

Passing along the edge of a pine wood, we came to Medwin-head, where Faed, the artist, lived. From here a cart-track goes to Fernyhaugh, Garvald and Dolphinton. But the spirit of the hills had gripped us, and we continued our way for Linton and the Carlops, over the Slipperfield Moors and the romantic road by the Siller Holes.

Relics of far-off times abound on every side. In the strath under Mendick (Menedict, 1165-90) are two giant cairns that point to some ancient fight whose story is lost, and the burial-place of heroes. A third cairn opened before 1775 contained an earthen urn with human bones, while a brass sword, stone and flint instruments, dagger blades and saws have been found in the district. Flint arrow-heads were here called "elf-shots," said to be used by witches and warlocks in their incantations and cantrips, while stone axes were regarded as uncanny things. Among a local collection is a claret jug given by gipsies in payment of a coffin made by a West Linton joiner. Three beautiful gold torcs, found at Cairnmuir in 1806, are figured in the *Archaeologia Scotia* (vol. iv, p. 217, Plate X). They were found, along with various other relics, by a herd-boy, who going early in the morning to his sheep, observed something glitter in the sun, and on scraping with his feet, brought the whole valuable treasure to light. It consisted of three gold torcs or collars for the neck ; a beautiful gold ornament, supposed to have been the head of a staff or sceptre, and a number of flattened circular gold pellets, each marked with a cross in relief. The staff head and gold beads or pellets are in the Antiquarian Museum, Edinburgh. The latter were once used as the primitive type of native minted currency. They resemble two segments of a sphere irregularly joined and appear to have been cast in a mould. Forty of the same simple class of early currency were found, along with an ornament of pure gold in Dolphinton Parish, which is said to have resembled a snaffle-bit of a horse's bridle (*New Statistical Account*, vol. vi, p. 57). No doubt it was a funicular torc (*The Archaeology and Prehistoric Annals of Scotland*, pp. 317 and 520).

Our next object of interest after passing the cairns is the Rumbling Well, "Thirsty Katie," out of which the Garrel is born, where pilgrims place their ear and listen to the water rumbling underground. The Garrel or Garvald means the *rough-flowing stream*, while the Medwin (Meduane, 13th cent.) is the *soft-flowing stream*.

In the hill called Kingseat is the source of another stream, the Polintarf or West Water, flowing through the lands of Slipperfield, a tributary of Lyne Water, the largest and longest of Tweed's affluents in Peeblesshire. These lands were conveyed to the Friars of Holyrood by Richard Comyn in 1165. In the seventeenth century they were part of the Barony of Broughton.

William Russell, minister of Stobo (1700–33), was another owner of the Kingseat property, who gained so much notoriety in the Church and parish by his recalcitrant and contumacious conduct that he became known as the "Holy Terror." On several occasions he defied the Church Courts, absented himself from the Presbytery, was admonished by the Synod and told to behave himself more submissively and respectfully to his brethren. He appealed to the Synod, was suspended, sharply rebuked and told that he would receive higher censures if he was not more dutiful towards the Presbytery and other Judicatures of the Church.

He was then called to account by the Synod for neglecting to pray for King George and the Royal Family. Not wishing to appear disloyal or defiant, he had prayed for the King as commanded, but in such a " suffling fashion " that suspicion was aroused, and he was summoned before the Presbytery. His defence was that he had always prayed for King George, and although not in express words, his congregation knew quite well what was meant. Later, Sentence of Suspension was intimated to him, and he was rebuked for his " disingenuousness and contumacious behaviour," and suspended for two months. The first minister sent to intimate the Sentence (Paton, Newlands) for not praying as aforesaid and his disregard of all Judicatures of the Church was met by a mob of women who told him that no one would preach there but their own minister. The second minister (Gray, Innerleithen) was obliged to preach in the churchyard, being denied access to the church, the porch being " choked with cart wheels, ploughs and the like " ; the church-yard stile was locked, no bell could be rung, and the beadle could get no response from the manse. The third minister (Wallace, Drumelzier) had no better success, finding the stile and doors shut. Going to the manse for the key, a servant maid told him the minister was from home, his wife was unwell, the parishioners had the keys and that he would not get access to the church.

Ultimately Russell repented, and declared to a Commission of the General Assembly " that he was sensible of his fault, and would endeavour through Grace to walk more orderly and with greater subjection to the Judicatures of the Church " (May 1722). Before going to Stobo he was deposed (1697) for contumacy in not going to the North when ordered by the Assembly to do so. The sentence was taken off by the Assembly in 1699 on promise of subjection.

In early life he was a member of the Troop of Horse con-vened in Tweeddale by Royal Authority in 1685 under command of the Laird of Drumelzier to suppress what was then called rebellion. He was called the "Tory-trooper" Minister. Dr. Pennecuik mentions him in his "Panegyric":

> Young Kingseat was a Tory Trooper then,
> Now Stobo stipend makes him Whig again,
> So frequently we see from cloak to gown,
> Prelate and Presbyter turn upside down.

His uncle, Rev. William Russell, "son of the Laird of Kingseat," was also minister of Stobo (1688–99). He was ordained at Easter Happrew farm-house (22nd March 1688) by a Committee of Synod, the reason being that for eighteen months there were two ministers in the parish—Episcopalian and Presbyterian, and no doubt the church was in the former's custody, as he was not deprived till 3rd September 1689. In this farm-house the first Presbytery of the Revolution Settlement was constituted (March 1688).

When Episcopacy was finally abolished, the parish ministers were commanded to cease praying for James VII and to pray for King William and Queen Mary. Some declined, and were ejected, including the above Episcopalian minister of Stobo, and William Hay, minister of West Linton. This William Russell's father, James Russell of Kingseat, took a leading part as an elder in the new Reformation. (The Church of Scotland was Episcopal 1610–38; the Second Episcopacy, 1661–89; the Revolution, November 1689; Act of Parliament—25th April 1690—restored the Presbyterian ministers who had been ejected for non-compliance with Episcopacy; Episcopalianism being abolished in the Church of Scotland in July 1689.) It was at this time that William Veitch, the Dunsyre Covenanter, became minister of Peebles (1690–94)—as against the Duke of Queensberry's presentee, an Episcopalian—without stipend and burdened with law expenses. He was eventually settled at Dumfries.

Another event happened in this momentous year 1690: the General Assembly met for the first time after forty years.

On the occasion of an enforced settlement of a minister (Rev. Thomas Findlater) in Linton parish church in 1731, a company of military was called in to protect the Presbytery amidst riotous scenes. Many years later, an old soldier wayfaring near the village was asked by an inhabitant (a son of the minister) what engagements he had seen, and made reply: "I ne'er had sic het work, or was sae near bate, as at the settlin' o' a minister, just abune ye here at Lintoun!" One of the first Secession Congregations in the South of Scotland had its origin at West Linton at this time. From 1760 till 1766 there was a schoolmaster at West Linton named Lancelot Whale. He became rector of Kelso Grammar School, and tutor to young Walter Scott, who afterwards referred to him as "a classical scholar, a humorist and a worthy man."

Slipperfield and Kingseat are names referring to the one estate, the one being the estate itself, and the other the mansion-house, now demolished.

After this dissertation upon these noted ministerial Tweeddale lairds, let us continue our walk. Although sunset is yet an hour away, we find that already the first effects of sunset are appearing in the western sky. Through light cumuli came colours rosy red that threw their kisses on far-away clouds. The Corbies' Crag and the massive head of Dunsyre Hill stood forth majestically. Black Mount cleaved the sky that changed momentarily, blues and greens and pearly shades blending with pink and purple and mackerel grey.

But it is from Linton golf course that the south-eastern view is most attractive, because of the semicircle of hills that stretch across the horizon from Byrehope Mount and Mendick to Coulter Fell and the Moorfoots, with Broughton Heights and the Heights of Glensax and Hundleshope in the centre. In the foreground stand the silent pine trees, characteristic of the Pentland landscape.

Sunsets and far views, how often they thrill us with their wonder and beauty. In the hearts of most of us there is always the desire for something beyond experience, the

Something far more deeply interfused
Whose dwelling is the light of setting suns.

The sunset lingered, then gave its parting gift. As we breasted the heights above Stoneypath on the old road to Carlops, slender pointed shoots of pine tree-tops were silhouetted against a band of crimson that flamed across the western sky above a vault of fairest green. Later, in the radiant blue there dawned the evening star, and amidst calm and tranquil beauty the day slipped away to rest. How precious is Nature's benediction at such times.

If freshness had marked the morning hours, wonder and awe filled the hours of twilight, and homeward bound, we pondered in our heart the rich treasure that the day had brought in our adventure across the hills in Tweeddale by Garval Syke and Medwin Water.

MR. ANDERSON

. . over 40 years at Glenormiston, Innerleithen

DARLINGTON
PUBLIC LIBRARY.

BROUGHTON HOUSE

DARLINGTON
PUBLIC LIBRARY.

HALLYARDS, MANOR

XXIII

RURAL VIGNETTES

I. THE FISHER, ROBERT O' THE "NEST"

A Tweedside Character

IT is a long time ago since "Robert" passed onward. It was a sunny day with every token of the coming springtime that he loved so well, the singing birds, the greening larches and hedges and the song of Tweed "glittering in the sunny beam," when among his ain folk his mortal remains were laid to rest in Caddonfoot kirkyard.

Robert Shortreed was a typical Borderer of the soft Lowland tongue, and for over forty years was the faithful and respected fisherman and keeper of the Edinburgh Angling Club at their quarters on the Tweed, and the guide, philosopher and friend of every Tweedside angler. At what date the Club was started is not exactly known; it was some time in the mists of Scotland's morning. But the Club took definite shape in 1847, rented a stretch of water near the famed boat pool of Yair, and had premises first at Betty's Cottage near Ashiestiel, then at Clovenfords House and afterwards at "Robin's Nest," near Fernielea, Robin Pringle being the previous proprietor of the "Nest," so called because it was flower-embowered and twig-enfolded, a cosy, snug little cottage with windows that opened to the sun and the scent of roses and mignonette, where the members found Elysium after a day on the river. Later, the Club moved to another cottage at Caddonlee, farther up the river, amidst surroundings of much beauty and interest "where every ruin is history and every glen is song." Round this second "Nest" gathered memories of happy days and merry evenings similar to those associated with the original "Robin's Nest."

Many eminent men were among its members, representing Literature and Art, Law, Medicine and Science, editors, artists and business men, most of whom resided in Edinburgh. Here to the "Nest" they came, "a place of rest, a refuge in time of trouble, a place of repose for weary heads, a little haven where human barques, more or less heavily laden with overwrought brains, cast anchor for a little while, and were still."

Recollections of the "Nest" are bound up with Robert. He it was to whom was first directed enquiry as to the state of the water and fishing prospects, and his reply brought just the tonic needed for brain-weary authors and lawyers, jaded artists seeking fresh inspiration and depressed professional and business men with the noise and din of town still singing in their ears. Here was caller air to renew vitality and bring new hope, and Robert's cheering assurance, "She'll fesh! Eh, mon! she'll fesh the day."

On further enquiry as to who were all at the "Nest," Robert in his native Doric would reply, "Ou, there's twa Samsons and the body Arkley and his clerk," under which cognomens were unceremoniously disguised two R.S.A.s, the Sheriff of Mid-lothian and the Sheriff-Clerk.

"Come awa', mon," he would say, "they're takin'," for "ay the spate comes doon the glen, and up the siller fish are soomin'." Robert was *persona grata* to all the members of the Club, and was allowed an intimacy and friendliness ever exercised with a native courtesy and decorum and never transgressed. His words were few and well chosen, he didn't chatter, he had a knowledge of values—the relative value of things, and so was wise ; and he was a power with the rod, and happy were those who came under his guidance and instruction. His humour was delightful, quaint and homely, and frequently unconscious.

Once when an over-anxious angler slipped, and narrowly escaped complete immersion, Robert, looking up, remarked, "Ye're no wat, are ye?"

If fish were slow in taking, he would advise his tyros to have patience, to fish "painfully," and if that failed was it not comforting to be told there was "nae head o' fesh in the water," and that "there micht be a happenin' beast" or "aiblins a transient brute"? He was ever anxious to help, his eagle eye saw everything, he could spot a fish or the faintest rise in response to the lightest fly better than anyone. He knew all about the leister too, and the mysteries of burning the water. He had his own ideas about the shape and plumage of "saumon flees." An English guest once thought to get the better of Robert by twitting him about what the salmon could possibly take such strange-looking things for, but the Scot was unperturbed and replied assuredly, " Waal, a fancy they tak' them for mate (meat)."

In a discussion about why a certain train had not stopped at the Club's private station as expected, much to the disappointment of one of the members who expected to travel by it, Robert contributed the remark, " Lord's sake, a was near sookit in."

His travels far from Tweed were not many, but on one occasion the President of the Club invited him to his country quarters on the Clyde, and a sail in the member's steam yacht was proposed as far as Rothesay. The day was breezy, and a sail was used, with the result that the yacht pitched a bit and had a considerable list to port and poor Robert grew white about the gills. On a suggestion that perhaps a glass o' grog would put matters right and restore Robert's equanimity, the parties proceeded to the cabin, but on looking down the steep stair, and seeing the confined space, he raised his head and remarked in no small discomposure, " Lord's sake ! Hoo wad ane get oot o' that gin she coups ! " History relates that Robert came up " powerfully refreshed," and ready to face the stormiest sea.

But it was on Tweedside, and at the " Nest," that he, " a gem o' men, a king o' Tweed," was most in his element. There were few experiences in the lives of members of the Club into which he did not enter, for it was together that they entered into feats of piscatorial romance, with " the music o' the birring reel that has charm for fishers a'," the tumbles and leaps o' salmon "noo deep in Tweed, noo i' the air," and the landing or the losing of the heaviest fish in Tweed, or the greatest beauty ever seen.

And after the day on the water, there was dinner in the " Nest " presided over by the Sheriff, the President or the much-loved Russel of *The Scotsman*, the wit and soul of many a stirring symposium, with racy and rollicking fun and humour, and songs and jovial hilarity. Under the swinging lamp that made the " Nest " resemble a ship's cabin, good cheer was partaken, good stories told, good toddies were drunk, and good tobaccos smoked. Ah, the memories of those days ! And when it was time to retire, Robert's kindly parting rose above the din—" Waal, gentlemen, guid nicht ; a fesh apiece the morn."

Such personalities, so leal, original and characterful, and all they stand for, never die, their memory lives on, their spirit survives.

II. THE PLOUGHING MATCH

THE CREATOR OF THE UNIVERSE DOES NOT ALWAYS SPEAK IN PROSE

No sky was visible, no moon or stars, only continuous blashes of wind and rain and sleet greeted the competitors as they set out in the darkness from lonely farms in southern glen and upland, to travel to the scene of the Annual Tweeddale Ploughing Match, eagerly anticipated for weeks past.

As the distance in many cases was considerable, and the rate of progression was slow in the newly painted cart that carried the plough, and drawn by one of the plough horses gaily caparisoned (the other horse following the cart), an early start was necessary ; and when the match began at eight o'clock it was not yet daylight, and already men and horses were dripping wet. But lack of sleep and damp clothing little daunted these hardy farm lads, little recked they of the outward conditions so long as the contest was in full swing ; and but a short interval sufficed for dinner during the eight hours that the match continued.

Wet and snowy weather of past months had left its mark on the field in the strath by Tweed's swollen banks ; the upper three inches were soft and sappy, but underneath the rich loamy soil was dry and firm, with hardly a stone in the length and breadth of it.

It is the general opinion that young men are taking a renewed interest in ploughing, taking their place along with the elderly and middle-aged men, and it was not the least inspiring part of the day's outing to study the serious expression on the faces of all the competitors. There was no joking or chaffing or light-hearted banter about these proceedings, it was too serious an occasion for that. Would that all professed workmen were imbued with a strain so serious. It was not the material gain that counted with these men. Rather was it the inward joy of striving to excel, to beat the neighbouring farm, the last year's winners, to do a job better than others, to do it as well as it could be done, a striving towards perfection into which was thrown the worker's utmost skill and his own priceless personality. God's field and God's work, so he reckons his daily round. Such are the underlying motives of this contest of these worthy sons of rural Scotland.

Among the "knowing" onlookers there was suppressed excitement. Here and there at the rig's end would gather a few of the ploughman's friends and critics, but the anxious worker paid little heed to quip and sally. Quite apart from his lock-fast jaw and serious mien, the movements of his back and shoulders and legs showed the almost tremulous, nervous strain in which he worked that he might excel.

As the afternoon wore on, the wind and the rain and the sleet continued at intervals, and many of the horses, as well as the men, showed signs of the strain. Sleek, glossy coats were wet and matted, some carried themselves less gallantly, their movements slow and wearied ; the strain was telling, and a farm hand near by expressed it fittingly—" No a day for either man or beast." Yet some of the horses with more breeding and reserve of strength than the others carried themselves as they knew befitted the occasion, with proudly arched neck, rhythmic movement of limbs and feet, and a steady look in their large soft eyes that seemed to say with confidence, " I know what it's all about ; I can finish it easily, comfortably ! "

For the final rig only one horse is used with the plough, and his companion standing by watches steadily the progress of his mate—as dogs do at sheep-dog trials—and as the plough neared the end of the rig to complete the day's toil, one horse whinnied to the other, and was duly answered, " All is well." An almost human touch marks this incident.

As daylight faded, and the wet earth gleamed steel-surfaced in the sleety rain, the last of the competitors moved off with plough and horses to the corner of the field where the carts were gathered. The family party was complete. The women folks with their bairns had brought flasks of warm tea and provender for the men folks, to fortify them for the return journey. All the competitors were discussed, and the judges' awards taken as the final word. " Tam did rale weel," says one. " I couldna hae done better mysel'," lightly adds another. " Aye," continued a third, " but the judges didna pit him first a' the same : he'll dae better next 'ear, he's young yet, you mark ma words," and so the discussion goes on, in the wind and the rain and the sleet.

In due course all departed for the long slow journey home. The stables had been lamp-lit when they left in the early hours of the morning; they were lit again when the cavalcade returned to the farm steading more than twelve hours later.

Although tired and weary, the ploughman must first see that his horses are attended to before he himself enters the house; and as he gives each horse a pat before he leaves the stable, he whispers in their ears, " Guid lass, Bess ; guid lass, Nell, ye've done a lang day's wark ; rest weel ; guid nicht."

And it was fitting that the champions, not for the first time, should come from one of the glens among the hills we have been visiting, ten miles and more away, where husbandry has been carried on for many centuries, and in which to this day may be seen evidences of an ancient village settlement, a glen where from very early times dalesmen pastured their flocks by the side of the stream, and made rude hut dwellings for their abode.

Although the ploughmen had gone home, the day was not yet done for farmers, judges and members of the Ploughing Society. They adjourned to the Farmer's Inn, and there under the lamplight one could study more closely these authentic rural types and faces, so full of character, and representative of old tradition, and when the evening meal was over, there began the social round of speech and song and story. All phases of farming life were discussed, and one member, in emphasising the antiquity of the ploughman's lineage, maintained that while Adam remained in the Garden of Eden he was a gardener, but when he was sent forth from the garden he became a ploughman : that while Abel was a shepherd, Cain was a ploughman : that the youthful Elisha was ploughing when Elijah cast his mantle upon him, and when it was remarked that he was ploughing with no fewer than twelve yoke of oxen before him, the members smiled. And the smile turned to honest laughter at Samson's retort to the Philistines, when they answered his riddle, thanks to the suborning of his wife—" If ye had not plowed with my heifer ye had not found out my riddle."

After listening for a while to an impromptu discussion on the proper way to plough a field, one member related a tale from the *Noctes* : " Aye," said Awmrose, the landlord, to the Shepherd —" It's most delightful to hear Mr. North and you bandying matters across the table ; ye take such different views of the same subject." To which the Shepherd replied, " That's just it, Mr. Awmrose. That's the way to exhowst a subject. The ane o' us ploughs down the rig, an' the ither across, then on wi' the harrows, an' the field is like a garden."

If the stories came slowly from bashful lads from out-by places, yet under the chairman's coaxing smile and winning way, they did come. The Rev. Dr. Gillespie's beadle-ploughman story was one of them : " Well, Andrew, how did you get on ? Did you get a prize ? " " Yes, sir, I got the sixth prize." " How many ploughs were there ? " " There were twenty-four, sir ! " " Only twenty-four, Andrew, and you have only got the sixth prize ! I'm ashamed of you, Andrew, and you ought to be ashamed of yourself." The minister kept nagging at Andrew until, losing patience, the latter at length rejoined, " Weel, sir, if ye had been at a preachin' match, wi' as mony at it, ye mightna hae been sae far forrit yoursel'." The minister went from the stables back to his own fireside.

. . . . .

The Victors' Return.—We were coming down the glen after a day among the high hills, when in the gathering dusk of a January night we met a procession making its way up the hill road, forming a vignette that left an indelible impression upon the memory.

It was composed of two farm carts gaily painted and shining in the half-light of evening, drawn by two noble animals, and led by stalwart servants. Each cart contained a newly-painted plough. Behind the carts walked a bunch of women folk and bairns. There was something arresting about the cavalcade that moved with such stately unison. The road was hilly, and the horses kept rhythmic motion, as with no uncertain steps they proudly climbed the hill. The men were silent, silent with the consciousness of an experience that meant much to them, but the women folk and the bairns chatted merrily.

The men with heads erect were first in the procession, for they were the victors ; then came the horses, for they had contributed to the success, and seemed to be conscious of it ; while the means to the victory—the ploughs—were carried high in the carts in the place of honour, and that full measure of the glory should belong to these, the women folks brought up the rear.

It had been a great day for the glen folks, for their heroes had matched their skill against many competitors from the surrounding countryside, and won the victory, proving themselves to be the best ploughmen in all Tweeddale.

There was something fine, something noble, about the men and the horses ; probably they were tired after the long day's trial, but they carried themselves like victors. What were the thoughts of these silent men, one wondered ; those of the women folk could be easier imagined, for they were proud of their men folk, and all the district would speak of their prowess for many days and months to come. It was a lonely road they were travelling ; they had already come several miles, and several miles still lay ahead of them before the lights of the farm dwellings up the glen came into view. But distance to them did not count : they travelled with high hearts. On the day of victory no fatigue is felt. How proudly they carried themselves ! The victors' return to the glen was witnessed by few ; there would be no excitement as the carts trundled into the farm-yard and the " lowsin' " began ; it would all be taken as a matter of course ; but the glimpse that we got of that simple procession in the gloaming, instinct with such life and vigour and true nobility, was that of real poetry, an idyll of Scottish pastoral life, that thrilled the passer-by.

XXIV

"THE CLIPPIN'"

SHEEP-SHEARING AT A TWEEDDALE HILL FARM

LAMBING-TIME, with its anxieties and arduous duties, is no sooner past than the season of sheep-shearing begins—first "laumin' tim'" then the clippin'"—although the exact time varies with the different breeds and the climate and the natural "rise" in the wool in the late spring; but from the middle of June till the end of July sheep-shearing will be going on somewhere in Tweeddale.

One of the essential conditions is dry weather, for wool cannot be cut when it is wet, and when the good appointed day arrives it usually means steady work from early morning till well on in the evening, or if the start has been delayed, till darkness is beginning to gather. If the farm is a large one the clippin' continues for several days at a time. Then there will be the neighbouring farms, and the more distant ones, where assistance is required, so that shepherds may be engaged for several weeks without a break at the annual sheep-shearing.

Before daylight there is a knock on the bedroom door, and up we spring. Heavy feet are moving about on the stone flags of the kitchen, latches are clicked, doors swing open on creaky hinges, and folks pass and repass the windows, a piece of furniture is dragged to the "floor-head," followed by a "reeshle" of crockery, and a tumbling of knives and forks. Then we hear the singing of the kettle, the "skirling" of the frying-pan. And what a breakfast! Here everything is massive—the quality of the home-fed bacon, the cheese, scones, flagons of creamy milk for the bickers of porridge, and the farm butter in which you can see the marks of your teeth !

It nears five o'clock, and as we sally forth the greeting of the shepherds' collies resounds in the quiet morning air among the hills of Tweeddale. But some neighbours are before us, and soon we join them in the walk up the hill by the burnside Already we are among the sights and sounds of Nature. Herds pay little heed to these, perhaps, but they join us in our admiration, and tell us many things which are common knowledge to them, but of which we are ignorant. On we tramp through the budding heather and the early brackens, varied with wild flowers and bell heather in purple masses, and here and there the wild saugh spreads at our feet, and the wild thyme and bog myrtle scent the still, sweet air. Swallows sweep across the glen, and wagtails flit about, and run on in front of us, while on the next bush is a " stonechacker." Farther up we meet the whaups and peewits ; golden plovers and blackcock creep out of the heather and fly away ; and rabbits and hares jump up and scamper off. Dogs have to be kept under control, or would neglect the work in hand. Soon " the Glorious Twelfth " will be here again. There goes one covey of grouse, there's another, and another—six to nine birds apiece, and strong on the wing.

All this time the collie dogs have been busy, gathering the sheep, directed by the stentorian commands and whistles of the shepherds—" Aye, dogs, like bairns, need whyles to be keepit in aboot, or they micht gang fair ower ye, they're sae delighted tae be workin'." A great number of sheep have been collected ; a bleating crowd, they are pushing on in front helter-skelter along the hillside track, yet kept well in hand by the trusty collies, as we draw near the faulds. Others have been gathering too, and we are all converging on one point from different directions. Hill sheep feed in " hefts," that is to say, a number of the flock go together, feeding over a certain area of ground, which may be divided or bounded by a hill-end, a hill-top, a burn or a cleugh. Confining themselves to this bit, they work downwards from the hill-top in the morning, and back again towards evening.

On clipping days each herd brings with him to the shearing-place the several hefts comprising the hirsel over which he has charge, and one of the hefts may represent, more or less, his day's clipping. Brought together, the sheep are put into the folds. Here the ewes, which of course are alone to be clipped, are separated, or " shed " from their lambs, and put into wooden pens. The hogg clipping precedes the ewe clipping. Covered in overalls—for clipping is not an overclean job, the clipper, armed with his shears, settles himself on the clipping bench. " The catcher " enters the pen, seizes a ewe by the horns and drags her to the clipper. She is then laid on her back, her head on his knee, and he quickly gets to work. To-day, many flocks are sheared with mechanically worked clippers, but most of it is done by the old-time hand workers. It used to be customary in the Borders to slip a noose of cord over the sheep's legs to keep them still, but nowadays the legs remain free—sheep are used to handling by the shepherd, and quickly get accustomed to uncomfortable positions, and full control of the sheep is retained by the shepherd with his strong arms and knees, and if the sheep's struggling is protracted, a word from the shepherd is often effective, and the ewes submit quietly.

Then the shearing begins, first around the head and neck, which takes a little time, for this slender-fibred wool around the neck is the choicest portion of the fleece, the snowy whiteness of the inner wool contrasting strongly with the weather-stained and dirty outer side. An incision is then made between the forelegs, and the clipper works downwards to the tail, which is cleared with delicacy and patience. Next the shears are run in concentric circles round the breast and flanks, first one side, then the other, without either cutting the skin or leaving unsightly tufts, always, if possible, keeping the fleece entire, and free from flaws. The trimming of legs and tail completes the process. The fleece is then spread flat on the ground by one of the workers set apart for this duty, the edges folded to the middle, with all the loose bits, and the fleece rolled up into a compact ball, and secured with the twisted bond ; string or twine loosely spun from the wool itself is sometimes used, but more frequently the fleece is effectively bound up with a rope twisted from the head wool, used to secure the rolled-up bundle, which is pitched into a heap to be afterwards packed into large sacks, duly sewn up, and ready for transport to the mill, where the fleeces are cleaned, sorted, spun and made into clothes. Blackfaced wool is rolled up with the outside of the fleece outermost ; Cheviot wool with the inside outwards, although the reason for this long-established custom I have been unable to ascertain.

Wool of Blackfaced sheep brings about 1s. 4d. per pound in these days, and Cheviot wool 1s. 8d. per pound, and a fleece of Scottish hill Blackfaced may yield from five to nine pounds of wool, so that the proceeds of the wool clip goes a long way towards payment of the farm rent. Hogg wool is more valued than wedder wool.

Shepherds are usually expert shearers, and clip their own

flocks. It is a hot and arduous job in the height of summer, requiring physical strength and considerable skill. Indeed the highly skilled work of shearing to a nail's-breadth and not drawing a drop of blood, demands dexterity of execution and quickness of eye, and in the hands of an expert each sheep may take only a few minutes, so skilfully and cleverly is the work done. Of course much depends on the quality of the new wool in the fleece, and when this is good and close the shepherd's task in wielding his clippers is easier and quicker. Cuts, if they do happen, are dressed with balsam and sulphur to keep the flies away, and repeated till healed.

After the ewe has been fleeced and branded or "buisted," she is sent scampering away to the other end of the enclosure, surprised and shivering, to be driven back to the hefts with tremendous clamour of bleating. And then of course there will be time for a crack and a joke and a store of reminiscences at the various intervals in the day's work, and time was when there was always a dram for those who wanted it. When herd meets herd there's much to say, and neighbour herds, and herds frae far awa', may never meet at any other time the whole year round than at a clippin', and much may have happened since last they met. So that the clippin' is always regarded as a pleasant event in the shepherd's life, a time of work, and a time of pleasant social intercourse, when the flood-gates of memory and experience are unlocked, an oasis in the long spell of lonely herding on mountain, hill and valley, where the only attendant company is the shepherd's faithful collie dog. "There's nae cheerier place than the rees on a fine clippin' day," remarked an experienced shepherd.

Last of all comes the walk back over the hill, and while we gratefully sniff the moorland fragrance of bog and heather, thyme and myrtle, not forgetting the peat reek and the wood smoke from the forester's cottage by the way, it is as nothing compared with the will with which we set ourselves to the farm-house meal that has been prepared for us, with its heaps of buttered scones, large cups of tea, sizzling rashers of home-cured ham, sweet and juicy, and fried eggs, the size and flavour of which are quite unknown to the townsman's meagre ration.

"I've seen mair fun at a clippin'," said an experienced herd to me the other day, when we were talking about young folks feeling the country life lonely—"I've seen mair fun at a clippin' than ever I saw in ony toun."

XXV

THE SHEPHERD'S COLLIE DOG

"There is in every animal's eye a dim image and gleam of humanity, a flash of strange light through which their life looks out and up to our great mystery of command over them, and claims the fellowship of the creature if not of the Soul."

(RUSKIN)

ALL who know anything of dogs and country life admire the Scottish collie, not only for what it is in itself, but for the high degree of its intelligent service to the shepherd. Yet little is known of the origin and early history of the collie. Perhaps Argus, the faithful hound of Ulysses, was a collie. Shepherd dogs were not unknown to the Romans, but they are not mentioned in the Bible, probably because they did not exist, and we know that the Jews regarded all dogs as unclean animals. It is no doubt to the descendants of the Anglo-Saxons and Normans, who founded British agriculture, that we owe the sheep-dogs. The moorlands and hills were good feeding-places for sheep, and dogs would then become necessary. That the sheep-dog is one of the most ancient breeds in Britain is certain, but the collie of to-day differs much from the rough ungainly animal of the sixteenth century. Goldsmith in the eighteenth century classified the "shepherd dog" as that from which all others were derived, and some enthusiasts still make this claim. Darwin said the type approximated more closely to the old feral type than any other domesticated variety. The collie as we know it to-day is probably the result of breeding during the last three centuries, and the present type was fixed only about eighty years ago.

Both the derivation and orthography of the name are disputed. Just as the dog that hunts the fox or deer is the foxhound or deerhound, so the collie may be the dog having care of blackfaced and black-legged sheep, from *col*, black. Chaucer speaks of "Colle, our dog"; and Allan Ramsay wrote in

1721, " a better lad ne'er hounded coley o'er the mossy bent."
There is, however, general agreement as to the outstanding
qualities of this true dog of Nature—intelligence, sagacity,
fidelity, usefulness. He may be superior in instinct to all other
breeds, and have reasoning power of a high order ; indeed he
seems to be born perfectly trained for the service of others,
whereas much care and trouble are entailed in training other
dogs for their destined work. Indeed his intelligence cannot be
over-estimated ; he thinks and acts for himself under difficulties
and conditions new to him. He feels the responsibility of his
charge, and often acts independently of special orders. A faithful
and worthy servant, a properly trained collie will do almost
anything required in the handling of stock. On the hills he is
indispensable, and even when beyond the range of shepherd's
voice and whistle, he will work by given signals and gestures,
or according to his own judgment, which is not often wrong.
His power of hearing, like his keenness of scent, enables him to
trace the shepherd's footsteps over the hills for miles till he
overtakes him, so highly is it developed. It is said the bitch is
more acute in hearing than the dog, though the dog may bear
the greater fatigue. Many shepherds prefer the former, finding
them more clever and more devoted, but requiring gentler
treatment.

The collie is happiest and best understood when working
with sheep ; his eyes sparkle, his ears are half-erect, as he listens
only to obey his master's orders. Even when not working he
sticks to his master. In the house it is often most interesting for
the stranger to watch him as he lies content if his master is there,
seemingly half asleep and half awake. But on the first sign of
master rising, collie is up ; his eyes brighten, and his whole
attitude is that of enquiring what is to be done.

In the *Noctes Ambrosianae* it is intimately described :

What gladness in the creature's een, gin ye but speak a single word
to him, when you and him's sittin' thegither by your twa sells on the
hill. Pat him on the heid and say, " Hector, ma man ! " and he
whines wi' joy—snap your thooms and he gangs dancin' round you
like a whirlwind—gie a whuslin' hiss, and he loups frantic ower your
heid—cry halloo, an' he's aff like a shot, chasing naething, as if he
were mad. Love is the element a dowg leeves in, and a' that's necessary
for his enjoyment o' life is the presence o' his master.

A real delight awaits all who would watch a shepherd's collie at work. You may be chatting with the shepherd on the hillside about his two dogs lying quietly at his feet, when suddenly the shepherd will notice that, away over the boundary of his hirsel, his neighbour's ewes have got through the fence and are on his ground. " Here, lassie," he will say to one of the dogs, " awa ower and turn aff they sheep." At once the collie springs to attention ; he understands what is required (but how, no one has ever been able to find out), rushes off at full speed down the hillside, over the burn, through a clump of trees half a mile away. A sharp whistle, produced by placing the first and third fingers between the teeth, given by the shepherd, and collie looks back for orders. The shepherd signals " hold west," and is obeyed immediately. Now she's out of sight amongst the bracken, the white and black, which, by the way, is the best mixture of colouring for effective working among sheep and lambs which are susceptible to colour effect, the head and tail appear inter-mittently ; then emerging she jumps the burn, and climbs the hill face. But by this time the sheep have heard and seen, and understood. They know the reason for the dog, and lose no time in getting back through the slap in the fence by which they had trespassed. The sheep are on their own ground now, collie's work is done, yet so delighted is she in her work that she feels she wants to do the job properly, so she gives the sheep a chase up the hillside. Then she lies down at full length, panting, facing her master and waiting the next order. Recalled by another sharp whistle, collie obeys at once. Satisfied, she leisurely trots back, takes a drink on the way, lies down in the water until the back is almost covered then comes up to where we are standing. Note how shyly, how modestly, she comes, and lies down on the heather beside the other dog, which has all this time been eagerly watching the proceedings. Perhaps she in turn has had her day, not having now the agility of former days ; perhaps there is harder work for her in store. A hundred miles a day is not uncommon for a shepherd's collie.

All the shepherd wants is " a guid worker " ; no fancy, show or highly trained dog ; and where there is mutual loyalty and sympathy, and proper care and treatment by the shepherd, he is greatly helped by his collie dogs, who will always remain faithful to him, ready to respond to every word, gesture and action. I have heard and read stories of shepherds who did not treat their dogs with that care and attention, especially in regard to regular feeding, that their faithful service, and ordinary human decency, surely demanded, but I have always regarded such stories with reserve, and as exceptions, because my experience among Border shepherds has been that they are fond of their dogs, although they may not show it, and treat them thoughtfully and well.

The collie dog is an interesting animal to study. It is the only dog that can control and hold sheep with its eyes, and it is wonderful how sheep and dog come to understand each other. This eye-control may vary; it can be too highly developed in some, while in the case of others they may be what is termed "loose-eyed." Each dog has its own peculiarity in disposition and character; like humans some will take to you kindly, to others it may be hostile or indifferent, and even among other dogs it will have friends and foes.

Training the young puppy is important. It is better to begin with the puppy and secure confidence. A recent authority (W. R. Seward) writes: "If a puppy gets among stock at too early an age he may get scared, particularly by bellicose ewes with lambs. This will tend to make him stand back and bark at them for the rest of his life." Take a puppy among sheep occasionally from the age of six months so as to note when it becomes interested and maybe keen to start work. Some do not allow puppies to see sheep until they are nine to ten months old and have greater speed and confidence. Barking, to be effective, should be tempered with judgment or sheep will become indifferent. A dog soon knows right from wrong, and should be handled accordingly—patted and complimented and allowed some play on the way home if training has gone well, or called in and put on a lead if he has been a "bad dog." A dog in training should never be beaten except for the sin of biting a sheep; and when off duty should be chained in a comfortable corner shady in summer and dry in winter (*Ministry of Agriculture Journal*).

No one studied his dogs with more care than James Hogg, the Ettrick Shepherd, and he told some wonderful stories about "Sirrah," "Hector" and "Lion."

One dark night 700 lambs took fright, scattered over the hills in three divisions, and soon were altogether lost. "Sirrah, my man," said Hogg to the dog, "they're awa." He couldn't

PEEBLES

DARLINGTON
PUBLIC LIBRARY

"A RIDDLE OF CLARET OR PORT" IS PRESENTED OUTSIDE THE TONTINE HOTEL, PEEBLES, AT THE SHOOT FOR THE SILVER ARROW

see the dog, but the dog heard, understood and was off. Hogg and his shepherds searched till daylight, but in vain, and on the way back confessed "it was the most extraordinary circumstance that had occurred in my pastoral life." Soon he came upon a number of lambs, and "Sirrah" standing in front of them, looking for help. It was now light, and Hogg concluded this at any rate was a portion of the lost flock, but later it was found that not a single lamb was wanting. The dog had been in charge himself from midnight till dawn, and if all the shepherds in the Forest had assisted him they could not have accomplished a task so difficult, or with greater propriety.

A shepherd early learns to travel up-wind when in search of lost sheep, for it assists the collie's sense of smell, and often develops a real faculty for finding lost sheep which, once acquired, may gradually improve.

"Hector," a son of "Sirrah," small, rough and shaggy, was, he declared, even a more interesting dog, with more humour and whim, but stupid in some ways. Yet how he loved, "Hector," and conversed with him. Inspiration came to him as he sat on the high hill-tops with this dog by his side, as he tells us in *The Mountain Bard* ("The Author's Address to his Auld Dog Hector") :

> For mony a day, frae sun to sun,
> We've toiled fu' hard wi' ane anither ;
> An' mony a thousand mile thou'st run,
> To keep my thraward flocks thegither.
>
> .   .   .   .   .
>
> Come, my auld, towsy, trusty friend,
> Let's speel to Queensb'ry's lofty height ;
> All warldly cares we'll leave behind,
> An' onward look to days more bright.
>
> While gazing o'er the Lowland dales,
> Despondence on the breeze shall flee ;
> An' muses leave their native vales
> To scale the clouds wi' you an' me.

As showing Hector's devotion to duty, Hogg tells of how he remained all through a wet night watching some wet lambs he had bought the previous day, and intended selling next day along with others, notwithstanding that he had been called by his master night and morning to come to the house. He evidently thought he dared not leave them, although hungry, fatigued and cold—he had driven them some miles in the dark—he had not even lain down, for only the small spot on which he sat was dry, and there he kept watch all night. Any other collie would have seen that the lambs were safe enough in the fold, but Hector didn't see this.

Hogg had to give up the office of precentor in Ettrick parish kirk because Hector insisted not only in joining him in church, but joining in the psalm-singing, causing much amusement among the congregation.

Then Hector knew exactly when the prayer at family worship was coming to an end, because a second or two before the close he rose up and ran barking round the room. Hogg's father didn't interfere ; he just smiled. Hogg traced the dog's idiosyncrasy to the fact that he was fond of watching and " pointing " the cat, and he evidently thought that when he saw all the household kneel down in a circle with faces couched on their paws, and in the same posture as himself, they were all engaged in " pointing " the cat. So he lay in tenters all the time, but his acute hearing enabled him through time to know the very moment when we would all spring to our feet, so that Hector thought, " I'll be first after her anyway, and before you ! "

Sometimes the dog knows what is being said in a certain conversation. If not, how are we to account for this story ?

One winter evening Hogg told his mother he was going to Bowerhope for a fortnight, and added, " But I'll not take Hector with me." " Na, na," replied his mother, " leave Hector wi' me ; I like ay best to have him at hame, poor fella." These were the words that passed. Heavy rain during the night caused Yarrow to rise in spate, and Hogg didn't start off till after breakfast, and before going he went to tie up Hector, but he wasn't to be found. " The deil's in that beast," said Hogg. " I'll wager that he heard what we were saying last night, and has gone off to Bowerhope, as soon as the door was opened this morning." " If that should really be the case, I'll think the beast no canny," said his mother.

Yarrow's spate was so big, Hogg had to walk up to St. Mary's Loch and cross by boat, and on nearing Bowerhope he saw that it was as he had anticipated. Large as Yarrow was, and it appeared impassable by any living creature, Hector had made his escape early in the morning, had swum the river and was sitting, "like a drookit hen," on a knowe at the end of the house awaiting his master, with great impatience.

Dr. John Brown knew all the dogs in Edinburgh, and had many stories to tell. He declared that the Scotch collie Wylie, "the wee fell yin that could do a' but speak," was the finest collie he ever saw, admiring her perfect shape, beauty and gentleness. She was the property of a Tweeddale shepherd, Adam Cairns of Newbie, Glensax, and when Adam came to retire after years of faithful service, he told the Doctor that he was going to Glasgow to live with his son. At once Dr. Brown said, "And what are you going to do with Wylie?" "'Deed," says the shepherd, "I hardly ken. I canna think o' sellin' her, though she's worth four pound, and she'll no like the toun." "Would you let me have her?" enquired the Doctor, and Adam, looking at her fondly, said, "Aye, I wull, if ye'll be gude to her." So Wylie came to live with the Doctor in Albany Street, Edinburgh. Then a curious thing happened. Every Tuesday night about nine o'clock, Wylie disappeared, and was away all night, coming back next day, wearied and covered with mud as if she had travelled far. She slept all next day. This went on for months, the mystery unsolved. "And always when she returned she would look up at us wistfully as if she would have told us if she could." Then one day, when the Doctor was crossing the Grassmarket with Wylie at his heels, two shepherds stopped and looked at her. "That's her; that's the wee black bitch that naebody kens." It seems she went to the markets every Wednesday, making her appearance by the first daylight at the "bughts" or sheep pens in the cattle market, where she helped the shepherds with their sheep and lambs. "She's a perfect meeracle; flees about like a speerit, and never gangs wrang, wears but never grups, and beats a' oor dowgs." Everyone knew her, and said, "There's that wee fell yin, we'll get them in noo." Often they would speak about her, and try to coax her to stop and be caught; but no, she was gentle and coy—she was off home.

Do such dogs need much training? Whyles aye, and whyles no; her kind needs nane, she sooks't in wi' her mither's milk. "Naebody wad ever sell a guid dog, and wha wad buy a bad ane?" remarked a shepherd to me, which reminds me of the time when John Tod, the Swanston shepherd, refused forty pounds for "Cheviot."

One day Tod had been to the market in Edinburgh, and had bought sheep from various dealers, and with different markings, and when bringing them home over the Burghmuir he discovered that two were amissing. Later he learned that a farmer at the Braid Hills had discovered two stray sheep among his flock. Tod applied to him. " Can you tell me their markings ? " asked the farmer. " No," replied Tod, " but if my dog can seek them out, will ye let me have them ? " " Yes," said the farmer. The dog got to work, and singled out the two sheep ; and shepherd and dog, with the sheep in front of them, kept smiling to each other as they went on their way by Fairmilehead to Swanston hollow. That was the day that John Tod, " honest John," immortalised by R. L. S. in *Memories and Portraits*, refused forty pounds for Cheviot.

XXVI

SHEPHERDS OF THE HILLS

" Sweet are the thoughts that savour of content ;
The quiet mind is richer than a crown."

(GREENE)

MANY estimable qualities are found in the character of
the shepherd. He has a philosophy of life wrought out
of his own personality and the solitary situation in
which his lot is cast. He is largely of independent mind, strong,
upright, honest, with a simplicity that has something of greatness
in it. Character is for ever destiny ; and his destiny is the reward
of duty nobly done.

Contentment is great gain, and not only is there a contentment in the herd's house in the glen, there is also happiness,
which is more than contentment, implying a striving, an activity
and an attainment, the reaching of a moral height. In many a
quiet Border glen and upland the shepherd and his wife live
together supremely happy in each other, each with work to do,
and together working unselfishly for each other and for their
family. One old couple I know are always making jokes at each
other's expense in such a delightful way that the memory of it
always makes the remaining ten miles over the hills seem but
half the length. Another Tweeddale shepherd, who came from
the wild remote hills of Kintyre, would watch for my coming
that we might talk together about his native district. Another
would recite to me, out on the hill-tops, his latest rhymes about
the " Hillside business," and often by the ruddy glow of kitchen
fires of Tweeddale shepherd cottages I have listened to the
reciting of original pastoral poetry that was real and genuine.
There are men with poetic feeling and fervour among our
Scottish shepherds, whose verses speak of the wonders of Nature
among the hills and valleys, of the singing of birds, the blooming
of sweet-scented flowers and music of hill burns, and of sun and
shadow on pastoral scenes, and on human life. Many also have
a love for classical literature and Scottish Covenanting history.

A shepherd from a lonely cottage far up among the hills came to the manse one night, where I have often stayed, and asked the minister if he had any books he could give him to read. The Doctor was at once in a difficulty. What books would be likely to appeal to this member of his flock whose cottage was six miles from the nearest habitation? He offered him two novels. "Na, na," said the shepherd, dignified, bearded, broad-shouldered, "I've nae time for the like o' that; gie me something that'll exerceese ma brains, Doctor." And he went away with a volume of Kant under his oxter, proud, contented, comforted.

A Tweeddale shepherd who had struggled hard with storms and drifts, hurricanes and tempests for fifty years and more enquired of Sir Walter Scott if he really believed in the fairies, as often when overtaken by darkness in the lonely wilds he felt some trepidation lest a party of the elfish creatures should fall in with him in their peregrinations from glen to glen. In almost every cleugh and ravine in Ettrick-head the fairies had been known to hold their revels. He had been reading Scott's novels and tells him that when herding on Penvalla (Broughton Heights) he had been agreeably entertained with *The Monastery*. "I am perfectly astonished," he writes, "how ye have acquired the Scottish dialect and phraseology so exactly. . . . I like best the *Legend of Montrose* and *The Monastery*, and Edie Ochiltree in *The Antiquary* is very good," and concludes with a tribute to Scott's native craftsmanship: "I can scarcely select one passage more beautiful than another, yet when ye say that Halbert alighted from the heart of the oak with as little injury as the falcon stooping for his meal, it is truly excellent. On a tranquil summer's evening I have sometimes witnessed the aptness of this comparison: the eagle, that noble bird, wheels her spiral course to such a height that she appears like a small dot on the clear sky; sometimes the eye loses her altogether: anon she appears like a speck of vapour wandering over the blue void; after taking a number of circles at that extraordinary elevation she descends by the same winding course she arose, but only in larger circles, keeping her wings as steady and expanded all the while as ever ye saw the arms of a mock-man that had been set up to fray the cows from a field of new-sown barley. When she comes near her favourite cliff she stretches out her legs to meet its ragged point, yet alights as safe and easy as if she had descended to the ground and meadow from only a few yards' elevation. So fell Halbert from his oak, and so stoops the eagle from her airy flight " (*The Private Letter-books of Sir Walter Scott*, pp. 321-24). The shepherd did not sign his name, but Scott endorsed the letter as from a shepherd. It was dated 24th June 1820.

The blasts of the world's turmoil, with its wars, persecutions, inhumanities, often cause deep sorrow and concern in the cottage in the glen, and one is frequently met with the question as to what it all means, and the reason for it. Antidotes to get away from all such ungentle things are eagerly sought by dwellers in these far country places, whom I have often found to be possessed of a refinement and delicacy of feeling and speech that are infrequently met with in these days among either " toun-bred or land 'art."

In conversation with a typical Tweeddale herd in his cottage one day I produced a copy of Professor Veitch's *Hillside Rhymes*, and asked if he would like to have it. " Aye, wad I," he replied, and, accepting it, he remarked, " I'd raither read that than a' that modern rubbish ; onything aboot Natur' ; aye, an' sheep," he added. Whereupon he brought forth an ancient leather-bound volume on *Sheep*. " Man," he confided, " I canna lend it ye ; I canna bear to let it oot o' ma sicht ! "

The quickest way to a shepherd's heart is by an interest in his work. The love of sheep is with him a consuming passion. He can tell where his sheep are likely to be at any time of the day. In the morning they come down the hill to the burnside ; then after a time they move up the hillside again, grazing as they go : and at night they are to be found on the highest part of the ground. Perhaps they feel safer there ; perhaps the hill may be more dry on the top. Indeed, the first essential in a good shepherd is love for his sheep, and a willingness to tend them constantly and carefully in all weathers, and at all seasons of the year. As he watches them grow and develop, he makes them his study, and considers how he can improve his stock by careful selection and constant, watchful care, striving to live up to the traditions of his calling with its high ideal of duty.

The real shepherd early realises his vocation ; for him there can be no other. " Hill herds, like poets, are born not made, they maun be brocht up til't," remarked an experienced shepherd ; and it is doubtful if this business can be learned efficiently if the inherited, natural aptitude be lacking. Meeting a middle-aged shepherd on a boggy part of an Argyllshire sheep farm one day, I enquired in the course of conversation if he lost many sheep in the bogs. " Ou, aye, whyles," he said. " Jist noo an' again." " How long have you been on the ground ? " " Oh, jist six months. Ye see, I took the place o' a man that got cauld at the Games, an' he's deid ! " " Do you like it ? " " Ou, aye, whyles, if it wasna for the walkin' ; it's a' richt for a young man, but for me, wi' ma rheumatics, I'd raither be diggin' a drain or warkin' aboot the fairm." Such a one could hardly become a good, reliable shepherd. He had a gamekeeper friend in Ross, who told him that in Ross he could always follow the sheep-tracks for they were easily distinguished and easy of gradient ; not so, those of the goats. " Where the sheeps will go, I will go," said his friend, " but the goats, the goats is awful ! " No, he would not care to be a gamekeeper either, and especially in Ross ! But I do not think he would have gone so far as the Irishman on Clare Island, when rabbits and hares were of recent importation, who spent two days rounding up sheep and could not catch what he thought was one of the lambs, and complained bitterly when he found " the divil was a hare."

The shepherd's knowledge of the varying aspects of Nature is almost unrivalled. His daily life makes him familiar with every changing mood of the glen, the hillsides and the sky, in each revolving season, from the first green shoots of spring till the heather blooms on the moors and hills, and autumn brings the " bent sae broon," and winter winds sae wild and waesome. The breaking light that betokens the sunrise, the Tweeddale shepherd terms " the sky " : he speaks of the " carry of the clouds " and the " rack of the sky." The " skaum " or darkening of the sky is the term he applies when the vapour shows thin before the sun. When through the mist the sun strikes and makes it glorious, he speaks of the " dry-ure " ; and the " scarrow of the hill " is when the evening sun slants down the glen, and the broad, deep-bosomed hills lie in the shadow. The gloamin' and the mirk, and in between these two the " weather-gleam " (" wuther-glum "), have associations all their own, and have given rise to tender feelings and aspirations in herds both old and young.

If the shepherd's work is hard, it is nevertheless performed in a wonderful world. Who that has ever experienced that first faint rustle of the dawn wind, as he leaves the cottage before sunrise, can ever forget it ? It seems as if the whole countryside is held in leash waiting for the age-long miracle, the rising of the sun. The eastern sky begins to grow pink, the moonlit sky changes from grey to a delicate egg-shell blue ; the larks are singing amongst the stars ; and then there follows all the glory and the wonder of the dawn, welcomed, as we have seen, by the shepherd not least at " laumin' tim'," when that first white film in the sky brings to him something of relief from physical pain, and to his tired mind and brain, after work in the sleet and the rain, the cold and the darkness, fresh hope and courage, that gives strength to his arms and renewed faith and confidence.

Few men work harder among Scotland's hills and glens than the shepherd and his dogs. I see him making his way home in the gloamin' time after his last round, with his long, sweeping, balanced stride, the tired dogs at his heels. As he nears the cottage, he sees the lamplight streaming from the open door, and it shines like gold upon the dark. As he angles his way in, puts his cap on the peg and his crook in the corner, no man earns more worthily his rest by the fireside, and the blessings of sweet repose—" innocent sleep ; sleep that knits up the ravell'd sleave of care . . . chief nourisher in life's feast."

The shepherd is observant and intelligent, and is a local authority on the old Drove roads, bridle tracks, boundaries and rights-of-way. He is interested also in the farm-yard, and will point out to you many things familiar to him ; for instance, the smile of contentment on the fat faces of the cows as they lie half-covered in lush grass chewing the cud, or flap a slow tail knee-deep in the river ; the bright eye, the haughtiness of the farm-yard cock, strutting about as if he was the centre of things. He pauses, one foot in air ; blinks at you, either gives a " Cock-a-leerie-law " or looks at you coldly first with one big eye, then the other, and with arched, disdainful neck struts proudly into the sunshine. Also, he's an optimist, he begins to crow long before the sunrise. Ducks are oddly comical, with more character and intelligence than ordinary fowls. They like a procession— left ! right ! left ! right ! barn, stable, stack-yard—and if you go too near they look at you with wicked, cynical eyes. In the mud among the sedge and slime, they gobble and peer, and say " Quack ! Quack ! " Yet they are friendly too, as they come waddling to meet you as you near the cottage door. Then there's the smell of hay, never more fragrant than at dawn in summer-time; the warm odours of stable and byre; low sounds of cattle, as they quieten down for the night; the rattle of chains, the cough, the sigh, the splutter of water; and, the drip, drip, dripping of the water at the well.

And the shepherd's children also know all about these things, and about sheep and lambs also; and know that a full-mouthed sheep has eight teeth (which includes two small ones on each side), and that the front teeth are used for pulling the grass into the mouth, while the back teeth are used for chewing.

" I've got a memory like a hen," I once heard a Tweeddale shepherd lad say. The Gaelic proverb reads : " A hen's head is a fool's head ! " And a Tweeddale lass defined patience : " Bide a wee an' dinna weary."

Big families were more common in former days. A hundred years ago there stood at the head of Manor valley a small white cottage, where there was ten of a family. Not that they all lived in the one " but and ben " at the same time, but as they grew up the older ones went out to service, and so there was always plenty of room for those at home. They had eight miles to go to school. There were no motor-buses then, but they had a donkey. Two of the children rode on the donkey's back half-way down the glen; then they dismounted, tied the donkey to a tree, and continued the journey on foot. Meantime the two who had set off on foot came up to the donkey, untied him, and rode the rest of the way to school. So the sixteen miles a day were made pleasant and interesting in companionship with the donkey. School was no drudgery or hardship, but was eagerly looked forward to.

In winter, snow filled the glen, and the children were taught by the tailor, who came to each herd's house for a week at a time, being engaged in making garments of home-spun cloth from the wool of the sheep of the herd's own hirsel. A boy began to help his father in those days at ten years of age; at fourteen he went out to his first place.

In those days of large families there was a greater faith in Providence. " The Lord will provide " was a text frequently found on the walls of shepherd's cottages; and so it was that, where the parents were well-doing, none ever went in want, and children grew up lusty and strong on good fairin' of porridge and oatmeal, Scotch broth, potatoes and milk, and were a credit to their parents and their country. From the shepherds' cots have gone forth some of the finest examples of Scottish men and women. Country children have a simple existence ; they know the changes in the woods that the seasons bring ; the miracles of Nature are known to them, and all the trees and animals are familiar and loved companions. Visiting the woods after the children have departed, I have sometimes felt as if the trees were sorry the children had gone.

It is now said that young folk will not live in the country, because it is too lonely. Those who find it so are better in the towns ; they are certainly not good enough for the work required of shepherds and others engaged on farms. Probably both home and school education have been lacking in making them self-reliant and interested in country life. On the other hand, there probably never were more young shepherds on the Border hills than there are to-day.

Lambing, shearing, dipping, trimming, tailing, care of feet, and so on, are tasks calling for manual skill and ability. Many are the tasks which the shepherd has to perform, which are incapable of mechanisation, even in this age of machines. To the right kind of shepherd there is no such thing as dullness or loneliness. There is too much work to be done, and Nature has too many things to teach for loneliness to find any place. Upon asking a successful shepherd in a far sequestered cleugh in the Cheviots why he had left his last place in the Moorfoots, he replied, " Ach, there was faur ower mony folk there."

Another shepherd who had recently arrived at a solitary cottage in the Lammermuirs of whom I enquired, in the course of conversation, how his wife would like the place, replied in astonishment, " Like it ! Like it ! She'll hae tae ! "

One winter day while crossing a range of hills I called at a shepherd's cottage, and while in conversation suggested to the good wife that, seeing the mornings were so dark, she would no doubt have a longer lie in bed ; but she at once scorned the idea—" Do ye no ken that a' the cocks an' hens are gaithered roond the door waitin' on me at sax o'clock o' the mornin' ? "

These stories represent, in part, the temperament, and the strength and independence of character of the shepherd folks in the glen.

In the cottage no one could be more appreciative of woman's work than the shepherd, who knows the love that tends and cares for his creature comforts. Visiting a cottage at the glen-head one spring day, I remarked to the herd that " Of course herds' wives are also hard-worked at laumin' tim'." " Ou, aye," he replied philosophically, " nae doubt, nae doubt, but their wark is mair ahint the scenes again." He, the herd, was at the forefront of the battle working among life and death, in dark and daylight, in rain and shine, in storm and calm, but the herd's wife, her wark was behind the scenes ! Bless her and her work, for it is as essential to the herd as the herd's work among ewes and lambs.

Many a herd's house has the wireless, and while this has brought a great boon to country folks, it has probably meant the lessening of interest in playing the fiddle, the flute and the concertina, although it is realised that a barn dance would be a poor affair without the fiddler.

In a cottage, far from any other habitation, a herd's wife was detailing how in times of need or trouble it was wonderful how there was always somebody about to help. " The other day," she said, " the wireless went off. I went to the door, and there on the hill I saw Jamie, the mole-cacther. ' Jamie ! ' I cried, and he came in. I explained what was worng, and, would you believe it, in five minutes Jamie had the wireless going as before, and a' wi' the help o' a bit matchbox he took oot o' his waistcoat pocket ! "

Truly there is neither loneliness nor dullness in the herd's cottage in the glen. And how refreshing it is to meet such frank, honest, guileless folk. " Aye," said one good woman when I called at the cottage far away up among the Tweeddale hills, " John's awa the day ; he's awa for a coo. Ye see John's awfu' fond o' his porridge, and he canna do without milk, and—we need a coo ! He was at the market last week, but they were ower dear. I hope he'll get ane the day." John got his cow all right.

On another occasion, at a herd's house at a lonely glen-head, the wife came briskly to meet me, for she had seen me coming up the glen, and on my enquiring for Wattie, she replied, " Wattie's awa the day ; aye, awa for a coo ; aye, an' he's drivin' her frae Hertree," over the hills by pass and cleugh and glen, " an' she's only a month aff her time, and canna be hurried ; she wad calve on the sixteenth o' next month. Ou, aye, but ye see, Wattie's gentle, he'll manage her a' richt, an' he'll be here afore nicht-tim'."

Unwelcome visitors seldom make their appearance, but the resource of the herd's wife is equal to most emergencies, as we learn from the story of " Jenny o' Birkhill," who was frequently left in the cottage alone with her little girl. A rough-looking fellow slunk into the kitchen one day, and made as if to help himself. " My man," said Jenny, " did onybody see ye come in here ? " " No," said the man. " Then deil a ane will see ye gang oot : lassie, gie me the axe ! " The intruder vanished in an instant.

The visits of well-intentioned strangers, however, are usually welcomed and valued by the shepherd folks. It must not be forgotten, however, that often by temperament, heredity and training the Scot is not easily moved to geniality or fervour, but he will ponder for long any philosophical or religious problem you may suggest to his mind. That such visits are welcomed and remembered by the shepherd folk there is ample evidence,

" It's a year ago last Monday ye last ca'ed," said a wise, ruddy-cheeked little body to me the other day when I called, as if to remind me that she had not forgotten. And impressions of conversations that were considered trifling and of little account are remembered long after the speaker has forgotten all about them. It is perhaps natural that it should be so, seeing that the shepherd's life is often spent in places where, save for an occasional visit to kirk or market, he sees few new faces, and hears no other voices save those of his own family and that of the herd whose hirsel marches with his own.

There must always be a certain romance about a calling that takes one out to the hills and open spaces. The hills are Nature at her bravest and best, and who can live beneath them without being imbued with their steadfastness and courage ? It is a calling with dangers and adventures, often hardship, suffering, loss, of men who serve faithfully, without servility ; and a calling requiring perfect physical and mental health. There is no need to wonder why the shepherd is honest, sincere, that he retains his sense of wonder and awe, reverence and simplicity. It's all the influence that comes from living among the hills. It is natural also he should ponder the ways of God with men, and have a deep and abiding faith in Providence, and love of freedom.

Little wonder it is that the spirit world is very real to the thoughtful and imaginative mind of such men, and that James Hogg could write :

> Our converse was with heaven alone—
> With voices through the clouds that sung,
> And brooding storms that round us hung.

It is almost impossible [he said] that the shepherd can be other than a religious character, being so much conversant with the Almighty in His works, in all the goings-on in Nature and in His control of the otherwise resistless elements. He feels himself a dependent being, morning and evening, on the great Ruler of the Universe. He holds converse with Him in the cloud and in the storm, on the misty mountain and the darksome waste, in the whirling drift and the overwhelming thaw. How can such a man fail to be impressed with the presence of an Eternal God, of an omniscient eye, of an Almighty arm ?

The Ettrick Shepherd regarded his daily contact with spiritual things as quite a natural thing ; he walked and talked on the hill with the Great Spirit of Nature, and was at home in this environment.

So long as a nation has men like our Scottish shepherds, there is no fear of degeneration or a decadent population. Of such was the first generation, and of such in all probability will be the last.

> By the soul only,
> The Nations shall be great and free.
>
> (WORDSWORTH)

In all my wanderings among the shepherd folk of Tweeddale and the Uplands, I have always valued their native graciousness, naturalness, friendliness and quiet humour, along with a native shyness and a certain difficulty in finding a true and correct expression of their thoughts.

The shepherd is not a man of quick or copious phraseology or verbal melody, such is difficult to come by on the solitary areas of the hills ; it is easier for him to think than to speak. So it is not infrequent that he has recourse to proverbs, saws and maxims to formulate his experiences of life, social, philosophical, humorous, which become the bank-notes of speech, circulated and honoured all over the countryside in the native lowland tongue, with its beautiful rhythmical lilt—the " sweetest, richest, subtlest, most musical of all the dialects of Europe." So wrote

John Ruskin to a Scottish lad about his native tongue—the old language of the Scottish Lowlands. Allan Ramsay's *Collection of Scots Proverbs* was dedicated to " The Farmers of the Dales and the Storemasters of the Hills." And John Buchan (Lord Tweedsmuir) in his Memoirs has spoken of " the soft kindly idiomatic Border speech " of the shepherds, these men of " the long stride and the clear eye—a great race—I never knew a greater."

Natural feeling, and the feeling for Nature, are valued gifts of all who love Nature and the hills, and are part of those larger gifts of liberty of thought, serenity of mind and fellowship of spirit which are the natural inheritance of those whose dwelling is among Scotland's hills and glens.

DARLINGTON
PUBLIC LIBRARY.

INDEX

DARLINGTON PUBLIC LIBRARY